René Blum and the Ballets Russes

RENÉ BLUM AND THE BALLETS RUSSES

In Search of a Lost Life

Judith Chazin-Bennahum

OXFORD
UNIVERSITY PRESS

OXFORD
UNIVERSITY PRESS

Oxford University Press, Inc., publishes works that further
Oxford University's objective of excellence
in research, scholarship, and education.

Oxford   New York
Auckland   Cape Town   Dar es Salaam   Hong Kong   Karachi
Kuala Lumpur   Madrid   Melbourne   Mexico City   Nairobi
New Delhi   Shanghai   Taipei   Toronto

With offices in
Argentina   Austria   Brazil   Chile   Czech Republic   France   Greece
Guatemala   Hungary   Italy   Japan   Poland   Portugal   Singapore
South Korea   Switzerland   Thailand   Turkey   Ukraine   Vietnam

Published by Oxford University Press, Inc.
198 Madison Avenue, New York, New York 10016

www.oup.com

Oxford is a registered trademark of Oxford University Press

Library of Congress Cataloging-in-Publication Data
Chazin-Bennahum, Judith.
Rene Blum and the Ballets russes: in search of a lost life /Judith Chazin-Bennahum.
    p.   cm.
Includes bibliographical references and index.
ISBN 978-0-19-539933-2 (alk. paper)
1. Blum, Rene, 1878–1942. 2. Ballets russes—History. 3. Choreographers—France—Biography. 4. Publishers and pub-
lishing—France—Biography. 5. Jews—France—Biography. 6. Holocaust, Jewish (1939–1945)—France—Biography. I.
Title.
GV1785.B53196C47   2011
792.8′2092—dc22   [B]   2010036763

1 3 5 7 9 8 6 4 2

Printed in the United States of America
on acid-free paper

I dedicate this book to Janet Rowson Davis, an English dance and television historian who introduced me to René Blum's important career. I would never have written about René Blum without Janet's kind suggestion years ago that I take over from her the hundreds of pages of research, including dozens of letters to libraries and institutions, reviews and programs of the Blum Ballets Russes and Ballets de Monte-Carlo performances, as well as all sorts of documents pertaining to Blum's literary and artistic career. Mysteries abound in his life, as World War II intervened and things disappeared with his violent death in the Holocaust. I hope that she takes pleasure in this biography, and that I have justified to some extent her boundless faith in me.

CONTENTS

NOTE ON TRANSLATION

All translations from the French are the author's own, except where otherwise noted.

FOREWORD

René Blum! I have known the name since childhood. I remember a half-heard conversation between grown-ups connecting him with a ballet company then playing in London and with his brother Léon Blum, later to be the first Socialist premier of France. Even then I wondered what being the brother of a senior politician could possibly have to do with running a ballet company. What indeed? It had a profound effect on René's life.

That was in 1933, my first year at boarding school. For my half-term treat, I was taken to see that company at the now-demolished Alhambra Theatre in London. The program was *Les Sylphides*, *Choreartium*, and *Le Beau Danube*. I still remember the in-drawing of breath as the curtain went up on the moonlit magic of *Les Sylphides*. I remember somber glimpses of *Choreartium* (not at all realizing the new ground this ballet broke) and the lilting fun and gaiety of *Le Beau Danube*.

At the end of the performance the audience burst into rounds of applause and calls of approval. I recall baskets of fruit and flowers being banked up on the stage and armfuls of bouquets being presented to the dancers. Little did I realize at the time that I was attending the last night, on November 4, 1933, of the now famous, much extended first London season of the Blum-de Basil Ballets Russes de Monte-Carlo.

What an occasion to introduce a child to ballet! If she was not already a balletomane—the word had not then been coined—she would soon become one.

In actual fact, it was some six or so years before I had any proper chance of building on that first amazing encounter. I had left school; World War II had broken out in Europe and I had donned a WAAF uniform (Women's Auxiliary Air Force, ultimately absorbed into the Royal Air Force). For the next six years, I served in various locations all over England. Although it seemed that one was out in the wild, it was usually possible to get to the nearby towns and cities and their theatres.

During the war there was an enormous increase in activity in all the arts, among them ballet. This was kept alive and developed by companies such as Sadler's Wells (now Royal) Ballet, Ballet Rambert, Mona Inglesby's International

Ballet, and Ballet Jooss, then based in Dartington, Devon, in the forefront with other smaller evanescent groups. Somehow I managed to see a sufficient number of these companies to build up a foundation of knowledge.

Throughout six years of war, England was virtually cut off from ballet activities in other parts of the world. When peace came in 1945, there was an inundation of ballet news and views in newspapers, periodicals, books, dictionaries, and encyclopedias, which included the sad but not unexpected news of the death of René Blum, at the hands of the Nazis.

There were many tributes to him praising his good taste, his knowledge of music and musicians, his love of art and his insight into modern art, his love of books, and of course, his running of the Théâtre de Monte-Carlo and his founding and running of Les Ballets Russes de Monte-Carlo, but much of it needed to be substantiated. I set about trying to do just that, and found myself engaged in an ever-expanding correspondence with sources such as the theatre at Monte Carlo, the French Institute in London, Jewish organizations in Paris, the *Encyclopaedia Judaica*, and occasionally ex-dancers from the company who had appeared under Blum's aegis at Monte Carlo, and so on. In due course, I delivered a paper on Blum at the 1988 conference of the Society of Dance History Scholars at Winston-Salem. This stimulated interest among the members and also my own desire to know more.

In continuing the research, it soon became evident that the project would need much more research in France and Monte Carlo by someone with time to visit these places and with a better knowledge of French than I have.

Over the years I contributed a series of articles on dance and ballet on British television to the scholarly magazine *Dance Chronicle* (New York) edited by George Dorris and Jack Anderson. It was Dorris who suggested that I approach Judith Chazin-Bennahum, a dancer, French scholar, and university professor in theatre and dance at the University of New Mexico, whom I had met briefly at Winston-Salem. In time, she agreed to take over my project.

For me, this has been a very happy association. Despite the geographic distance between us, she has always kept me in touch with her progress by phone, letters, and visits, telling me of her most recent discoveries, the people she met, the centers she visited. In no way would I have been able to do what she has done. I am so glad that her researches have come to fruition, that her book is now being published, and that the name of René Blum is finally established.

Janet Rowson Davis
Bournemouth, United Kingdom
2009

ACKNOWLEDGMENTS

My first thanks go to my husband David, my cherished collaborator in this seemingly vast memoir. He accompanied me in this quest to many locations—Paris many times, New York many times, Jerusalem to the Yad Vashem Holocaust Museum, several times to London and Bournemouth, to conferences in Limerick and Banff, to Monte Carlo where we stayed close by in opalescent Beaulieu. Most importantly, he also researched and wrote the portions of this book dealing with politics and economics, and spent many long hours editing several versions of this manuscript. *Abrazos* to all our children and grandchildren, who happily stood by us during this book's gestation process.

Melinda Jordan and I have worked together on several other books; she helped me through the perplexing initial stages of shaping and transforming the manuscript into a cohesive oeuvre. Her unfailing eye and penchant for direct clarity led to its becoming a readable document. George Dorris, the former co-editor of *Dance Chronicle*, brought together Janet Rowson Davis and me. Throughout the text's development, he was a gentle mentor, privileging the subject under discussion, heightening its significant meanings, and eliminating extraneous material. My brother, Rabbi Joel Chazin, gave me courage all along, and cared so much about the outcome of this book. Roselyne Chenu, like a sister, is the author of a number of beautiful and provocative works, and was always ready to assist me with questions concerning research in Paris.

Very good friends, including Noel Pugach, generously helped answer puzzling Holocaust questions. Malka Sutin, who survived the Holocaust, nurtured and cheered me along. Lynn Garafola encouraged me to ponder issues surrounding the complex negotiations with personalities of Blum's time. Nancy King Zeckendorf put us in touch with Charles Gordon, an entrepreneur, and his talented wife, the ballerina Nadia Nerina. It was Charles, one balmy day in Beaulieu, who heard our story about Blum and advised that the title should be "In Search of René Blum." Judith Brin Ingber, Dawn Lille, Linda Tomko, and Janice Ross all felt a deep connection to this subject and proposed useful and cogent ideas. Jacques Delacave indicated an important Le Touquet connection; Jeanine Belgodere aided me in getting through some of Proust's dense prose; Walter Putnam kindly suggested that I contact Anne-Sabine Nicolas, who decoded and translated dozens of Blum's hurried, at times scribbled, letters; Claude Conyers, formerly of Oxford University Press, was there to encourage me whenever I called on him. Eva Lipton and Katita Milazzo both agreed to look for information about Blum in the Holocaust archives on their visits to Germany. Karen Butler knew that Vuillard had painted Blum and kindly sent me information as well as a photo of the intriguing portrait. Ilan Greilsammer, author of a biography of Léon Blum, offered counsel about looking for René's lost manuscript and letters. Judith Berke, the poet and our cousin, cheered me on for the long haul. Amira Mayroz suggested some books on music that gave me insight into the musical culture of the 1930s. Sondra Lomax facilitated my liaison with a photo library in Texas. Laurent Hyafil, the son of Francine Hyafil, sent me his very touching, personal writings about growing up in post-Holocaust France; and Coralie Hyafil, Francine's granddaughter, spent many hours seeking documents in Parisian archives that might shed light on Blum's educational record. Jack Anderson, Elizabeth Souritz, and Kathrine Sorley Walker warmly offered to be consultants whenever possible.

The many hours of research in libraries across the world were aided and abetted by some of the most selfless and supportive people, the librarians. I am profoundly grateful to Romain Feist of the Paris Opéra archives, as he provided me with dozens of clippings and many other sources for the Blum book; Bénédicte Jarasse of the Paris Opéra library researched Blum's educational background; Cécile Coutin of the Bibliothèque Nationale has become a warm, amicable supporter in this endeavor. She led me to the Blum archives at the Arts du Spectacle and continually offered valuable advice; Valerie Gressel took time to show me how to navigate the Bibliothèque Nationale Mitterand collections; Charlotte Lubert as well as her colleague Véronique Fabré at the Archives of the Société des Bains de Mer in Monte Carlo kindly and continuously located letters, contracts, and photos germane to this project; Dominique Parcollet from the Centre d'Histoire de Sciences Po provided wonderful materials from the Léon Blum collection. Severin Hochberg and Paul Shapiro of the United States Holocaust Museum in Washington, D.C., helped me in my attempt to track down the autobiography of René Blum, which remains lost. Other librarians and curators who spent time amicably assisting me were Yehudit Shendar of Yad Vashem Museum in Jerusalem; Jane Pritchard and Revinder Chahal from the Victoria and Albert Theatre collection; Micah Hoggat at the Houghton Library and Harvard Theatre collection; my wonderful colleagues the late Monica Moseley, Pat Rader, Charles Perrier, Jan Schmidt, and Alice Standin at the

Jerome Robbins Dance Collection at the New York Public Library for the Performing Arts; Eva Ayala Canseco and Pablo Berrocal at the Museo Soumaya; and Judith Hansen and Nina Kay Stephenson from the Fine Arts Library, and Nancy Pistorius from the Zimmerman Library at the University of New Mexico.

Also very sympathetic were the ballet dancers who gave their valuable time to be interviewed for this book—Christiane Algaroff, Frederick Franklin, Natasha Krassovska, George Zoritch, Leo Kersley, and Adda Pourmel. I found great new friends in the relatives of René Blum—Francine Hyafil, her son Laurent, Françoise Nordmann, Antoine and Chantal Malamoud, and Sophie Lavigne. Without their warmth and their hospitality over the years, I could not have delved into his world and oeuvre. I also owe a great deal to Joan Bybee for suggesting the remarkable Clay Beckner whose keen eye for detail and warm soul helped me to put the finishing touches on this manuscript. Coming into the home stretch, I am grateful for the staunch support of Mica Rosenberg, Rick Stinson, and Gabe Waters. Finally, I would like to say that I am enormously grateful to my editor at Oxford, Norm Hirschy, whose initial letters of encouragement gave me such hope. I relished the grace with which he chided and guided me through this process.

PORTRAITS OF NOTABLE PEOPLE IN THE MAKING OF THIS BIOGRAPHY

Francine Hyafil

We met on the Boulevard Montparnasse, near the Hotel Central on the Rue de Maine. She picked us up in her sporty French car to take us to her sunny and upscale apartment in Boulogne just outside Paris. As we drove, she immediately started criticizing Ilan Greilsammer, author of a biography of Léon Blum. She believed that he exaggerated Léon's attention to religion. She was right, although Léon never denied his Jewishness. Francine was warm, witty, and colorful, with a deep love for life and laughter. She spoke in clear punctuated phrases and was very definitive in her opinions. She always served us the most delectable dishes of her own making. We discovered later that she had written a diary of the war as a young woman. Her journals of earlier times described her family and the halcyon days holidaying in northern France. They became idealized in her memory. Her memories of the Occupation were not so jolly. They told a grim tale of her family's perilous journey to the Free Zone, and her father's desperate attempts to house and care for his family. Francine also brought to life the trials of her grandfather Lucien. She tells the stories with rich and vivid

Figure A.1
Snapshot of author with Francine Hyafil, great-niece of René Blum. Photo by David Bennahum.

details. It was her mother, Jacqueline Lancrey-Laval, who helped preserve the memories, writing for those interested in Léon and René about the facets of life so often ignored by biographers. Jacqueline additionally responded to Janet Rowson Davis's queries about the early life of René Blum.

Françoise Nordmann

Invited for tea with Françoise, "Oncle René's" niece, we spent lovely warm afternoons enjoying her sweet coffee cakes. Her quiet elegance and grace pervaded all our meetings. Her husband Roger has died since our initial meeting. At that first luncheon, he told us breathtaking stories about his escape from the Germans. Apparently, he was about to be arrested by the Nazis; in a fortuitous moment, as one of his guards looked away to light a cigarette, Roger ran and successfully hid from them. I naively asked why the authorities had wanted to arrest him. He said rather forcefully, "Because I was a Jew, that's it." Françoise and Roger married during the war, while René was interned at Compiègne, where he wrote them an endearing and heartfelt card of congratulations. Françoise and Roger lived on the Boulevard Vincent Auriol. It seemed no accident that they resided there as Auriol was a great friend and political advocate of Françoise's uncle, Léon Blum.

The huge piano in Françoise's living room, a small space filled with book-shelves, meant a great deal to her, as her father was a sophisticated musician, playing it all the time, as did their visitor, Uncle René Blum, who lived right below them in a smaller apartment on the rue de Tocqueville. Françoise recalled the gentleness and kindness of her uncle, who invited her to the ballet in Paris and in Monte Carlo as often as possible.

Antoine Malamoud

It was a pleasure to meet Antoine Malamoud, the great-great-grandson of Léon Blum, at one of the oldest restaurants in Paris, La Procope. He showed up with a helmet in hand, his motorcycle parked nearby. The restaurant, a snazzy place now, was formerly a café frequented by the most brilliant intel-lectuals of the Enlightenment, such as Voltaire. The rendezvous spoke to Antoine's innate sense of good taste and care for fine food and wine. I had the feeling at our first meeting that he was accustomed to supporting heavier players, writers who were recognized political historians working on biographies, for example, of Léon. He was charming and open, not fully cognizant of René's broad and rather brilliant accomplishments, and I sensed an ironic wit that erupted quickly when he was amused by some-thing I said. Antoine's father was an Asian specialist; his mother, Cathérine, was a favorite daughter of the son of Robert (Léon's son) and Renée (his wife) Blum. Though Antoine's livelihood depends on his job with a phar-maceutical company, he's a fine writer who has contributed an introduction to Léon's *Derniers Mois*, and helped with other publications, and recently a film, about his great-great-grandfather. He was kind enough to send me copies of some of René's writings that appeared in publications similar to *Vogue* magazine. I suspect that they colored Antoine's opinion of René. We also shared some wonderful dinners with his lovely wife Chantal, an owner of a children's bookstore.

Sophie Lavigne

I received a telephone call out of the blue several years ago. Sophie Lavigne told me that she was the great-great-granddaughter of Marcel, René Blum's brother, born after Lucien the eldest. She explained that she had created a website for the Blum family, something I did not know about, and that she heard I was writing about René. Might I share some of the information I had discovered? It was a joy to hear her voice, and to know that there was someone else searching the past, rather than "moving on" or trying to escape it. Sophie came to our little studio apartment in Paris with a bundle of postcards that her father had received from his mother Simone. They were all addressed to René Blum, and Sophie wanted me to be able to use them for my research. The three of us jumped into a cab to pick up Julien, her five-year-old son, and then went to the Montmartre cemetery where her grandparents were buried, and where there was a plaque dedicated to René Blum. We walked from Julien's school to the cemetery where so many distinguished figures are buried. Apparently, Sophie and Julien visit the cemetery rather often; many cats abide there and Julien loves to seek them out and to chase them. The plaque to René Blum was blackened and impossible to read, but Sophie was trying to arrange for a cleaning of the stones. What is so impressive about this young lady is her clarity, her brightness, and her intelligence. Her long journey back in time to discover her roots has been a bit arduous, but rewarding.

Christiane Algaroff

While working on the book in Paris, my husband and I lived in a little studio next door to Madame Algaroff, a former dancer with Les Ballets des Champs Élysées and the Nouveaux Ballets de Monte-Carlo. She married the well-known dancer Youli Algaroff, who studied with Kniaseff, danced as a soloist with the Lyons Opéra in 1944, and made his debut with Les Ballets de la Jeunesse (1946 and 1948–1949). As a freelance dancer, and principal soloist, he created roles in Charrat's *Jeu de Cartes* and Lifar's *Chota Roustaveli*. He later became a ballet producer. Christiane told stories about dancing in Lyons during the Occupation. In another apartment nearby lived a young man who would return home very late at night and barely communicate with Christiane and her roommate. He was suspected of being a Jew, and one day he disappeared and never returned. She thought he'd been taken to the nearby Fort Montluc where the Nazis were known to have tortured their victims. She also recalled dancing in a ballet in which Boris Kochno had been the dramaturge. While the dancers waited in the wings before the curtain went up, they always knew when Kochno in his dark suit would approach, as they smelled the perfume, Bandit de Piguet, that he used, and it was an unfailing clue for them. She said he was known as a rather dark character.

INTRODUCTION

René Blum's radiant life was lost in the Holocaust. From the moment he was arrested in Paris on December 12, 1941, his intimate possessions, letters, valuable artwork, and books fell into the abyss of war. Like many Holocaust victims in Europe, his resplendent reputation was ignored; it was as if in remembering him, too many were painfully reminded of the forces of evil that murdered him.

By the time René Blum became a celebrated impresario of theatre and ballet for the Théâtre de l'Opéra de Monte-Carlo, he was already an established editor, publisher, and literary critic. It remains a mystery why few contemporary dance historians have divulged the story of Blum's youthful and lifelong successes. A well-known man about Paris, his charm, wit, and close relationship to his brother, the brilliant Socialist politician Léon Blum, added a note of distinction and elegance to his reputation.

Filled with a burning desire to excel as a ballet producer, René Blum wrote to his paramour Josette France that he was unable to spend a weekend with her: "I am driven by a demonic force inside myself that pushes me to work endlessly and without respite."[1] This obsessive streak propelled Blum to seek and to achieve recognition in many areas of the arts, and after the tragic death of his friend Serge Diaghilev, to bring back to life the glorious Ballets Russes de Monte-Carlo.

Born to a prosperous Jewish merchant family, all five of the Blum brothers witnessed with awe and fear the Dreyfus affair. Their lives began during la Belle Époque in the late nineteenth century, a period that brought prosperity and stability to much of the Jewish community in France. The Blums thrived with the growth of urban industrialism, yet would be altered forever in the blistering atmosphere of a France torn asunder by hatred and anti-Semitic accusations of treason. Like bookends to René Blum's rich and productive life, the Dreyfus affair marked the beginning and the Holocaust the end. He was sixty-three years old when he was picked up by German and French military police and taken to die in Auschwitz. But despite the final horror, the Blum brothers, especially Léon and René, succeeded in living rich, productive lives.

René was sixteen years old when the Dreyfus affair began, and as the affair played out from 1894 to 1906, René and Léon never seemed to fear for their own careers despite their tight connection to the literary and artistic salons of the Jewish community. As an outstanding young lawyer, Léon worked for the defense of Dreyfus and Zola. Denunciations against Jews for being foreigners and "un-French" certainly affected the Blums, whose parents were from German-speaking Alsace, yet they responded with a fierce nationalism, truly believing in the French ideals of Liberté, Égalité, and Fraternité.

Following in the footsteps of Léon, who served as an editor for the famous literary journal *Revue Blanche*,[2] René met the most famous artists and writers of his generation, such as Edouard Vuillard and Stéphane Mallarmé, by spending most of his time at the offices of the *Revue Blanche*. This initiation helped him to feel comfortable in the presence of artists, to understand and to promote their ideas.

René's lifelong, unyielding commitment to contemporary artists was recorded in a book of homages (*René Blum 1878–1942*) published soon after his death.[3] They remain testaments to his belief in the power of French culture. René produced the works of theatre writers such as Romain Coolus and Colette, as well as retaining designers, composers, and actors for his productions at theatres in Le Touquet, Pigalle, and Monte Carlo.

In his ten years as co-editor for the chic Parisian journal *Gil Blas*, Blum projected a singular personal warmth, engaging in conversations with his readership on such diverse issues as the critic's prejudices against what was considered popular performance, or the duty of the critic to explain to the public what he saw, and thus to stimulate discussion. In his criticisms, he wrote about the playwright's unique ability to connect with the audience and to convey direct, honest emotions without design or literary trappings that might interfere with their authenticity. He maintained that no matter the reputation or history of a particular theatre in Paris, such as the Odéon, it must belong to its "quartier" and present dramas that appealed to those who lived there; he believed that the best theatre should be rooted in communities.

His inherent good taste and intelligence, and important connections led him to arrange for the publication of Proust's first novels in the series *A la Recherche du Temps perdu*. Blum's exceptional sensitivity to Proust's unrecognized genius catapulted the solitary and eccentric author into fame, if not fortune. Other writers benefited as well. For example, Blum was not only the friend of the mercurial author Gabriele D'Annunzio; he was his collaborator in translating one of his most famous novels, *Forse che sì, forse che no*.

In his prologue to one of the first Cubist exhibitions, Blum wrote about how important Duchamp, Archipenko, and others were to the strategies of the early moderns. On a more practical note, he created an early union of writers and artists that defended their basic interests, an effort that was truly original and professionally essential. Blum's articles on art and theatre remain sound and inspired aesthetic discussions, exploring the most basic issues confronting visual artists as well as dramatists.

Blum's sensitivity to popular culture was at the heart of his skills as a producer. He adored the diverse geographies of contemporary films as well as the popular culture of the circus. Along with his colleague Ricciotto Canudo, he became president of the Cine Club of France (1920), and a passionate proponent of film as an art form as well as a profitable industry, exploring the power of cinematic imagery. In Monte Carlo, he presented many films for his lyric drama program and arranged for an orchestra to accompany these visual spectacles. He was one of the first people to realize that film could also serve as a memory, especially for ballet, as dance is so ephemeral. He encouraged his choreographer Massine to film rehearsals of his works.

From the tender age of twenty, as part of his attraction to the everyday making of art, Blum promoted the sale of decorative art. French business seemed hostile to fresh forms in the arts and crafts, except for the work of a few audacious artists. Blum founded a publishing house, Les Éditions Choumine, where in a series of documentary works he introduced the artists who, twenty-two years later, were to ensure the success of the Paris Exposition of Decorative Arts in 1925. Blum was one of the architects of this exhibition, displaying his passion for fashion, crafts, and the publication of art books that he avidly collected and wrote about. Some of the era's most famous artists designed illustrations for classic and modern tales in these beautiful books.

Love of arts did not preclude love of country. In 1914, though already thirty-six years old, Blum enlisted in World War I, and was assigned as an interpreter to the English 19th Quartermaster Squadron (Equipages); he remained "under the colors" for the duration of the war. Not least among his accomplishments was the distinction of earning the Croix de Guerre for his courage under fire during the battle of the Somme. He knew of the paintings in the Amiens Cathedral and had the resolve to systematically remove a number of magnificent artworks under intense enemy fire. He also volunteered to recover other works of art lost in the military zone.

After the war, he took over the management of the publishing house Librairie de France, where he helped issue a series of works devoted to great writers such as Flaubert, Verlaine, and Daudet, with illustrations by prominent contemporary artists. He also published encyclopedias, most notably a sports encyclopedia in two volumes, which represented the most outstanding and complete work on sports of the time.

Blum made his most inventive and valued contributions as a purveyor of and publicist for original and classical theatre and dance. In Monte Carlo he staged 140 different productions, including 40 premiere productions of English dramas such as St. John Ervine's *Anthony and Anna*, which was first produced in Monte Carlo and had a run of 1,200 performances in London. He knew that for years George Bernard Shaw had been unappreciated by French audiences, but decided that the luminous Russian actress Ludmilla Pitoëff would make a brilliant Saint Joan; Shaw's *Sainte Jeanne* received superior reviews in Monte Carlo, and afterwards it took Paris by storm. He recognized Marcel Pagnol's exceptional talent and presented *Jazz*, Pagnol's first play to become an immense success.

One of Blum's striking attributes was his ability to edit and rework plays and operettas in performance. He knew how best to present the scenarios, with a careful eye to his audience and to the theatre where they were performed, adding musical scores that were appropriate for the dramatic intention. And he was a superb writer, enhancing or taking out dialogue to insure a play's success, yet always sensitive to issues of copyright and the author's wishes. Several productions carried his pseudonym René Bergeret. He co-wrote under his own name one or two plays, most notably *Les Amours du poète* with Georges Delaquys. The play was about the great poet Heinrich Heine, who fell madly in love with his cousin Amélie. The reviews in Monte Carlo and Paris spoke glowingly of the thoughtful way Blum integrated Schumann's Dichterliebe music, a charming choreographic pantomime by George Balanchine, Heine's exquisite poetry, and his own dialogue. Unfortunately, Blum's crushing schedule made it impossible for him to create more of his own original works.

In the history of dance, Blum is revered for having saved the Ballets Russes from probable extinction after the death of Diaghilev in 1929. A close colleague and "student" of Diaghilev's during the many years the Ballets Russes played in Monte Carlo, Blum realized that the ballet had to go on despite the death of its founder. He quickly began to reassemble the important artists in the company, rehiring in 1932 Serge Grigoriev, who possessed a keen knowledge of repertoire, as ballet master. Blum also brought in George Balanchine as master choreographer and teacher, Léonide Massine as a dancer and choreographer, Bronislava Nijinska and Boris Kochno as artistic advisors, among others. He made the unfortunate choice of Colonel de Basil as his co-director, soon regretting that decision as the Colonel proved an unreliable partner. He was unable to disengage from the Colonel until 1936.

Blum nurtured and encouraged the making of many important works in the ballet repertoire, drawing on world famous painters, designers, and composers. The debut performances of his company included Balanchine's exciting *Cotillon* and *La Concurrence*, and soon after, Massine's unique symphonic innovations *Les Présages*, *Choreartium*, and *Seventh Symphony*.

Several years later, Blum formed his own Ballets de Monte-Carlo, and hired Michel Fokine as the director of ballet. During that time Fokine created *L'Épreuve d'Amour, Les Éléments*, and *Don Juan*. Over the years, Blum's companies toured London, Paris, and many European cities, and traveled to South Africa as well. Most importantly, they experienced huge success across America, so that when it became clear that Europe was to fight another war, Blum sold his company to the American impresarios Serge Denham and Julius Fleischmann. Retaining shares in the company, Blum traveled with them, watching rehearsals and performances until 1940 when the war broke out and he chose to return to his family in Paris. There he began a film about Molière, only to find himself trapped by the Vichy government, unable to work as a result of the anti-Jewish racial laws during the German Occupation.

Perhaps more precious than any other quality, Blum had a gift for loyalty and friendship. The homages written for Blum after his death included many compliments, as well as long lists of his accomplishments. But foremost among the encomia were descriptions of his warmth, gallant generosity, and lack of self-interest. Georges Huisman, state councilor and former general director of fine arts for the French government, recalled that in 1936, at the height of Blum's career, he asked Blum to run two of the most important theatres in Paris: the Opéra and the Opéra Comique. Blum declined, saying that as long as his brother was prime minister, he must remain in Monte Carlo, so as to avoid any suggestion of family privilege.

In another essay, the astonishing artist Jean Cocteau paid tribute to Blum's unique qualities of kindness and devotion. Cocteau wrote about Blum's "grace and ardor," more suited to someone who lived in a fantasy world than to someone preoccupied with the most practical details of life. Blum and Cocteau would take "interminable" nocturnal walks through Paris, in conversation until daylight came. On these long wanderings, Cocteau discovered Blum's generosity, and his ease in accepting others' secrets and confessions. Blum helped Cocteau "to forget the cold and egotistical world." He found comfort in Blum's long perorations on art.[4] Others as well noted Blum's gentle soul and empathy as something more than vague sentiments; Romain Coolus ascribed to Blum a "perspicacious intuition that women possess in the highest degree, a tenderness that enveloped all of René Blum's being, something of the grace and delicacy of women."[5]

Thus, Blum not only lived a life in the service of art and beauty, but also gave many fellow artists courage and modeled an exalted view of human relations. How tragic that we lost him to the Holocaust along with his autobiography *Souvenir sur la Danse*, a detailed history of his contributions to ballet history, and meditations on his life and art. I hope in this book to bring back to life this marvelous man whom the world should remember and know better.

CHAPTER 1

Childhood and Youth

The Formation of an Intellectual and Aesthete

René Möise Blum was born in Paris, the city of light, on March 13, 1878, the youngest of five boys. Above a bustling, heavily populated mercantile street in an apartment at 151 rue Saint-Denis, his parents, Marie-Adèle-Alice Picart and Auguste Blum, raised their sons in a loving and inspiring household. Historian William Logue characterized Saint-Denis as a "long depressing, urban street where small merchants lived frugally above their businesses.... It was a place more populated than popular, and haunted by memories of worker rebellions."[1]

Auguste had grown up in Westhoffen, a city in Alsace southwest of Strasbourg, but moved to Paris in 1848 in search of better opportunities.

At first employed by Moïse Léon, Auguste soon opened his own wholesale silk and ribbon store. He had several business partners; when they retired, he bought out their shares and become proprietor along with his brothers Henri and Émile. According to historian Serge Berstein, as the market for women's clothes grew in the late nineteenth century, "A brisk business for Blum Frères developed in rubans, soieries, velours, tulle, dentelles."[2] Taking advantage of the hearty growth in industrial Paris, Blum Frères managed to stay in business despite changes in women's fashions. However, when Auguste died in 1921, the company was already failing, and the 1929 market crash dealt the final blow to the family's finances.[3]

The original store stood in the old neighborhood of Les Halles, the famous food market where dozens of peddlers filled the streets. The Paris of the Third Republic, into which the Blum brothers were born, was undergoing enormous changes that would create the modern city of Paris. After 1880, gas lights, elevators, steam heat, toilets, and baths became the norm in new apartment buildings, soon to be followed by electric lighting and an

Figure 1.1
Auguste Blum's home in Westhoffen, Alsace-Lorraine. Courtesy of Centre d'histoire de SciencesPo.

underground metro system. The French celebrated this new metropolis in the expositions of 1878, 1889, and 1900, the last of which attracted 50,860,801 visitors.[4] British historian Alistair Horne noted that this figure equaled more than the whole population of France. The world came to Paris because, as Colin Jones, also a British historian, said, "The expositions celebrated the cult of technology and industrial production."[5]

Admiration for the machine age was not universal; some writers and artists questioned the values that had destroyed the old Paris in order to create the new, and decried the deprivation suffered by the workers in the suburbs. The central part of the city, with its magnificent department stores, parks and promenades, and, above all, the Eiffel Tower (erected in 1889 to celebrate the centenary of the French Revolution), could not hide the poverty of the enlarging *banlieues*, workers' suburbs that surrounded the city. Jones commented that Paris "retained its ability to defy interpretation and to divide opinion. Dispute over the meanings of the city had become a debate over the nature of modernity, a debate in which non-Parisians the world over were free to participate. . . . The period of La Belle Époque was thus also that of the fin de siécle."[6]

Social issues continued to plague both urban and rural areas. The esteemed English historian Alfred Cobban wrote that "France evidently remained under the Republic what it had been under the Monarchy and the

Figure 1.2
Portrait of Auguste Blum. Courtesy of Francine Hyafil.

Empire, a socially intense and conservative country."[7] Political tensions swirled beneath the modernist façade of the Third Republic, whose constitution had given the vote to all adult males. "From the ashes of the Commune," on the left, a new Socialist movement developed.[8] The first Labor Day celebration on May 1, 1890, attracted some 100,000 workers. By 1895, the Confédération Générale du Travail (the CGT) had begun campaigning for worker rights such as the eight-hour workday. The left grew increasingly militant as anarchists turned to violence.

René Blum's eldest brother, Lucien, was born in 1870, Léon in 1872, Marcel in 1874, and Georges in 1876. Eventually, Lucien, Marcel, and Georges worked in the office of Blum Frères, but René and Léon had other dreams.

A family friend, Thadée Natanson, described Auguste as a shrewd, upright Jewish merchant who cared deeply for his business. Modest and known as a lover of nature, especially flowers, Auguste had a conciliatory disposition; kind and diplomatic, he was particularly attracted to clear

Figure 1.3
Portrait of Blum brothers. First row from left: Georges, René, and Marcel; in back: Lucien and Léon.
Courtesy of Centre d'histoire de SciencesPo.

thinking, to facts and a precise way of looking at things. Although financially acquisitive, he was discreetly and anonymously generous and chari-
table. He sought constant instruction and learning; quite gifted in
languages, he knew Hebrew, German, French, and understood English.[9]
René seems to have inherited many of Auguste's talents and his equitable
disposition.

In 1869, Auguste married Picart, whose family was originally from Alsace, and whose mother, Henriette, owned a bookshop on the Place Dauphine, not far from the Palais de Justice, where lawyers and students of law brought their texts. Widowed at a young age, Henriette had a strong character and a passion for poetry and literature, especially the writers Victor Hugo and George Sand. She had republican sentiments, hostile to the regime of Napoléon III, that led her to sympathize with the Commune and with the hope for a just society. Therefore, having inherited these values from her mother, early on Marie-Adéle taught her sons the humanistic and Jewish values of charity and justice. Léon later told a story about his mother that echoed these precepts:

> She was the most just being I have ever known. I have never encountered anyone else with such an intensity of scruple. She carried the sentiment of justice to melancholy extremes. . . . Have I ever told you the story of the apples? I was raised with a brother a little older than myself. When my mother gave us apples for a snack, she did not give each of us a whole apple. She cut two apples in half and gave each of us one half from each apple. It was only in this way that the division seemed equal to her.[10]

René's mother and grandmother reflected the new voice of French feminism as articulated by Marguerite Durand, who established the journal *La Fronde* in 1897. This was a period in which women once again strove for the right to vote and the right to divorce. Under the façade of la Belle Époque, politics, class, and gender divided society, and René's grandmother and mother exemplified the new woman who espoused workers' and feminists' causes.[11]

French middle-class Jews of the late nineteenth and early twentieth centuries often did not observe restrictive culinary habits, nor did they necessarily hold to the Sabbath. They were eager to be French, to work when it was necessary, and not to structure their lives with religious obligations. But René's mother affiliated with orthodoxy and kept a kosher home, in part as the neighborhood stores sold kosher products. Lucien wrote in his diary, "When I think about my mother's piety as a Jewish woman, I can only imagine that she was the epitome of what one means when one uses the word piety in any religious sense."[12] He added that when his mother wished for something, she always added, "If it pleases God," as a token of her faith.[13] As the family professed a deep and abiding dedication to equality of opportunity, regardless of birthright, it is no wonder that Léon became a Socialist.

René's niece, Françoise Nordmann, and great-niece, Francine Hyafil, recalled that Marie-Adèle Picart also emphasized Friday evening meals as important family gatherings. She knew the Sabbath prayers, and tried to imbue her children with a sense of Jewish culture. All five boys were trained

a nos chers enfants

Figure 1.4
Portrait of René's parents—Auguste Blum and Marie-Adèle Picart. Courtesy of Centre d'histoire de SciencesPo.

in Hebrew for their bar mitzvahs, and the holidays of Pesach (Passover), Rosh Hashanah, and Yom Kippur were part of their parents' ceremonial calendar. Yet none of the young men professed to be religious; they all sought an assimilated life, despite their strong "esprit de famille" and their close ties to other Jews. Their mother welcomed their friends and was considered a warm conversationalist. In a letter to his mother in 1890, the writer André Gide, a close friend to Léon and René, spoke of "maman Blum" who kept him convivial company while waiting for the busy Léon, who tended to be late for appointments.[14]

Madame Katz, Auguste's sister Tante Ernestine, also had a profound influence on the brothers. Much younger than René's mother, and without children, she showered a great deal of love and affection on the young Blums. Her intelligence and beauty were enhanced by a marvelous gaiety and sense of humor.

Since little is known about René's youth, we must piece together the facts as they are described by family members and make assumptions based on their experiences. From what his niece Françoise and his great-niece Francine have said, the Blum brothers seem to have been educated in similar ways. As the youngest in a large family, René was coddled and adored, and apparently not held to high standards. He was considered a bit fragile, yet imperturbable. Léon's literary entourage designated René "le Blumet" and "l'Infortunio," appellations that arose from his being the youngest brother, and from his melancholy nature. Indeed, his destiny seemed wrapped up in these diminutive titles. Léon became an attorney and a Socialist politician, while René sought his fortune in theatre and the arts.

René's niece, Jacqueline Lancrey-Javal, described his education as following in the footsteps of his older brothers, especially Léon, and explained that René continued on to "une école commérciale" after the lycée, rather than to a university.[15] Like his brothers, he attended elementary school at the Pension Roux, a boarding school on the rue d'Aboukir near his home. The Blum boys were sent from their parents' tiny apartment to learn basic French in pre-schools. Lucien recalled the school he attended where he was put when he was six years old: he remembered being afraid in the sleeping quarters, in spite of their lovely view of the gardens. Every morning a clock would wake them up; "The *maîtres* were kind, but the food was mediocre." Sunday morning, Lucien's parents fetched him and brought him home, sending him back in the evening with a box of chocolate cookies that should have lasted the whole week, but that he consumed by the next day.[16] After the Pension Roux, the boys boarded at the Pension Kahn at 26 rue Francs-Bourgeois. Apparently, they all hated the schoolmaster, M. Kahn, "and his idiotic son who put on grand airs."[17] René moved on to the Lycée Henri IV and later enrolled at the Lycée Charlemagne (in an old seventeenth-century *hôtel* near the Bastille).

The brothers Blum all appreciated language and poetry, especially Lucien, Léon, and René, but Georges had more scientific interests. He completed his medical studies in 1904 with a thesis on diphtheria. Not finding a medical internship discouraged him, but he was able to serve as a physician at the front during the entire First World War. For most of his life, he played piano, sang, and enjoyed entertaining the family with his music.[18]

René was especially musical. His friend Georges Huisman, who became an important artistic advisor in the government, a conseiller d'etat and general director of fine arts, said of René's knowledge of music, "He knew in detail every score and kept a complete record in his memory of all the most

Figure 1.5
Portrait of Blum brothers. Seated from left: René and Lucien; standing from left: Marcel, Léon, and Georges. Courtesy of Centre d'histoire de SciencesPo.

distinguished instrumentalists and singers."[19] It is thus not surprising that the René Blum archives at the Bibliothéque nationale in Paris contain dozens of scores with Blum's notations.

The musical and artistic bent of the Blum brothers was enhanced by their language abilities. Jewish families from Alsace spoke German and Yiddish at home, but knew it was essential to read and write in French. When the Blum boys were growing up, it was assumed that German would be their second language and that fluency in English would be an excellent addition. Anthony Eden, the British foreign secretary, visited Léon at the Quai Bourbon in 1936 when Léon was prime minister. Léon was unsure of his English, so his great-niece Francine, who at the age of fifteen knew quite a bit of English, served as his interpreter. Léon was never able to speak English fluently, whereas René saw its value and learned it early on. His knowledge of English eventually led René to be posted with an English battalion as an interpreter during World War I. Later as a ballet producer traveling with the company to England and America, he felt comfortable speaking with the press and negotiating its affairs.

The eldest Blum son, Lucien, who wrote reams of poems and verses, was sent at a very early age to England to learn the business of selling silks and ribbons. He never finished his baccalaureate, taking over the Blum Frères business when his father died in 1921. In his seventies, he wrote, sadly, "Truly, I regret every day that I only wrote for the theatre as an amateur."[20] But from René's earliest writings, it is evident that the youngest boy would not let anything interfere with his desire for a career in the arts.

Acceptance into the system of high schools, or "lycées," in Paris was essential to the career of any respectable middle-class youth, especially a young person who wanted to join the city's lofty intellectual circles. Central to academic training in France was a commitment to a classical education. Latin and Greek texts were foremost in the curriculum and the crowning glory, it seemed, was the philosophy "Bachot," or baccalaureate, that promised a position in higher education or in the government. The degree's emphasis on language and literature, with its close study of carefully selected texts, prepared René for his career in journalism and subsequently in the theatre, although no record exists that he actually passed his "Bachot." Like his brother Léon, he learned to look critically at works of literature and dramatic pieces, and to write clearly and precisely about them. He shared with his brother an idealistic streak, not for politics but for a world in which the arts were produced freely and enjoyed, without economic or governmental constraints. Beyond that, René had a gift for friendship, and his relationships with artists and schoolmates at top academic institutions endured throughout his life. They were his entrée to Parisian society.

By the sea in Brittany, Normandy, and Bordeaux, the brothers, their friends, parents, and several large Jewish families joined together for the summer holidays. By the end of the nineteenth century, the Blums had country homes in Enghien and at Val-Changis near Avron, just northwest of Paris. Enghien offered a quieter and gentler life style, with many frequent guests, especially musicians such as Alfred Cortot, Reynaldo Hahn, Pablo Casals, Jacques Thibaud and occasionally Maurice Ravel and Gabriel Fauré.[21] All the Blum brothers made a point of gathering with their siblings on such occasions.

In her charming autobiography, *Le Pain Polka*, Thadée Natanson's niece Annette Vaillant recalled those sweet summers by the sea in 1910, 1911, and 1912, at Criquebeuf near Villerville in Normandy. As a young hostess, she attended to the needs of her family's guests—E. Vuillard, Romain Coolus, Sam Aron, Pierre Bonnard, Catulle Mendès—and listened to their many stories of love and romance. Vaillant reminisced, "And always there was the eternally young René Blum."[22] "Among our most amicable friends was René Blum, our 'Blumet' engaged at the very Parisian *Gil Blas*. I see him climbing up the path from the beach in the company of a very young actress who seemed to have just escaped from a Gainsborough portrait, and who was just opening in a Max Dearly show."[23] Annette's father was Alfred Natanson and her mother the actress Marthe Mellot, who was portrayed often in Vuillard's paintings and later appeared in René Blum's theatrical productions in Monte Carlo.

During these summers by the sea, life was carefree and everyday concerns suspended. Buoyancy and mirth lifted spirits and countered the dreariness of Paris's gray skies and winter rains. At Val-Changis, Suzanne Pereyra, the future wife of Paul Dukas, and her sister Thérèse, who became the second wife and great love of Léon Blum, often visited together. Cortot, Casals, the writer Tristan Bernard, and the controversial and sensual Misia and her then husband Thadée Natanson gathered there as well. Misia was to become an ardent admirer and supporter of the ballet impresario Serge Diaghilev—indeed, "his best friend," as her biographers Gold and Fitzdale declared.[24]

On important holidays, the Blum family visited a nearby synagogue on the rue de la Victoire in Paris; the five brothers would come together, if only twice a year, to remember their parents after they had died. Years later, in 1941 during the Occupation, Lucien wrote in his diary: "We all met at 8 am on the rue de la Victoire for the anniversary of our father's death. The synagogue was badly heated and the absence of music created a depressing atmosphere. The Rabbi gave an emotional sermon for the new month. We returned home in the company of Georges and René, who brought with him the unedited manuscript of *Faust* by Edmond Rostand."[25]

As young men, both René and Léon adored the excitement and charm of a dizzy social life, especially dancing, as organizing balls was one of Léon's specialties. Leading a cotillon, revolving in a quadrille, and whirling around to a merry waltz tune were chief among his favorite evening pastimes. In one biography of Léon Blum, Fraser and Natanson narrated a story:

> The French Foreign Minister, M. Ribot in the early 90s was working in his room in the Quai d'Orsay. Suddenly the door opened and a couple of youngsters burst in, they saw the minister, cast a glance round the room and murmured an apology and disappeared. "Who on earth are these impertinent youngsters?" "Oh that's only Little Bob and his brother René. He is organizing the ball that takes place here tonight and must have mistaken the room."[26]

René loved to dance and to entertain others by quoting poetry or acting out different classical roles. When René and Léon left the all-boy atmosphere of their school, Léon was eager to play the man-about-town and quickly fell in love with the "young and tender fair sex." He was called "Little Bob" after a character in a popular novel by Madame Gyp. Being young and clever, he meandered in and out of Parisian society where he danced, smiled, and talked his way into every conceivable circle, and was the very image of impertinent charm.[27] One can only imagine René following in his admired older brother's path.

Finding entertaining pursuits, though, was only a small part of the Blums' activities. They cared deeply about social issues, and the Socialism that engrossed the family, despite their entrepreneurial undertakings, drew Léon to the celebrated Socialist Lucien Herr, the librarian at the École Normale, which Léon attended. They met in 1891, when Herr was twenty-seven years old and Léon nineteen. Herr was an Alsatian Catholic who opted for La France in 1870 when Germany acquired Alsace. Attracted to the writings of Hegel, he encouraged his young disciples to read the German philosopher's works. Although Herr was a librarian and not a teacher, he held court over an entire generation of young and elite college students, or "normaliens," those who had attended the École Normale and were destined to assume power in France then, as they still do today. Prestige, ideological dominance, prerogative, and vested authority were the gifts bestowed on graduates of the École Normale. Herr, who reigned over the books and the ideas purveyed in them, excited, distracted, and amused the young men. Even though Léon was for a brief time a "normalien," he was careful not to be swayed by Herr's leftist politics. It was only after Léon opted for a law degree years later, at the University of Paris, that the two became good friends, and Léon an acknowledged Socialist.

The Dreyfus affair galvanized Léon, the Socialists, and motivated French citizens; it was Lucien Herr who brought Léon Blum to the defense of Dreyfus. The case became the center of a political struggle between two forces: traditional French society (as represented by the army, the Catholic Church, as well as the surviving elements of the old aristocracy, who were against the Revolution, the Third Republic) and the modernizing influences of a new technological society. Jones observed that "tensions at the heart of politics over mass politics and women's rights were given a new ethnic and political focus in the mid-1890s by the Dreyfus Affair."[28]

Alfred Dreyfus was born in 1859 into a wealthy, assimilated Jewish family from Alsace that settled in Paris after the war of 1870. He studied at the École Polytechnique and entered the army as an engineer. In 1892, he was appointed to the general staff where he was the only Jew. In the fall of 1894, Major H. T. Henry accused Captain Dreyfus of being a spy for the Germans based on a secret military document, the "bordereau," or memo. French military intelligence in Paris discovered that the memo had been sent by a French officer thought to be Dreyfus, to Colonel von Schwartzkoppen, the German military attaché. Dreyfus was arrested and tried in a military court martial. Unfortunately for Dreyfus, the members of the court were given secret military documents that were later discovered to be forgeries, and that were never revealed to Dreyfus's attorney. Convicted and sentenced to life imprisonment on January 5, 1895, he was demoted and degraded publicly, with the anti-Semitic press inciting the populace, and he was then exiled to Devil's Island in French Guinea. This happened despite the fact that the German ambassador to France declared Germany had never had contact with Dreyfus.

The new head of French Intelligence, Lieutenant Colonel Georges Picquart, had sensed independently that something was amiss in the accusations made about Dreyfus and his eventual conviction. In March 1896, French Intelligence discovered a letter that General Schwartzkoppen had written to a French officer of Hungarian origin, Major Ferdinand Walsin Esterhazy, that made it clear Esterhazy was a German agent, and that he might have written the memo that convicted Dreyfus.

Major Henry then forged additional documents to prove to his superiors that the court martial had been justified. Considered a threat by the officer corps, Picquart was dismissed from his position and sent to a remote post in Africa. However, before he left, he sent a summary of the facts to his friends, which in turn reached the leftist Senator August Scheuer-Ketner, who proclaimed in the French Senate that Dreyfus was innocent and openly accused Esterhazy. The right-wing prime minister F. J. Méline did not believe that Dreyfus was innocent and tried to obscure the evidence. Esterhazy was tried and acquitted, while the courageous Picquart was punished with sixty days of imprisonment.

While Dreyfus continued to languish on Devil's Island, on January 13, 1898, Georges Clemenceau, the editor of the newspaper *L'Aurore*, published an open letter from Émile Zola to the president of the republic, "J'Accuse," which sold 200,000 copies. Because the officers of the general staff believed that the honor of the army was more important than any one officer's innocence, they threatened to resign if Dreyfus was retried and acquitted. Zola wrote that "the Dreyfus court martial may have been unintelligent, but the Esterhazy court martial was criminal."[29] Zola was tried on a charge of defamation; Léon contributed legal assistance to his defense.[30] Anti-Semitic riots broke out in France and in the French North African colonies, and Zola fled to England for eighteen months to avoid imprisonment. By then France had split into two camps. The Ligue des Droits de l'Homme advocated for Dreyfus; the Ligue de la Patrie Française held against him, led by Paul Déroulède, who asserted, "A single case of injustice involving one Jew was not sufficient grounds for staining the honor of the army."[31]

In the summer of 1898, public protests led to a reopening of the case. Henry's forgeries were detected and he was arrested, only to commit suicide in his cell at the Mont Valerian fortress.[32] Dreyfus was brought back to France for a new military trial, and he was once again convicted and sentenced to ten years. Shortly thereafter, he was pardoned by the president of the republic. In 1904, after a fresh investigation, he was finally exonerated. In 1906, he was restored to the army as a major, and later served with distinction in World War I.

The Dreyfus affair increased the chasm between the left and the right, conservatives and liberals, the Church and the republic, leaving a bitterness that undermined French society until the debacle of the Second World War and the Vichy regime of General Maréchal Petain, leader of France under the Nazis. Although not fully appreciated even by those close to the affair, anti-Semitism was becoming an important force in France. The consequences went on for years; a writer and editor of several journals, Fernand Gregh, described the Dreyfus affair as a civil war "where the French deployed forces that broke old friendships, divided families, reconciled 30 year enemies, and briefly led to a redefinition of parties."[33]

Until the Dreyfus affair, René's brother Léon had considered anti-Semitism to be a social matter. As the American historian William Logue explained: "More importantly, the affair brought the first full-scale political attack on Jews in modern French history, but Blum's experiences had not prepared him to see the nature of this attack."[34]

Léon, and probably René, were too intellectual and too assimilated to see themselves as anything but French. Yet Léon certainly became more aware of his Jewish identity and more sympathetic to Jewish values, especially justice, which were in harmony with the appeal of Socialism. It is not known to what extent René was influenced by anti-Semitism. However, when he wrote for the theatre, he took the pseudonym M. Bergeret, the name of the protagonist who decried Dreyfus's cruel treatment in a novel by Anatole France.

Léon later wrote a book on the Dreyfus affair. His brothers, along with Léon's close colleagues Jean Jaurès, Lucien Lévy-Bruhl, and Lucien Herr, all believed passionately in the innocence of Dreyfus and were convinced that this belief could engage others' sympathies. According to Léon, "Our certainty was pure, solid and serious, and we were convinced that the whole world would spontaneously agree with us as soon as they understood what we already knew ourselves."[35]

Gregh recalled in *L'Âge d'Or* that he wasn't the only writer and artist of his generation who believed that Dreyfus was not guilty: "We were all young people of the same opinion. A group of us met together two or three times above the Café des Variétés to plan our strategy." Included were Elie and Daniel Halévy, Jacques Bizet, Louis de la Salle, Marcel Proust, Robert de Flers, maybe Robert Proust (brother of Marcel), and Jacques Bonzon.[36]

The two Halévy brothers, Bizet, de Flers, Léon Yeatman, and Louis de la Salle collected signatures on behalf of Dreyfus. Dr. Proust, Marcel's father, was a confirmed anti-Dreyfusist, and a personal friend of almost every minister in the government. Father and sons barely spoke as a result. The "manifesto of 104," signatures proclaiming Dreyfus's innocence organized by Marcel Proust and his friends, was soon followed by statements from many professors at the Sorbonne, including Proust's schoolmaster Darlu and Paul Desjardins, whose philosophy lectures he had attended when studying for his *licence en droit*. Not unexpectedly, the egotistical Proust proclaimed proudly: "I was the first Dreyfusard."[37] As Léon and René made their way into the Parisian upper class, their social ties to important businessmen, influential politicians, and the intellectual elite were potentially dangerous for them. Anti-Semitism was rife in the ministries, the government, and the Church. The Dreyfus affair unleashed such virulent feelings and struck to the heart of French life. It was a defining period in French history and in literary history as well, since it pitched the great authors of the time against one another in unexpected ways. The young and impressionable René must have felt the daunting consequences of this event.

The bourgeois salons were either neutral or Dreyfusard. According to the critic George Painter, "The Affair, it might be claimed, had begun at the salon of Mme. Bizet-Straus which became the general headquarters of Dreyfusism." Geneviève Straus, the widow of Georges Bizet, was capable of sacrifice in the cause of truth, and Painter said, "Her beauty resided in the sincerity of her expression, the fervour of her eyes ('like black stars,' said

Abel Hermant) and the elegance of her dress." She created a salon where people came because they had intelligent things to say.[38] Straus hosted the aristocrats Prince Auguste d'Arenburg, Comte d'Haussonville (Mme. de Stael's relative), Princesse Mathilde, Louis de Turenne, Lord Lytton, Lady de Grey, and later, the Marchioness of Ripon and Reggie Lister. Fernand Gregh described Mme. Straus as "a very intelligent and spiritual woman. She was deliciously female, especially as her mind brought together a certain kind of common sense elevated by an astonishing gaiety. She would often articulate the most profound thoughts in the most innocent way."[39] The daughter of Ludovic Fromental Halévy, composer of the celebrated opera *La Juive*, she married her first husband, Georges Bizet, in 1869. Soon after Bizet died in 1875, she married Émile. Judaism played a major role in her life, especially when the Dreyfus affair shocked French society. With her help, Proust gathered signatures of 3,000 artists and writers to bolster Dreyfus's case.

Mme. Straus's husband Émile Straus devoted his life and his enormous wealth to the clothing and social career of his wife. Her noble guests were loyal to her despite the tensions caused by the Dreyfus affair, and continued to attend her home on Saturdays. There the first *Aurore* petition was organized to gain signatures in favor of Dreyfus's innocence.[40] Her friend Joseph Reinach was one of the chief agitators for Dreyfus. Unfortunately, a few were opposed to Mme. Straus's political views. For example, Mme. Haussonville began to pronounce Mme. Straus's name as "Schtraus," to emphasize her Jewish heritage.[41]

Proust's meetings with the famed Guy de Maupassant took place in the salon of Mme. Straus, which Maupassant frequented in the late 1880s. For a time, Maupassant was in love with his hostess and he made her one of the heroines in his last novel, *Fort comme la Mort*. Painter observed that "Mme. Straus's wit is important, for Proust made it his chief model for the celebrated Guermantes wit."[42] In another monumental encounter, Proust met Oscar Wilde at Mme. Straus's where, as Gregh noticed, the two men eyed one another with complex curiosity.[43]

At a particularly crucial time in the course of the Dreyfus retrials, Anatole France called on Proust; he asked Marcel to secure from Mme. Straus the influence of one or more big names in her salon, preferably that of the Comte Othenin d'Haussonville.[44] But sadly, Mme. Straus had developed a facial tic, and had seen her salon suffer grievously for Dreyfus's sake. She was already approaching the intermittent nervous exhaustion by which she was to be tortured for the remaining twenty-eight years of her life (her mother, sister, and aunt died insane). She lost heart and gave up this monumental project. Painter remarked that her demise was not unlike Proust's. "During the last year or two, she lapsed into "a state of vague neurasthenia . . . and was condemned to solitude, silence and darkened rooms."[45] Later, she was committed to the sanatorium overseen by Dr. Widmer, where both René Blum and Proust visited her occasionally; located near Montreux in Territet, it was called Valmont.

The "Jewish salons" attracted a lot of attention, and curious outsiders tried to fathom the ways that Jews managed their religious obligations. An interesting story by André Gide in his *Journals* commented on the way Jews described themselves and their religion. When Gide presented his play *Saul et David*, Alfred Natanson was quick to say in a casual conversation, "Besides I have never read the Bible." Taken aback, Gide, a devout Protestant and a Sunday School teacher, responded:

> It's odd the way all educated Jews I know make a point of honor of never having read the Bible. . . . What the devil are they afraid of finding in it? Nothing annoys me more. It's like Schwob [a famous scholar and writer] spreading papers over his mirrors. And this allows them not to admit their uglinesses; yes, but by the same token they miss their beauties. I must discuss this with Blum.[46]

Like many young men of his generation, René Blum frequented the places of business, cafés, and theatres where his family and friends gathered to discuss events of the day, as well as their artistic preferences. Léon took René with him to the offices of *Revue Blanche* (1891–1903), one of the foremost arts and literature journals in France, launched by the Natanson brothers, Thadée and Alexandre. There, Léon published sophisticated dramatic and literary criticism along with Proust and other distinguished writers. *Revue Blanche* became René's after-school hangout, his "club." As he said in 1924,

> It is at *Revue Blanche* where almost all the famous writers in literature began their careers. When I was a young man, I recall meeting in the editorial room situated just above the first floor, Henry de Régnier, Paul Adam, Romain Coolus, Tristan Bernard, Mallarmé, Gide and many other writers making their debuts. Indeed, it was at *Revue Blanche* that many of the Impressionist painters also became celebrities: Seurat, Bonnard, Vuillard, Roussel, and Toulouse Lautrec.[47]

Claude Debussy, its resident music critic, signed his columns Monsieur Croche.[48] Henry de Régnier, the most admired poet of his young generation, also contributed to the *Revue Blanche*. His first books thrilled readers for their decorativeness and full splendor, in addition to a sense of mystery that gave way gradually to an acute psychological insight. As Gregh noted, "He was an eighteenth century man on which was superimposed a symbolist poet."[49]

Thadée Natanson knew René during this exciting period, and much later said that the young man met all these great people, such as Vuillard and Proust, but did not flaunt his friendships with them. He remained innocent growing up and did not promote the various literary and artistic currents surrounding him for his own advancement. Natanson found him incorruptible in this naiveté, a quality that he retained throughout his life.[50]

At this time, Thadée and Misia Natanson owned large country and city homes that provided lovely refuges for artists from the *Revue Blanche*, settings in which they could engage freely in intense conversations. There they chatted, played cards, argued, and reveled in one another's company, while Vuillard painted halcyon moments at the nearby villages of Saint-Jacut, Pouliguen, Villerville, Loctudy, and Cabourg.[51]

Vuillard, as well as Bonnard, painted many *scènes intérieures* and portraits of his friends, especially of Thadée's complex and ardent wife, Misia. The author Belinda Thomson surmised that the haute bourgeoisie intelligentsia were the sites where "Vuillard felt most at home. . . . He was also fascinated by the most exuberant, luxurious world when he associated with the aristocratic Lautrec and with 'the sensual Jewesses.' "[52] Vuillard painted a fine profile portrait of young René sitting at his desk, deeply absorbed in his writing while on holiday at one of those summer haunts.

Throughout his life, René lived in the shadow of Léon, trailing along beside him as a theatrical and literary critic, especially during Léon's precocious

Figure 1.6
Portrait of René Blum by Edouard Vuillard. Photo by Javier Hinojosa. Courtesy of Collection Museo Soumaya/Carlos Slim Foundation, A.C.

Figure 1.7
Blum brothers as adults. From left: René, Lucien, Marcel, Georges, and Léon. Courtesy of Francine Hyafil.

debut at the age of nineteen at *Revue Blanche*. Finding himself a home at *Revue Blanche*, René frequented the Bibesco brothers and began to know quite well Léon's friends such as the writers Fernand Gregh, Robert Dreyfus, and Marcel Proust, whom Léon originally met at the Sorbonne.

Proust's career began to blossom when he contributed short sketches to the respected but short-lived journal *Le Banquet* (1892–1893). *Le Banquet*, named for Plato's *Symposium*, was as Logue observed, "a slender poetry review of high aesthetic and typographic quality."[53] With the assistance of André Gide, Paul Valéry, and other mature writers, it produced a mere twelve elegant volumes of only one hundred copies each, all printed on deluxe paper. Proust's friends rather thought that he was a talented amateur. "He seemed to us far more anxious to find a way into certain drawing-rooms of the nobility than to devote himself to literature," commented Robert Dreyfus.[54] The publication was very favorable to foreign literature and Dreyfus did much to praise important Scandinavian writers. Its contributors were among the greatest poets of the time, including Paul Verlaine, Leconte de Lisle, José Maria de Héredia, Stéphane Mallarmé, and Algernon Swinburne. The writers varied in style, from Parnassians to Symbolists, and did not see themselves as rebels, but as artists who sought beauty in its essence.

When the *Revue Blanche* closed in 1903, René, with little discernible income except from his family, continued to live in the lofty circles of the Parisian artistic and literary intelligentsia, and especially in the Jewish salons of the period. He also became a theatre editor for *Gil Blas*, another prominent Parisian publication, known for its brilliant and witty columns. With the repercussions from the momentous Dreyfus affair, Léon chose a career in law and politics, but also became a regular reviewer of books for *Gil Blas* and the magazine *Comoedia*. René and Léon attended theatre productions with their eldest brother Lucien, as he too had a love and appreciation for live theatre. A prodigious writer, Léon joined the staff of the Socialist and later Communist newspaper *L'Humanité*, which devoted space to the arts and printed Léon Blum's column, "La Vie Littéraire." Reviews came out once a week, but while René's preoccupations rested with changes in modernist views of art and his passion for theatre, Léon's calling for politics and justice increased, and his belief in Socialism influenced his critiques of books and plays.

Like René, Proust loved the attention he received in fancy homes. The melancholic Proust was a charming dinner guest, lighthearted and ironic, especially when making imitations of the revered Anatole France and the infamous character Robert de Montesquiou. Proust impersonated not only their gestures and their words, but also their very souls. Gregh noted that when Proust play-acted, "What one heard for long periods of time were not only the words, but also the spirit of these people—it was exactly Robert de Montesquiou, and perfectly Anatole France."[55] Proust's talent for acting causes one to wonder to what extent he "played" at being a neuresthenically ill child to receive the attention he craved.

Proust adored Robert de Montesquiou, about whom he spoke most favorably, yet he took vengeance when he based his character Baron Charlus on Montesquiou, and thereafter, as Gregh fulminated, "nailed him to the cross of infamy for ever after."[56] Baron Charlus was the chief vehicle for the author's lengthy, detailed but compassionate treatment of homosexuality. Although Robert de Montesquiou is almost forgotten, from 1894 to 1910, he was the subject of many conversations and paintings, one notably by James Whistler for whom he sat dozens of times. He gave glittering parties, regarded as centers of tout Paris snobbism. René Blum had many opportunities to meet de Montesquiou and was quite taken by his flamboyant and outrageous display of androgynous sexuality. Blum revealed his sensitive liking for de Montesquiou in quite sentimental, even loving letters written to de Montesquiou when Blum served during World War I.

In his novels, Proust chose outlandish titles and names for his absurd characters, while his lovelorn male protagonists were "dazzling, young, heros of independent means"; he plumbed the "psychology of snobbism and love and jealousy in high society." Painter bemoaned the fact that "it was alarming to see in one so young so total a disenchantment, so final a disbelief in any values more real than those of the social marionette show he described."[57]

The majority of Proust's friends were engaged in love affairs with women: La Rochefoucauld, Antoine Bibesco, Georges de Lauris, the duc d'Albufera, Radziwill, and the duc de Guiche (who was half Jewish). The Marquis, later duc d'Albufera and Antoine Bibesco found that falling in love with actresses was an interesting hobby. However, Proust was more attracted to men.

One of René's closest friends, the eminent playwright Georges de Porto-Riche, told Antoine Bibesco as well as René Blum that reputations would suffer if they saw too much of Proust, citing Proust's odd, openly homosexual behavior.[58] And Léon Daudet gossiped maliciously that Proust's "ill health was due to taking morphine," a completely false statement.[59] Conservative thinkers seem always to stir up trouble when they fear the sexual proclivities of their winsome friends.

Proust encountered the Bibesco brothers at the Sorbonne in 1900, while attending Henri Bergson's lectures. Painter described Prince Antoine Bibesco's reaction to meeting Proust: he saw a "pale, slightly stooping young man, with unkempt black hair and black lacquer eyes who offered and quickly withdrew a drooping, childishly flabby hand."[60] Painter depicted Antoine as a "virilely handsome young man of 23, with stern chiseled features, implacable eyes, and a slightly cruel twist to his thin lips."[61]

Antoine's brother Emmanuel was René's fellow lycéen, a descendent of a princely Romanian family; Proust made friends with Emmanuel Bibesco, nicknamed L'Almée, "the dancing girl," for his tall, slightly effeminate, lissome shape, and sensual eyes. Emmanuel did not marry and unfortunately committed suicide at a young age. Antoine (1871–1951) became an attaché at the Romanian embassy in Paris where he was also known as a successful womanizer. Antoine introduced Proust to Comte Bertrand de Salignac-Fénelon, an intriguing young man who provided inspiration for the Marquis de Saint-Loup, one of Proust's major heroes.[62]

Another member of the family, Princesse Marthe Bibesco, was a beauty. Born a Lahovary, she married her cousin, Prince Georges Bibesco, in 1905 at the age of sixteen. Marthe's tribute to René in a 1950 collection of homages resounded with pity and sympathy for all of Blum's suffering at the end of his remarkably energetic life.[63] A cousin of Antoine and Emmanuel and of the famed writer Mme. de Noailles, she was linked through her husband's family or her own with Mme. Greffulhe, Montesquiou, Guiche, and just about everyone of note in Parisian society.[64]

Up the road from Proust's home on the rue de la Courcelles lived Hélène Bibesco, Marthe's cousin and widow of the Romanian prince Alexandre de

Bibesco. She was a virtuoso pianist whose salon was filled with famous musicians, artists, and aristocrats such as Liszt, Wagner, Gounod, and Saint-Saëns; there, Fauré played piano duets with her. In 1901, her guests included the writers Anatole France, Pierre Loti, Jules Lemaître, Maeterlinck, Georges de Porto-Riche, the composer Debussy, and the painters Bonnard, Vuillard, and Redon. The Blums, as well as Proust, were invited to her salon through her niece Mme. de Noailles, and her nephew Constantin de Brancovan.

Paris was a world of salons where small groups of devotées, or "plaideurs," came to meet and talk about their readings and inclinations, both political and social. It was in these weekly, sometimes monthly, gatherings at wealthy, influential homes that René built a world for himself, separate from that of his brother. The tall, rather regal René hobnobbed comfortably with writers and artists whose work he would promote and produce in the 1920s. As René Blum grew up, he fell even more in love with books and those who produced them, such as Georges de Lauris and Edmond See, and spent long evenings with Bertrand de Fénelon, the Bibescos, Marcel Proust, Tristan Bernard, and de Porto-Riche.

From these early ties, René's future in the theatrical arts was secured, as people who knew him liked and trusted him. In these circles René had the good fortune to converse with some remarkable personalities, and develop generally his own identity as a literary and artistic being.

In another recollection of those days, the writer Paul Reboux[65] recalled in the 1950 homages to Blum: "René was the fine artist—tender, amused, comprehensive, sensitive to all manifestations of art and with an excessive optimism." Reboux continued exultantly:

> He was magnificent, even though his finances were limited. He never wrote anything or did anything for money other than what he loved doing. He was a journalist, but he played the role of an amateur, the charming friend of openings of books or exhibitions. He was not a pedant, nor did he like obscurantism. He was always kind, with clemency and urbanity.[66]

In his memoirs from the same period, Fernand Gregh discussed his colleague Léon Blum and also mentioned his rather striking younger brother René, calling him "Le Fantasio" and "Le Fortunio."[67] But, as Gregh noted later, thanks to Tristan Bernard, René's appellation became rather prophetically "L'Infortunio."[68] Why might the young René, man about town, be associated with the Fantasio of Alfred de Musset, whose prose comedy *Fantasio* had been performed in 1866? We find in de Musset's Fantasio a tinge of the heroic, as well as the spunkiness of a renegade, and one senses that the young René impressed his "copains" with the same qualities. Furthermore, he possessed the easy-going, blithe spirit of a youngest child.

The French diplomat Philippe Berthelot (1866–1934), who moved gradually from director of political affairs to general secretary of the Ministry of Foreign Affairs, often visited the Blums' homes and established a fervent correspondence with both René and Léon Blum. All of the Blums were close to Philippe and his brother René Berthelot, the sons of the famed chemist Marcelin Berthelot. It was Philippe who introduced Léon and René Blum to Anatole France at Madame Caillavet's salon (her maiden name was Léontine Lippman), which France attended regularly. Logue surmised that "France, for his part, appears to have been attracted by Léon Blum's intellect."[69] The Caillavet salon became a center for Socialist politicians, especially Jean Jaurès. At her Villa Saïd, Mme. Caillavet also took on the Dreyfus cause, and Tristan Bernard and Anatole France strategized about how to spread the project to other circles.

In his tribute to René, the writer Romain Coolus reiterated that "above all activities, it was the theatre that most captivated René, such as Antoine's, Théâtre Libre, and Lugné Poe's Théâtre de l'Oeuvre."[70] Antoine and Lugné, discoverers of talented authors and artist designers such as Vuillard, were brilliant examples for René. From this moment in the early twentieth century, René imagined the possibility of bringing creative talents to the theatre. Coolus felt that Blum did not realize his own talents as a dramatic writer until he took over the theatres at Monte Carlo and Le Touquet, where he edited and rewrote a number of the plays in production.

Some of the authors with whom Blum collaborated lived with conflicted feelings about Jews, not really liking them as part of their French nationalism, but sensing the absurd and unethical madness of the accusations against Jews at the time. For example, the writer Colette was casually anti-Semitic, as was her mother. A friend of hers, Renée Hamon, "would observe that a lingering sense of anti-Semitism was 'native.'"[71] During the years of the Nazi Occupation, while some writers were vicious anti-Semites, many others courageously abandoned publishing since all articles had to be submitted to Vichy censors for their stamp of approval. Yet all writers were to some extent "collaborators" simply by virtue of their living through the war.[72]

Colette had no qualms about situating her work in the most pernicious editions of the pro-Vichy, pro-German press.[73] One of the supreme ironies of Colette's life was that her last husband, Maurice Goudeket, was a Jew; he was interned with René Blum for six weeks at the concentration camp in Compiègne, but was saved from deportation by a close friend of Colette, Misia Sert's third husband Jose Maria Sert, who collaborated openly with the Nazi regime.

The prestige of salon life in Paris exerted a passionate effect on fashion, the arts, and even ballet audiences. As a needy impresario for his Ballets Russes de Monte-Carlo, Serge Diaghilev's prime objective was to overwhelm the valuable salon devotées with notices about his precious company, and thereby acquire the funds, as well as the notoriety, the Ballets Russes needed in the late 1920s. The same salons frequented by Proust and the Blums were touted as cynosures for the chic ballet crowd. As Lynn Garafola aptly noted: "For Diaghilev and other entrepreneurs of modernism, these cross roads of Right Bank fashion and contemporary art defined the narrow world of their ventures: here, reputations were launched, commissions awarded, and audiences mustered for a theatrical debut."[74]

René Blum's affinity for contemporary style, as well as his appreciation for all that the Ballets Russes came to be known for, provided the foundation for his later project of recreating the Ballets Russes in Monte Carlo. Perhaps it was inevitable that he should find his way to Monte Carlo, where he would absorb the "look, the style and the tone," as Garafola discerned, "that Diaghilev promoted and that audiences relished."[75]

CHAPTER 2
René Blum, Man of Letters

For more than a decade, René Blum worked at the celebrated literary journal *Gil Blas*, first published in 1890 and closed at the onset of World War I. It is not clear exactly when his administrative work began, but his name figured in columns from 1903 to 1913. Blum's articles, reviews, and plays reflected his complex inner voices, revealing a personality that sought to stimulate journal readers, all of whom would have had great respect for his opinions. His theatrical and artistic columns conveyed a profound interest in criticism and analysis. When editing and writing, he created intellectual debates that revolved around practical issues for playwrights, directors, and producers. He often displayed an interest in questions about aesthetics or acting styles. The reader senses his desire to grapple with important suppositions and to hear opposing views. The French love of discourse and polemic was instilled in his very being.

Brought up during the late nineteenth century, Blum recognized the deep, injurious forces that divided France during the Dreyfus affair, and witnessed his brother Léon's passionate legal appeal in support of Émile Zola's famous letter "J'Accuse." Yet René also had to cope with the shock and disappointment of having his friends Edgar Degas and André Gide turn against Dreyfus; although Gide, in time, did come to his senses. Many famous writers were anti-Dreyfus as well—Jules Lemaître, Paul Valéry, René Bazin, Ferdinand Brunetière, Charles Maurras, Pierre Véber, and Léon Daudet, the son of Alphonse Daudet.

René's delight in theatrical styles such as vaudeville and operetta mirrored the popularity of these forms at the time. Tristan Bernard and Georges Courteline, about whom he wrote, were certainly models for him. He liked to take a light approach to performance as he enjoyed the display of wit and comedy, and the charms of music and dance. But he also appreciated tragic drama and classical theatre; during his final year, as he wandered the streets of Paris before the French militia and the Nazis took him, he was rereading Euripides.

In his formative years René developed a sense of popular culture, and of what excited and moved larger audiences. This later made him an excellent producer at theatre sites such as Pigalle, Le Touquet, and Monte Carlo, where vacationers tried to escape from the din and seriousness of city life. In scenarios for plays and operettas, Blum's writing assumed a bittersweet quality that bridged the realities of misfortune with the laughter of experience, so that audiences could react to romance with wonderment while always knowing that things may not turn out for the best.

René was also deeply affected by his brother's unique attraction to the debates surrounding many social issues including love and marriage. Léon published *Du Mariage*, a volume of essays on contemporary social mores that needed reforms, in 1907. These were, essentially, attacks on bourgeois conventions. He believed that love and marriage were possible, but insisted that sexual education was the key to a good marriage, suggesting that women needed to have sexual experience before marriage, that the prejudice for virginity had to be erased. Léon felt that women, as free agents, should also be permitted their dalliances during marriage, and that sexual appetites should not be responsible for destroying marriages; such casual liaisons were, he believed, distinct from marital friendships. Léon detested the authoritarianism and inequality observed in too many French marriages. All these ideas sent a shock wave through the more conservative elements of Parisian society.[1] It is ironic that René remained the only Blum who did not marry.

Naturally, René relished the controversies and reacted through the prism of theatrical plays and dramatic presentations, not only because the stage in France was a brilliant mirror of social politics at the beginning of the twentieth century, but also because he saw life in broad and dramatic terms. Both Léon and René were theatre critics, and understood the depth of the importance of "le théâtre d'amour," as Lacouture noted:

> Somewhat later, André Gide in a singular metonymy, would call Jewish Theatre the central theme of Léon Blum's book *On Marriage*. In effect, the theme was borrowed from a reply by a woman in love in Georges de Porto-Riche's play. The heroine suggested that in imitation of men, women should also experience without constraint premarital love.[2]

Many painters were also drawn to the theatre, especially Vuillard, who adored the wealthy Natanson and Hessel salons as well as the writers, critics, and dramatists like René who convened there. Vuillard found designing sets and backdrops for contemporary plays challenging and empowering, especially in light of the vogue for Symbolist ideas.[3] René was a frequent visitor to Lugné Poe's Théâtre de l'Oeuvre, founded in 1893, which brought Ibsen's controversial Scandinavian dramas to the Parisian public.

Vuillard's paintings exhibited something of the brooding moods found in those productions. He also linked his weekly visits to the Natansons and the Hessels with theatre audiences. For example, in his *Journal* for November 7, 1894, Vuillard referred to the Jewish salonnières set against the evening at Lugné's theatre—"all those sensual Jewesses, their silks shimmering in the shadows."[4] Attending the theatre was a major diversion for the haute bourgeoisie, and they relished all sorts of performance events, including the circus, popular middle-class comedies of the boulevard theatres, and avant-garde plays. When Joseph and Lucy Hessel entertained, they often invited Jewish writers such as Romain Coolus, Henry Bernstein, and Tristan Bernard. Bernard later married the actress Marcelle Aron, a cousin of Lucy Hessel. Tristan Bernard's play *Le Petit Café* was chosen by Vuillard as the subject for one of his decorations at the Théâtre des Champs-Élysées, where the Ballets Russes gave some of its most triumphant performances.[5] Apparently Vuillard, a bachelor who lived with his mother, carried on a love affair with Lucy Hessel, his patron, for forty years.[6]

While working for *Gil Blas* as an editor and overseer of theatrical events in Paris, Blum met and befriended many different kinds of artists, just as he did when tagging along with his brother Léon during the latter's *Revue Blanche* days. These relationships, whether personal or professional, served René well when he began to produce for both the theatre and the ballet. But the *Revue Blanche* closed its doors in 1903, whereupon many artists and writers sought new publishing venues for their essays. To fill the gap, in 1908, André Gide and others founded *La Nouvelle Revue Française*, which formulated the literature of the avant-garde. The NRF has been one of the longest-lasting journals in French letters, and marked the beginning of Gallimard, one of the greatest French publishers.

In one of René's first columns as editor for the October 9, 1903, issue of *Gil Blas*, he invited sophisticated readers to meditate on the profession of criticism, as a notorious argument had developed between a particular Parisian critic and the director of the Théâtre Antoine. The column was entitled "Polémique entre François de Nion et Théâtre Antoine."[7] Director Antoine had become fed up with what he considered critic François de Nion's partial and negative judgments that created a prejudice against Antoine's productions. Antoine wrote de Nion that he did not like his "tone," that he no longer requested his opinions of performances at the Antoine, and that going forward de Nion was barred from attending Antoine's theatre. In turn, François de Nion went to the Circle of Critics and protested, asserting that he was always impartial, and that surely he need not be an "admirateur" to keep his job. Antoine denied any personal dimension to his reaction, insisting instead that he had been taken aback by "sa critique," meaning the words that de Nion wrote. Antoine also denied that he sought the repression of this critic. But, he wondered, why should the critic have the right to say whatever he wished? Not timid about this discussion, René Blum asked, "What are the rights of critics? . . . Where do they begin and end?" He acknowledged that directors tended to believe a critic, who, regardless of solidarity with other critics, must be more sensitive and open to the work of the director.

On October 11, 1903, other directors began to respond to Blum's query. The angered director of the Théâtre de Vaudeville agreed with Antoine and exclaimed, "What if a critic doesn't like the light form of vaudeville?" He went on to say, "The critic shouldn't enter into philosophic discussions about a fun evening."[8] Some directors deemed it important to ask the critic if he or she is truly impartial or "désinteressé." Another director asked, "What do you think about the independence of the critic?"[9] Blum asserted that he was never told to influence his colleagues at *Gil Blas*. He suggested that the director and the playwright have different temperaments from that of the critic, a different "esprit." Though a review might not be utilitarian, the critic was still an important force in the performing arts. Blum declared that critics were not there to publicize, but rather to tell the public what they saw and to stimulate discussion, if necessary. He concluded that we must thus respect the critic's opinions, and recognize that many artworks may not be defended easily. Blum wrote that the critic is a rallying voice, a herald for the avant-garde. He found Antoine's irritation incomprehensible, and believed that it was important to have an enlightened view of art along with a profound sense of taste. In a mood of compromise, Blum affirmed that "though the critic might be wrong at the moment, all will finish well, and the Circle of Critics will bring the two sides together."[10]

Blum does not seem to have done much writing between 1903 and 1912. Reading the letters of Proust reveals that he was very much "the man about town" while continuing to build his reputation as an editor and critic for *Gil Blas*. One of his more curious articles for *Gil Blas* appeared in the February–March 1912 issue and centered on "le droit d'adaptation" or authorial copyrights. Blum asked his readers to respond to the concern that many authors rewrote novels and old plays, and then put them on the stage without any recognition of the original author. He remarked that "it is only with difficulty that one can cite a theatrical work in the past twenty years that is truly new and reaffirms a dramatic invention that hasn't already been seen many times."[11] We see here the legalistic side of René, perhaps inspired by his brilliant brother's legal talents. Blum testified that "we even see exact replicas of former plays and yet still there is no mention of the author who inspired it. This is a question of law, and of moral law."[12]

In the same article on *droits d'auteurs*, Blum asked for readers' responses to questions about copyright and the taking of plots from well-known books or plays without acknowledging their provenance. Blum argued: "Shouldn't there be some protection for these works?"[13]

The famed essayist Émile Faguet responded, saying that "it doesn't matter, the old works take care of themselves."[14] On March 1, the comic writer Georges Courteline acknowledged that "it is of no importance to Maupassant if someone steals the plot for his *Le Bel Ami*."[15] The dramatist Albert Guinon resolved that it was too difficult and delicate a question to banter about carelessly in these journalistic columns; it was better to seriously consider creating two new laws that resolved these problems: one addressing the issue of financial rights, and another dealing with the issue of rights of intellectual property or "pensées."[16] Grumon believed that the experts should reconcile the problem.[17]

The writer Romain Coolus[18] added that a bad adaptation only affects the bad writer, the one who stole the original; "le livre reste," he said, meaning that the book would survive in any case.[19] Agreeing with this assessment, the producer/director Paul Gavault stated that there was no risk for the older work.[20]

Author Albert Flament saw no danger to the original piece, but noted in the March 3 issue that the new adaptation should be "bien faite," well made. Flament contended that a carefully written theatrical adaptation would not harm a work of art. When another writer found out that a well-made play was based on Maupassant's *Le Bel Ami*, he promptly picked up the original Maupassant story, never having read it before, and concluded that "no one can ever hurt the power of such a great work of art."[21]

In a detailed letter in the March 9 *Gil Blas*, writer Alfred Mortier said he was a partisan of adaptations, of imitations, and even of plagiarism! All great artists steal ideas. He argued: "After all, one could easily show that there is not one modern play's plot that does not have its origins in an earlier work." One of the very few writers to protest adapting a classic work was the writer and critic Edmond See. He stated that he was against "all scenic adaptations of a chef d'oeuvre, and against any liberty taken by heirs or adapters."[22]

Ricciotto Canudo, the film expert with whom René established the first "Club du 7ième Art" (Cinema Club of the 7th Art) in 1920, was in favor of adaptations, but regretted that recent plays tended to lack imagination. In the March 16 *Gil Blas*, he exclaimed, "They are throwing themselves like vampires on works of the past, for lack of any good ideas."[23] One of the last letters concerning copyright came from René's brother Léon, the lawyer, writer, and theatre critic. Léon believed there should be a law respecting the rights of authors, especially when their works entered the public domain. Léon stated that it would be most beneficial for the author to announce how he wished to protect his writings, and for the public law to devise new ways to ensure the integrity of the author's works long after his death. Léon acknowledged that these were very prickly questions that required much thought. He complimented René for inspiring the *Gil Blas* debate, and for endorsing the opinion that society should safeguard great writers such as Shakespeare and Cervantes.[24]

In his response to the other writers, René suggested that after fifty years, authors who have stood the test of time should be protected by the creation of an organization, such as La Société des Gens de Lettres (A Society of Men of Letters), to oversee their classic works.[25] This lively debate endured for two months.

Continuing to develop articles and edit the journal, Blum also participated in events in Paris that did not necessarily pertain to theatre. His knowledge of and excitement about modern art were astonishing. In the fall of 1912, René wrote the prologue for the catalogue for one of the first exhibitions of Cubist art, which had its early stirrings in 1907 in the works of Picasso and Braque. René's experience with the bustling and vibrant intellectual life of the *Revue Blanche* had brought him into contact with some of the most celebrated painters and artists of the time. Several became close family friends, such as Pierre Bonnard and Edouard Vuillard. In October, René wrote the *Preface to the catalogue Salon de la Section d'Or, du 10–30 octobre 1912 (Catalogue avec une Préface de René Blum, Paris Galerie La Boétie, 64 rue de la Boétie)*. Some of the most renowned modern artists were exhibited, including Alexander Archipenko, Marcel Duchamp with his "Nu descendant l'escalier," Juan Gris, Marie Laurencin, Fernand Léger, Sonia Lewiska, Francis Picabia, Dunoyer de Segonzac, and Alexandra Exter, the constructivist, cubo-futurist.[26]

In his preface to the exhibition catalogue, Blum criticized the previous year's exposition of their paintings as having failed to properly show their work due to limited space. However, he affirmed that "in this gallery, they take on, in its totality, 'toute leur signification,' so that the brilliance of these radical works could be fully appreciated."[27]

He described the "unique turn of mind" that motivated these artists, so they disengaged from traditional and longstanding strategies, and freed themselves to envision life as they wished. "If you stop in front of these works," he wrote, "you would be shocked by the vivid colors and lack of restraint. The paintings are not easily categorized and do not owe anything to traditional works."[28]

Blum advised the spectator not to expect to find mere academic divergences from established schools. Rather, he made it clear that "there was a distancing of sensibility, and added to that is the imagination which permits all kinds of varieties, authorizing all the forces of art, favoring the most audacious combinations, the most unexpected connections." Blum concluded, "All of these elements create a harmony that is filled with tensions and contrasts and allows the artists to surpass the borders of impressionism and the formulas of Monet."[29]

Blum celebrated the painters' freedom, not constrained by one moment or one color. He valued their aesthetic and their nuanced and visionary understanding of form, and appreciated the similarities that existed in the technical approaches of some of the artists, but did not see them as contradictory. Rather, Blum foresaw an affirmation of their unique personalities, the individuality of their beings. He commended the newness of these artists' conceptions, but warned that the public might be hostile to them. He said that if the painters "do not have the felicity to convince the public, and cannot enjoy the fruits of their initiatives, will they then have the distinction of blazing the trail toward a new dimension, and 'l'honneur d'une renovation'?"[30]

In sum, Blum's commentary here is much more than an introduction to radically new styles of painting. It is a credo about art and an affirmation of the artist's flame and purpose, a prophecy for the future century and the gifts to be given by those whose imaginations overflow with vision.

During the exhibition's run, Blum and a friend, Jean Pellerin, wrote a one-act comedy under his pseudonym, René Bergeret. Pellerin belonged to Le Groupe Fantaisiste, poets who banded together in 1911 and thought the time had come to introduce gaiety, charm, and irony into French poetry. The subject of the play, the passion for a certain kind of "taste," fits remarkably well with the preoccupations of Blum's articles in *La Gazette*. It is interesting to note that Blum took the pseudonym Bergeret from a character in an Anatole France novel. Monsieur Bergeret figured in a keen satire comprising four books (1897–1901) that reflected on the Dreyfus affair and the endemic anti-Semitism in France. On opening night at the Théâtre Fémina on October 12, 1912, the play was dedicated to René's friend Pierre Muller and entitled *Le Goût du Toc*. *Toc* is an idiomatic expression for sham imitations, like paste jewelry.[31]

The play's four characters have names worthy of a Molière piece: Madeleine, Fernand, Flageolet (kidney bean), and Arsène. The play opens in an elegant small apartment, a *garçonnière*, where Fernand hastily brings out a vase of flowers and sprays perfume on the chairs while his friend Arsène suspiciously watches him, noting that elegant gentlemen never pay too much attention to their homes, but rather have servants who take care of such matters, and that perhaps it might be better to find a "woman of the world" who knows about beautiful objects.

Fernand declares that he "knows how to recognize a woman of the world," and that soon one will be visiting him. The bell rings and he welcomes the attractive Madeleine, who can only stay five minutes as her husband awaits her. She proceeds to gaze at the apartment's appurtenances and to criticize everything in sight, saying that the furniture and other provisions lack harmony. Reluctantly, she provides a card with the addresses of merchants who, she claims, will sell Fernand the perfect desk and the most gorgeous rug. Instantly, Fernand falls madly in love with Madeleine and her taste or *goût*. Once again, the bell rings and Madeleine is moved to the next room while Fernand greets his good friend Flageolet. They begin to gossip about their new girlfriends. Flageolet breathlessly tells Fernand about his glorious girlfriend who understands theories of design. Fernand quips nastily that she probably learned to converse about aesthetics by reading Galeries Lafayette catalogues. Eventually, Flageolet reveals that he purchased a Louis XVI desk that his girlfriend had found in a "passage" (or a series of elegant stores), the same passage that Madeleine described. Flageolet shows Fernand a card with addresses scrawled on it.

Fernand hints that he wants to be alone and Flageolet leaves. Madeleine saunters out from her hiding place, having heard the whole discussion. She makes the startling admissions that she did seduce Flageolet into buying her furniture, that she is a widow, that she was a maid for a consul with whom she had a baby, and that he subsequently married her. But Madeleine has no fortune and must find ways to survive without compromising her social status. This climactic confession inspires terrific anger in Fernand. He tells her that he has good taste and does not need her services. The play concludes with Madeleine's rapid-fire and wicked comment: "Yes, you have taste. However, it's a taste for the FAKE!" In this slight comedy, Blum and his co-author tackle the deep crevices that separate people in society: those who are poor but wish to be something special, and those nouveaux riches who have money but lack the necessary knowledge of an experienced or clever buyer. This was a monumental topic at the beginning of the twentieth century, a period during which materialism would triumph over experience and good taste. Beneath the surface of this light and amusing play, Blum perhaps anticipated the future.

La Gazette du Bon Ton (The Good Taste Gazette), a vanity publication for Parisian intellectuals, aesthetes, and lovers of fashion, seemed another appropriate outlet for Blum's articles on theatre, how to enjoy it, and what to expect.[32]

The honesty and insight of Blum's critical writings remain fresh today. Like his brother Léon when he wrote for the *Revue Blanche*, Blum utilized the current plays in Paris theatres as a jumping-off point to muse on theatrical writing and performance. In his column for *La Gazette*, "Le Goût au

Théâtre," Blum was the consummate teacher, calling forth the well-rounded approach honed in his many years of living in the theatre. He loved both old and new plays. He offered some homespun advice—that we usually leave the theatre with an impression, either good or bad, and that we form this impression before our critical senses have a chance to go to work. Often, we may not be able to understand why we either love or hate a piece. Thus, there may be a *mésentente*, or mismatch, between our "sensibility" or feelings and our "intelligence."

Blum surmised that we might not understand our first impression until our intelligence and our sensibility achieve a balance. Or they may not be in balance for a reason. Subsequently, Blum wrote a review of Émile Verhaeren's *Hélène de Sparte*, which he called "a poetic presentation whose words are both seductive and robust, yet sinuous and inspired."[33] Blum spoke highly of the well-orchestrated and eloquent music, as well as the costumes and décor by Léon Bakst, inspired by the brash colors of the Orient. Bakst's use of contrast was so immediately perceptible that thinking about those elements would not help to explain our astonishment. But, Blum declared that this was not always so. Sometimes the disparities in the effect caused a certain malaise, giving us a brusque sensation of discontent. Blum's tone was modest and helpful. He asked the reader to be sensitive to immediate impressions and then to analyze how the elements of a production came together and worked in concert. As examples, he questioned why *Hélène de Sparte* moved the audience, or how the collaborations of Debussy and Maeterlink in their work for *Pelléas et Mélisande* melded together to create a harmonious entity that emphasized the beauty of every detail. Blum also highlighted Sacha Guitry's play at the Vaudeville theatre, noting that one is hard put to discern whether its delight comes from the charm of the actors or the spirit of the dialogue. He complimented Guitry on the subtle beauty of the improvisation. Blum concluded his column by praising M. Antoine's reprise of *Le Malade Imaginaire*, which displayed all the fantasy and wit found in Molière's plays.

In the December 1912 issue of "Le Goût au Théâtre" in the *Gazette* (no. 2), Blum analyzed Paul Hervieu's comedy *Bagatelle*. He praised Hervieu's ability to express deep feelings by presenting dramatically understated conflicts imbued with an irresistible vigor. Blum remarked that "the comedy never stooped to vulgarity, sustaining its heightened noble style with a firm personality."[34] However, Blum added that Hervieu's efforts also tended to detract from the truth of his characters, and he reminded the reader: "The art of the writer consists in amplifying his thoughts to the point that the drama attains its greatest intensity. It is at this instant that the writer substitutes himself for his characters and takes control over their words in their name."[35] Blum cautioned the lyrical poet not to reveal himself too obviously in his protagonists, because, he said, "The process of creating true to life characters must remain invisible."[36] Blum reproached the producers, declaring that Hervieu's *Bagatelle* lacked the production values worthy of such a fine play; the set and decors suffered from a poverty of vision. In a visit to the Renaissance theatre where the costumes and scenery designs were gorgeous, he found that the current drama, a clever play by Paul Gavault, *L'Idée de Françoise*, lacked inspiration and rarely satisfied the viewer, despite the magnificence of the setting.

In the same article, Blum extolled Jacques Rouché for the care he had taken in mounting *Le Grand Nom*, and for the playwright André Marty's psychological study and clever parody. Authors M. de Flers and M. de Caillavet wove a seemingly ordinary tapestry in *l'Habit Vert*, with brilliant scenes featuring a classical music lover who hears a slow waltz. Savoring the sound of the gentle melody, he is drawn to the arena of popular culture, the music hall, ruining his reputation for high art. If this play brought together a perfect confluence of diverse dramatic elements, another by Lucien Besnard, *Diable Ermite*, fluctuated in style between two genres that never seemed to meld, despite the elegant writing of M. Besnard. As one reads through the great variety of Blum's critical writings about theatre, one is struck by his effort to find the core of art and truth beyond the plots, the settings, and the direction.

In the January 1913, no. 3, issue of *La Gazette*'s "Le Goût au Théâtre," Blum described his response to Henry Bataille's *les Flambeaux*. He confessed to feeling a dull sense of irritation as the major characters seemed weak and lacked truthfulness. But gradually, the audience was attracted to the rare beauty of Bataille's writing and rich psychological treatment of the conflicts that afflicted both heroes. Blum favored the heroine who best responded to the author's sensibility. He spoke about the designer's careful taste, but faulted him for pushing too far in his desire for exactitude through minute details. Similarly, Blum was not pleased with the "Oriental" tale *Kismet*, a story that had been greatly appreciated outside of France. He thought the scenes lacked interest and excitement, despite author Lucien Guitry's usually perfect taste. Blum wrote that Guitry forgot a play is not seen from the stage, but rather from a seat in a theatre.

When Blum reviewed Émile Vedel's *Faust*, he was delighted by the gorgeous and lush production images. The beautiful decors, rich orchestral melodies, and numerous costumes were stunning, but he asked, "What happened to Goethe's thoughts?" as he found the literary genius sadly lacking.[37]

After having criticized the luxury deployed by Vedel's production, Blum was enchanted by the simplicity of the director Lugné-Poe's presentation. In front of a simple back curtain unfolded a mysterious play by Paul Claudel. No artifice prevented the audience from being moved by Claudel's pure poetry in *L'Annonce faite à Marie*. His luminous, unaffected play flowed rhythmically from start to finish. Blum ended his meditation by emphasizing the importance of suggestion displayed in this important work.

Subsequent issues of *La Gazette's* "Le Goût au Théâtre" were written by Lise-Léon Blum, the first wife of Léon Blum. Her columns were predominantly about Diaghilev's Ballets Russes performances in Paris, and her opinions and comments were shaped by a dedication to beauty and a profound regard for these breathtaking and fascinating productions. Like René, her expertise in music enhanced the depth of her appreciation for ballet in general.

The next appearance of René Blum's name in print occurred in the July 12, 1913, issue of *Gil Blas*, when he published once again an inquiry directed at those of his readers who were important contemporary playwrights and musicians.[38] He asked: (1) What are your hopes for a vacation this year and where do you think you'll spend it? (2) What works are you preparing for next season, and in which theatres will they likely play? One wonders why Blum seems so interested in people's vacation plans, but we must remember that for the French, vacations are sacred and offer vital moments of reprieve and rejuvenation, representing a sensibility or perhaps a rationalization that is very different from that of other nationalities. His shrewd questions elicited a number of responses.

Some of René's friends, such as Romain Coolus, Albert Guinon, and Isidore Lara, responded with verve. Charles Muller penned a lacerating letter, and like Camille Saint-Saëns, he chided Blum, asserting that his vacation plans were of no interest to the public. But Saint-Saëns informed readers that he was planning the performance of a new piece, *Timbre d'Argent and The Promised Land*.

The famed actor/writer Sacha Guitry, for some obscure reason, entered into a long disquisition on the use of the nominative *tu* and the practice of "tutoyering." In the French language, the use of the second-person pronoun *tu* to denote a more familiar and warmer relationship provoked questioning thoughts on the complexity of human encounters. In the early twentieth century, it was not uncommon for husbands to say *vous* to their wives. Gabriel Fauré ignored this tangent and wrote that he hoped to spend time in Italy's Dolomite Mountains to compose music, rather than taking a specific vacation. He was also creating a piece of music for a play. Between July 12 and August 27, many artists answered Blum's queries, creating a lively repartee among the readers of *Gil Blas*.

In his last contribution to *La Gazette*, on October 13, 1913, Blum titled his column "Le Gant" (The Glove), named after a celebrated operetta of the Second Empire that, in all seriousness, touted the chic glove and the boot as denoting a well-clad gentleman. Blum made fun of his pretended ignorance when he chose a glove or a suit. What had become of those nostalgic, sartorial times when the famed dandy Beau Brummel employed five people to help him dress? When one looked longingly at boots made of alpine kid or Scottish deer? Worse still, when one pondered the destiny of gloves? What charmer today would pay attention to how the glove fits the hand? Blum quipped that in the modern world we hardly take notice of our clothes; we wear what might fit our older brother, or his older brother. What could be more expressive, more personal, than the hand whose palm contains our lifeline?

Blum then made a plea for someone to initiate a renaissance of the glove and meditated on styles of gloves that might appeal. For example, for the utilitarian, one might create a glove for travel that had the map of one's tourist destination engraved on the palm. And for the lighthearted, why not crocodile gloves for a change, especially to gather roses, and lace and embroidered gloves for the frivolous? For the modern Madame de Sévigné, why not gloves with nail polish on the tip of each finger, or gloves with lashes, or gloves for fishing, for a walk in the mountains, for the bath, or just for intermission at the theatre or at a concert? Blum remarked that fantasy provided a liberal way of thinking about fashion.[39]

He then imagined a range of scenarios during which gloves took center stage, for example, when the dawn rises, or when celebrating triumphs or disappointments, or to arouse secret movements of the soul. Contemplating one of these possibilities, Blum sketched this situation: "In the palm of your right hand, sir, you will take care that your monogram might be vividly obvious to the eye. The impertinent person whom you slap in the face would not deny the outrage. He would not dare accost the woman you love, nor would he contest your literary tastes."[40] If you were fitted with gloves, there would be no doubt that both men and women as arbiters of fashion will allow you free reign, so as to enjoy the beauty of your gloves. And with this last frivolity, Blum ended this absurd discourse on "gantsmanship."

In the March 10, 1914, issue of *Gil Blas*, Blum wrote an obituary for a relatively young, 54-year-old gentleman critic, Adrien Bernheim, who, Blum wrote, "devoted himself generously to the theatre." He began his career in journalism during the epoch of the journalist and politician Camille Dreyfus, and wrote penetrating critiques despite his rather delicate position as a theatre censor who needed to read all new scripts and recommend revisions, depending on the infractions. Apparently, he became a commissioner for all theatres that were supported financially by the government. Blum ended his homage by offering generously "notre respect et notre affliction."[41]

Just before the outbreak of war, blissfully unaware of the debacle that was soon to destroy the peace of Europe and his beloved *Gil Blas* along the way,

Blum on June 20, 1914, interviewed the artistic director of the Odéon Theatre, Paul Gavault, a playwright who authored *la Tante d'Honfleur*.[42] Blum
asked Gavault what the true role of the director of the Odéon was. Blum
remarked that Gavault called the Odéon the theatre of the grande bourgeoisie, as well as the theatre of students, but Blum argued that these terms
did not really characterize the true purpose of the historically celebrated
theatre. Gavault listed all the plays that would be produced the following
season: Dumas père's *La Reine Margot*, Victor Hugo's *Marie Tudor et "93,"*
Henri Murger's *Vie de Bohème*, Dumas fils' *La Question d'Argent* and *Un père
prodigue*, and several foreign plays by Ibsen and Gerault.

Blum believed that the Odéon should be a district theatre of the "quartier," with a large neighborhood presence. He added that Gavault had
the wisdom to eliminate the poor plays by substandard authors, and at the
same time include the classics that represented "Les grandes écoles," or the
classic traditions. Though Gavault did not seek out unusual pieces, he tried
to interpret classical dramas such as Molière's *Tartuffe* in original ways.
Blum concluded the article with a personal reminder for Gavault. He
advised him "to keep on using the best intentions in choosing works; and
not to forget to generously welcome young writers."[43]

After he returned from the First World War, Blum continued to write
articles and give lectures. He took over the management of the publishing
house La Librairie de France, where he participated in the publication of a
complete series of works devoted to the greatest French writers such as
Flaubert, Verlaine, and Daudet, with illustrations by the most prominent
artists of his generation. He was also instrumental in the publication of several important reference works, such as a sports encyclopedia in two large,
abundantly illustrated volumes that were well-reviewed at the time.[44]

The Diaghilev Ballets Russes, now situated in Monte Carlo, resumed its
fulgurant productions in Paris after the war, despite some setbacks. Several
stars of Diaghilev's ballet, such as Anna Pavlova and Ida Rubinstein, chose
to set off on their own to explore separate careers. About mid-summer
1919, Jacques Rouché, the director of the Paris Opéra, received what he
called "an exuberant letter from that weather-worn dramatist, Georges de
Porto-Riche."[45] Porto-Riche, a very close family friend of the Blums, had
met the composer Gabriel Fauré at the home of the musician Alfred Cortot,
another close friend of the Blum family. Blum brought together Fauré,
Porto-Riche (the librettist), and Jacques Rouché to create a piece for Ida
Rubinstein, who had worked with the designer Léon Bakst in 1910 on the
ballet *Schéhérazade*. They hoped to collaborate on a new work and to revive
the ballet at the Paris Opéra, but to no avail. Another attempt at such an
association occurred in 1925, although again, nothing came of the hoped-
for collaboration. Nevertheless, it showed, once again, the generosity of

spirit and willingness to go out of his way for others that René Blum demonstrated his whole life.

Ida Rubinstein loved and worked with the Italian poet Gabriele D'Annunzio, who had fled to France to escape his creditors. They collaborated with Debussy on the musical play *Le Martyre de San Sébastien*. It was during this period that René became friendly with D'Annunzio and translated one of his most famous novels, *Forse che si; forse che no* (1910). When D'Annunzio returned to Italy at the beginning of World War I, he favored Italy's fighting with the Allies, but later he developed a political philosophy that espoused Fascism and supported the rise of Benito Mussolini, much to the surprise and distress of René and his brother Léon.

For years, during and long after the time he worked for *Gil Blas*, Blum attended a monthly dinner event with well-known contemporary literary personalities who became his close friends. The astonishing list included Tristan Bernard, Mme. Geneviève Straus, Gus Bofa, Jean Cocteau, Colette, Romain Coolus, Georges Marie-Courteline, M. Curnosky (a famous gastronome), Roland Dorgelès, Robert Dreyfus, Dunoyer de Segonzac, Henry Duvernois, Léon-Paul Fargue, Ph. Gaubert, Georges Pioch, Georges de Porto-Riche, Paul Reboux, Edmond Rostand, Rosemonde Gérard, Samuel Rousseau, Alfred Savoir, Edmond See, and Edouard Vuillard.

After World War I, the reading public developed a fascination for decorative books, or *livres de luxe*. Having developed a lifelong respect for the printed page, and an equally passionate interest in art, Blum adored walking through book fair exhibits in Paris, and writing about those volumes that captured his interest. The "Salons d'Automne" at the Grand Palais best demonstrated French bibliophilia. Salons, of course, were venues for people to meet and interact that had begun centuries before, and reached their peak development during the eighteenth century. They provided opportunities to discuss works of art, science, and literature or French culture. But, the salons also held periodic exhibitions of painting and art and, at that time, art books and stamps. Blum's first column, "Le Carnet du Bibliophile" (Notebooks of a Book Lover) appeared in 1920 in *L'Amour de l'Art* (vol. I, no. 7), a chic arts magazine.[46] He disclosed the excitement that books and stamps caused among booksellers and art afficionados. And he underscored the fact that these works fetched sky-high prices. A new fashion from England had arrived, that of the premiere or first edition, a deluxe volume with beautiful illustrations, a tradition that had been lost after the Romantic period in the nineteenth century. There now appeared a new school of lithographers, aquatinters, and xylographers, which assured a place for the illustrated book.

In his article in *L'Amour de l'Art*, Blum explained how difficult it was to create such a book, to place the pictures felicitously, to choose the correct paper, to arrange the text on the page, and to find the image that was compatible with the spirit of the book. Blum also criticized the reality that often the mediocre sold as well as the excellent. Blum applauded certain works, such as Paul Claudel's *Protée*, illustrated by Jean-Gabriel Daragnès, Gérard de Nerval's *La Main enchantée*, and Rémy de Gourmont's *le Livret de l'Imagier*, among others. For books that contained the art of painters, Blum cited Charles Morice's *Gaugin*, abundantly illustrated by Floury, and *Renoir* and *Bonnard* by George Besson.

In his next "Carnet," Blum returned to the subject of the salon and reported that the books were placed at such a distance from the visitors that it was impossible to get a good view, and also that, in the vastness of the Grand Palais, the lighting was too dim.[47]

Blum subsequently recovered his good humor and congratulated the curator, M. Bernouard, who organized the "Section du Livre." Blum favored Lucien Vogel's *Gazette* and declared that any of his pages could have been featured in this exhibition. We recall that Blum wrote articles on *Le Goût au Théâtre* for Vogel. Blum cited the names of several others, especially the admirable pages of M. André Doin's *Les Fleurs du Mal* by Baudelaire, and M. Doyon's *Les Trois Contes* by Villiers de l'Isle-Adam. Blum believed that certain authors, such as La Mettrie, Bossuet, and Chateaubriand, had been neglected, and he heaped praise on current reproductions of their books.[48]

Along with his passion for book making, Blum was interested in modern ideas of printing. Writing for "Le Carnet," he pointed out the startling difference in taste before and after the Great War. Before the war, there were timid attempts to make exquisitely illustrated books, but the technology was still undeveloped. The war brought new mechanical processes that changed photographic illustrations for the better, via the trichrome process and the new Rembrandt method in black or bistre, printed by Hachette, a publisher that created some beautiful issues of the journal *L'Illustration*. Blum discussed Lucien Vogel's *La Gazette du Bon Ton*, whose very modern tone, with its reviews of art, fashion magazines, and stamp albums, documented the breadth and depth of taste in France. The typography was careful, the articles lively. Yet Blum opined that postwar publications were disappointing. He sensed an old-fashionedness in writers and artists, a sense of déjà vu. He acknowledged that Parisians had changed and were no longer interested in such subjects as Dandyism. Blum pointed out that M. Dufet and Mme. Davenne had created *Les Feuillets d'Art*, a perfectly original publication. Yet even with its fresh approach, the magazine suffered unfortunately from a lack of unity, a sense that each page was isolated from the next, though with excellent execution. The printed score of a melody by Ravel alternated with an architectural piece on the Hotel Biron, or the painter Van Dongen. In short, this diversity was bewildering. But, like Vogel's *Gazette, Feuillets* still had astonishing elegance.[49]

The depth of Blum's knowledge was illustrated in a later issue of "Le Carnet du Bibliophile" in *L'Amour de l'Art* (1920), where he remarked that during the summer vacation months, the ardor of book lovers abated and catalogues of new books and sales slowed down, yet the whole of the 1921–1922 year astounded everyone with its plethora of beautiful publications.[50] He then singled out several projects of outstanding importance, in which the designers and artists of the books' illustrations were featured. Edouard Champion edited the complete works of Stendhal, and the publishers Ollendorff and Conard offered the complete works of Hugo, Balzac, and Vigny, whose publication had been interrupted by the war. Blum recommended facsimiles by Marty in which Floury illustrated several poems by Tristan Corbière, as well as books on Degas, Willette, and Gaugin, and a superb volume dedicated to sculptor François Rude. Listing several other books of interest, he finished his article with bravos to journals such as *La Gazette de Bon Ton, Feuillets d'Art, Goût du Jour, Guirlande*, and *Monsieur*, praising them for their continued dedication to beauty and art.

In "La Section du Livre au Salon d'Automne" that reviewed the 1921 book season, Blum once again rebuked those individuals responsible for the placement and arrangement of the book exhibits. He found the exhibition too crowded, the publications mediocre, and the lighting dark and unpleasant, making the works difficult to view. He cited the famed artist Dunoyer de Segonzac, who had the questionable honor of organizing the objects in the exhibition. Blum was displeased that the exhibition organizers had substituted slim plaquettes for the larger 300- to 400-page books that were too costly to bind. In addition, he suggested that certain publishers were overrepresented, a fact that would discourage amateurs with good intentions.[51]

Blum admonished publishers who mostly reprinted classic writers and ignored new and younger writers. He found that the anecdotal illustration was supplanting the simple typographic illustration, and claimed that the basic rules of printing were often neglected, with the layout of pages not meeting the elementary standards of the profession. He put into words those abuses that were predominantly artistic or technical, and assailed publishers who printed books primarily for profit, rather than making books that articulated new ideas and were visually attractive. Blum realized that in the future the success of beautiful books or *livres de luxe* would require a very limited printing or a mass public. The rest of the article discussed the finest examples of deluxe books, especially those by Dunoyer de Segonzac, a close friend of René Blum, and a painter and aquafortiste of great talent, best shown in his moving pictures for the writer Roland Dorgelès' *Croix de Bois*.

Until his untimely death at Auschwitz, Blum sustained a complex and deep relationship with Tristan Bernard (1866–1947), a grizzly old man twelve years his senior and a fiercely committed comic writer. René knew him, as a close friend of the Blum family, on several levels. Bernard wrote many successful comedies, vaudevilles, satires, and caricatures of middle-class life. Blum was so intrigued by Bernard's talent that he arranged a conference on December 20, 1924, in Monte Carlo that focused on Bernard's contributions to the world of theatre. In the published documentation of the conference, Blum began his discourse by praising Bernard's most recent play, *Le Prince Charmant*, as performed at the Théâtre de Monte-Carlo, in which the gray-bearded Bernard played a challenging role that made him, as the critic put it, "the most celebrated of comic actors.[52] Blum discussed how Bernard's comedic talent was unique, in the vein of Mark Twain, and commented that "Bernard twists or reforms reality in a particularly clever manner."[53]

He remarked on Bernard's similarity to Dickens, and how Bernard had worked for a while in an aluminum factory, there discovering the ways of workers and the *petit commerçants* or small shopkeepers. Blum recalled Bernard's success at the Lycée Condorcet, and how his life experiences had formed his artistic approach. Trained as a lawyer, Bernard discovered quickly that his personality was not suited to the law. He loved the theatre and literature, and enjoyed writing for *Revue Blanche*. René presented a sentimental memoir of his own days at *Revue Blanche*, and recollected that he had spent a lot of time in the editorial room where he was fortunate to meet many writers, including Henry de Régnier, Paul Adam, Lucien Mühlfeld, Romain Coolus, and Félix Fénéon, as well as celebrated painters such as Bonnard, Vuillard, Denis, Roussel, and Toulouse Lautrec, who painted a portrait of Bernard.

According to Blum, Bernard relished spectacle, all sorts of spectator events, and even wrote sports columns about different competitions. Blum wrote that his relationship with Bernard began years before, when Blum was growing up in Paris. Bernard apparently took him to the Buffalo Velodrome on Sunday mornings to watch the bicycle races, something that enchanted the young René.

Blum disclosed that one of Bernard's most exceptional talents was his memory for poetry. He also wrote his own poems about the simple beauty of nature in the Parnassian manner. Blum was impressed that Bernard was able to quote very long poems by Hugo, de Vigny, and Verlaine, and read several poems by Bernard at the 1924 conference, observing that Bernard had a talent for fantasy as well as irony. Blum knew how meaningful it was for an audience to hear poetry read aloud, so that the metaphors could sing spontaneously. One of Bernard's poems was dedicated to the poet Catulle Mendès, and another told a fable in the style of La Rochefoucauld about a giraffe, a parrot, and an opossum. To conclude his discussion about Bernard's poetry, Blum read the sonnet *Les Trois Cortèges*, a parody of one by Joséphin Soulary, to the gathering.

Blum noted that Bernard found success as early as 1899, and became known for his skeptical view of life's foibles and failures, underscored with a deep sense of goodness. He discerned the subtlety in Bernard's writing, adding that "Bernard always told the either comic or tragic truths often disguised by the most deceptive circumstances and in the style of Maupassant."[54] He deduced that Bernard's stratagems were similar to those of the pointillists, building on a series of successive strokes with great care and discretion. Throughout this meditation, Blum pointed to Bernard's work, and showed how comedies, poetry, and parody functioned and illuminated French society. He explicated Bernard's theatrical processes, and described how Bernard deployed in his sentimental scenes a poetic grace, a *delicatesse*, a sensibility, and a thoughtful measure of sentiments worthy of de Musset and Marivaux. Blum supported his argument by listing the titles of plays that bore out his analysis.[55]

At the end of this literary salute, Blum narrated a story that was both typical and appalling. Bernard invited some friends to what he discovered to be a mediocre restaurant. He found the meal indigestible and the atmosphere too pretentious. When the bill arrived, he told the waiter that he was one of the owner's confrères or colleagues in the business. As Bernard started to leave, the owner asked him what restaurant he ran, and Bernard replied: "I am not a restauranteur." Surprised, the patron said, "You told us you were an owner of a restaurant." Bernard responded with an example of his sarcastic and bitter humor, "Yes, I did, that makes me a liar and a thief, just as you are!"[56]

Five years later, Blum wrote the preface to a publication by Bernard, *Mathilde et ses Mitaines* (1929), a short and eerie novel in the style of Edgar Allen Poe. In the preface, Blum constructed a dialogue between himself and Bernard, telling Bernard that he had debated the merits of the novel with a group of Bernard's afficionados who deplored this new ghoulish genre of writing, with its corpses, daggers, underground passages, and disguises. Blum contended that Bernard distilled this tale with great sincerity and truthfulness, and argued in favor of Bernard's challenging new style, citing his exceptional skill in placing characters in a believable setting, so that their most abnormal gestures and actions were justified. The characters in Bernard's novel weathered exploits similar to those of real detectives and exhibited qualities of both heroism and timidity. Blum concluded his preface thus: what Bernard wanted to bring to the audience was a fun, if somewhat scary, experience, and the pleasure of a good read, and on both fronts he succeeded.[57]

For years, Blum also maintained a relationship with the writer Georges Courteline, admiring his reverence for the French language as well as his strong dramatic character portraits. He organized a commemorative conference soon after Courteline's death, and in his commentary predicted that Courteline, along with Tristan Bernard and Georges Feydeau, would be regarded among the most cherished comic writers in French literature. Bernard and Feydeau still grace the French stage; Courteline is all but forgotten.

Blum began his commentary by describing the difficult experiences that Courteline had suffered as a youth. Born Georges Moinaux in Tours in 1858, he did not excel in his studies and was therefore unable to pursue an academic career. He secured a job in administration that suited him, but soon left that work to become a writer. Founding a publication in the tradition of Parnassian poetry, *Paris Moderne*, Courteline met Catulle Mendès whose poetry he admired but whose literary reputation has not endured. Courteline also interacted with the poets François Coppée, Paul-Armand Silvestre, and Paul Verlaine, the charming genius of late-nineteenth-century poetry. At *Paris Moderne*, Courteline wrote delicate verses, some of which Blum read to the public. Recalling long dinners on Friday evenings in Montmartre with Paul Reboux, Roland Dorgelès, and Georges Pioch, Blum remembered that Courteline would read aloud exultantly Victor Hugo's poetry and pound the table for punctuation. Everyone in the café looked shocked and wondered why this little man seemed angry, not realizing that it was only his poetic enthusiasms. Anatole France often dined with the group and insisted that Courteline was the purest writer of his epoch.

After two years, *Paris Moderne* closed its offices, forcing Courteline to find work with the journal *Les Petites Nouvelles*, and after that with *L'Echo de Paris*, an important and exclusive literary paper. There he wrote fantasies that brought him considerable success. During World War I, he pondered philosophical issues, including empathic essays about life's challenges. Courteline rewrote and corrected everything he had ever written, rather than creating new works. Blum noted that this obsession with perfection pervaded his later years. Courteline disregarded fame and disliked the attention of the "tout Paris" crowd; Blum thought Courteline's best feature was his lack of snobbism. He believed that Courteline would be remembered for wonderful humor that made his audiences laugh spontaneously and energetically without shame. Anatole France wrote insightfully that with Courteline the "comic turns quickly to sadness when it is human."[58]

With his usual generosity of spirit, in 1934 Blum arranged for Flammarion's publication of an anthology of Courteline's short stories. The most shocking first story, "L'Oeil de Veau" (The Calf's Eye), recounted the tale of a young boy who is sent away to the provinces to attend high school. He is assigned to a friendly mentor who takes him out every other Sunday. When the young boy earns high grades in his courses, his protector rewards him by cooking up a *tête de veau* or veal's head soup, a rare treat. When the child is served a bowl, and notices the eye of the young cow floating in the soup, he is horrified. The cook insists that the child eat the eye, literally forcing him to do so. The child never forgets that the eye is in his stomach, where it will remain until his dying day.

Although primarily a producer and critic, Blum was an excellent playwright. His pseudonym, Bergeret, was printed once again in the program for *Le Capitaine Fracasse*, a *comédie lyrique* with new compositions by Mario Costa, adapted from the picaresque novel by Théophile Gautier. This light comedy debuted on December 9, 1930. We no longer have the libretto; however, we do know that Gautier's story told the tale of an impoverished Baron de Signonac who lived during the era of Louis XIII. He fell in love with Isabelle, whom he was destined to follow even when she joined a group of traveling actors. Without any resources, he became one of the actors, Capitaine Fracasse, a lively and brave Italian soldier. He inhabited this role in more than one way, protecting Isabelle through many swashbuckling adventures. Eventually, Isabelle revealed that she was the daughter of Prince Vallambrosa, whereupon de Signonac swiftly married her, and became the governor of a province, saving them both from a life of bohemian penury.

Another play that touted René Blum's name was *Le Plancher des Vaches* by Jean Sarment, although it is unclear whether Blum produced it or co-wrote the text. A comedy in three acts and four tableaux, it was performed at the Théâtre de Monte-Carlo on November 21, 1931, and later played in Paris at the Théâtre Antoine on February 10, 1932.

Blum's position as purveyor of light comedy and operetta at Le Théâtre de Monte-Carlo, a job he acquired in 1924, fueled his interest in writing for the theatre. His close relationship with the comic playwright Georges Delaquys provided the inspiration for their collaboration on a performance that took place in Le Théâtre de Monte-Carlo on January 5, 1932. Robert Schumann (1810–1856) had created a musical score based on the verses of the German poet Heinrich Heine. He called his cycle of sixteen songs *Les Amours du Poète*, arranged with an internal narrative that centered on Heine's unrequited love for his cousin Amélie. The scenery, designed by Alphonse Visconti and Georges Geerts, and the costumes devised by Georgette Vialet, were simple but evocative. No doubt it was Blum who proposed that George Balanchine choreograph a sweet pantomime for four women and two men from the Ballets [Russes] de Monte-Carlo to the song "Le Pauvre Pierre" in Act 3.

The musical play as adapted by Blum and Delaquys engendered many kudos from the press in and outside Monte Carlo. The Parisian publication *La Petite Illustration* paid little attention to plays that were not performed in Paris, but decided to feature and publish the play *Les Amours du Poète* for two reasons: because it was a great success in Monte Carlo, and to encourage the possibility that it might be restaged in Paris, which did indeed happen. *La Petite Illustration* detailed an introduction to the play offering comments from newspaper critics. For example, M. André Corneau in the *Journal de Monaco* applauded the play's poignant treatment of lost love as the protagonist waits to hear just one passionate word directed toward him from his cousin Amélie.[59] Mindful of Marivaux's *On ne badine pas avec l'amour* (Love is not to be trifled with), Corneau spoke about the heightened moment in the fourth act when Amélie discovers the protagonist's worship of her every move. All is unveiled, each seeing clearly into the heart of the other, recognizing the ineluctable pain of love.

The critic's adulations stopped when Corneau discussed the way Schumann's music was arranged, and observed that Heine's poetry, written twenty years before Schumann's music, seemed to lose its sense and meaning. The music was not written for the Blum/Delaquys play; it was designed to work with Heine's prodigiously emotional songs. Yet, in this particular lyrical play, the critic sensed sincere respect for and veneration of both Heine and Schumann.

Other Parisian critics highlighted the play's grace and charm. In *Comoedia*, Gabriel Trarieux congratulated Blum on his choice of Delaquys as a collaborator. He thought that Heine's youth, a mere eighteen years, deprived him of a certain common sense, and that Amélie would surely choose a bourgeois lover with the potential for wealth rather than a neophyte poet. The play, according to Trarieux, excelled in psychology and in its dialogue; he predicted that its success was assured.[60] In *Le Figaro*, Henri Rebois commented on the perfect alliance of three genres: "the lyricism of the *Intermezzo* songs created by Heine; the music *Dichterliebe* by Schumann; and the most poignant expression of Heine's secret thoughts."[61] The most eloquent review, from the journal *Excelsior*, seemed too impressed by the fact that the prince and princess of Monaco were at the debut and participated in the vibrant and enthusiastic applause. The writer also assumed that the play would be restaged in Paris. *Excelsior* affirmed Blum's and Delaquys' interpretation, "especially the highly literary value of such a spectacle, bringing together the picturesque musical elements that the public rarely experiences. It is a victory of high dramatic literature that brings great honor to the French stage."[62] *L'Eclaireur de Nice's* Charles Lamy also praised Blum and Delaquys, asserting, "Thanks to them, I know well, tomorrow will reopen les Reisebilder. Beyond his poems, they will see Heine smile."[63]

The critic for *Le Petit Niçois*, Adrien Radoux, testified to the cult of Heine, saying that "he adopted Paris as his home where he was buried in Montmartre. Blum and Delaquys have created more than a theatrical piece, they have erected a tomb for the poet, a memorial where all those who believe in poetry can meditate and where the heart creates a place for dreaming."[64] Radoux noted that "Blum conceived the scenario, where he profoundly imagines an ideal union of love and friendship with a tristesse that was masked by a layer of humor. There was an ovation when the curtain fell on the last act."[65] Finally, *Le Journal des Débats*'s Étienne Bricon endorsed the play as a "poetic slice of life in the grand style, infused with a deep sense of humanity."[66]

Blum had worked with Delaquys several years before in 1927, when his-play *Le Marchand de Lunettes* was performed in Monte Carlo. For some time René had been thinking about creating a lyrical drama based on Heine's life, and he and Delaquys spent August and September 1931 combining text, music, and movement for their new project. The team researched Heine's life and loves, examining the sources of his humor, lyricism, and grandeur. It is ironic to recall that the romantically inclined Princess Alice, wife of Monte Carlo's great oceanographer Prince Albert I, was the niece of Heine, who ran off with a musician.

In *Les Amours du Poète*, the story begins in a local café where young Heine and his student friends chant a revolutionary song, imagining a world without tyrants and a life that is happy, free, and proud. Heine sings a love song in which he confesses his ardor for a young beauty, with sighs that are aroused by chirping birds and lovely flowers. He admits that the object of his marvelous tenderness is indeed his cousin Amélie. Both his friend and his mentor warn Henri that she is not the sort of woman for him, and that Amélie's father, his uncle, is a ferocious guardian. Henri replies that despite these obstacles, he will declare his love for her on the morrow. The plot thickens when a young man named Friedlander arrives from Königsberg, claiming that he is Amélie's fiancé. Somewhat oblivious to this unforeseen rival, the poet Heine seizes the opportunity to sing a sad and poignant tune about the complications of love.

A jolting intrusion occurs when a platoon of Prussian soldiers march into the café to threaten and arrest young students. Beginning the play with a revolutionary song clearly articulates the poet's radical sympathies. But conservative forces for the status quo are present as well, such as Friedlander who warns, "Down with revolt, long live order, discipline and authority."[67] Friedlander is supported by Amélie's merchant father Salomon, who despite his political views generously puts up the money to extract the students from jail, including Heine. Nevertheless, Salomon worries about his nephew's "lack of good sense, position or fortune."[68]

Heine ignores his uncle's chastising and expresses his intention to marry Amélie. When Henri finds himself alone with her, he overwhelms her with his romantic yearnings and eloquent poetry. She is quickly persuaded that he is crazy and full of childishness, and she calls him "just a big baby."[69] He protests that there is nothing wrong with him, just that he loves her. She berates him for not revealing his intentions to her and, more importantly, his hopes for a profession. She shocks him by admitting that her father has affianced her to M. Friedlander, whose prospects are much more serious and promising. Heine becomes inconsolable and, with Schumann's penetrating intermezzo playing in the background, bemoans his wounded love.

The centerpiece of the play takes place in a large salon, with friends and family in a circle watching Balanchine's pantomime for Jean, Marguerite, and "Le Pauvre Pierre." This Hamlet-like divertissement, told in Heine's poetry, cruelly confronts Heine with his own shallow existence, and the scene leaves him miserable. His paramour cousin chastens Heine, saying that he always writes about such sad things. Long discourses on the nature of love and suffering ensue, but even in this misery, Heine senses that he may one day become great and immortal. Indeed, in time, Heine's startling poetic talent became apparent, despite his lovelorn feelings and lack of fortune.

After many years, Amélie and Heine meet once again. We learn of her maturity, her children, her orderly life, and of Heine's worldwide fame as a celebrated poet. She reaffirms that a love affair between them could never have been possible. Knowing he must soon leave on a voyage, Heine departs as she plays a wistful tune on the piano. Heine returns to the café where he says goodbye to all his friends. The stage darkens as Heine thanks a group of young women who encircle him for their sweet regards, fervor, and gentle love. They depart slowly and the curtain falls. Blum's romantic piece reflects the latent idealism and artistic yearnings of its authors.

A sad repercussion of *Les Amours du Poète* was that it brought to light René Blum's personal misfortune in his affair with Josette France, an actress in his company in Monte Carlo. After a short period of time, she lost interest in him, despite the fact that they had a child together, leaving him lonely and isolated. While Blum's private life echoed the distress of their arguments and her deceit, he continued to find and identify theatrical performances that amused audiences and gave them many pleasurable evenings.

Blum often reworked older operettas that promised more substantial entertainment, and made serious revisions that brought new life to a worn out story. The most important criterion for Blum was a strong score. The opera *L'Étoile* by Emmanuel Chabrier was a lively farce with a scenario originally by Leterrier and Van Loo. For the 1936 version, the libretto was rewritten by René Bergeret (Blum) and Guillot de Saix.

According to the *Journal de Monaco* on January 4, 1936, their interpretation tried to reestablish a more orderly sequence of events for a scenario filled with inconsistencies and disarray. Blum and de Saix changed names and swapped old "truisms" for newer wordplay and metaphors. The jokes still kept to their wild fantasies and absurdities, but in the end the critic quipped that "one cannot turn copper into gold."[70]

In this production of *L'Étoile*, the music radiates joy with amusing melodies, unlike many operettas. The story takes place in the faraway, magical land of King Ouph who, on his birthday, is required to present to his people a spectacle in which a poor devil is sacrificed in honor of the king. A pathetic character, Lazzuli, on the appointed day strikes the king by mistake and thus becomes the sacrificial lamb. All sorts of silliness ensue, but Lazzuli survives the ordeal, so that the king forgives, forgets, and remains a hero in his own kingdom.

When meditating on the resonating factors in Blum's critical oeuvre, one immediately notices the authenticity of his approach to his subjects, and an open and direct conversation with his readers. He assumed that art has a natural and essential effect in everyone's life, and that dialogues about aesthetics should be engaged in daily and fervently. Though his articles were strident at times, he was primarily an advocate for the surrounding culture, and for his colleagues in the theatre, literary, and art worlds. Although he had great respect for original thinking, he left no writings about more adventurous and experimental theatre artists such as Alfred Jarry and Antonin Artaud. His creative ventures tended to have a utilitarian purpose, acquiring plays and operettas that he believed needed strategic changes to please the current audiences. His original works had both winsome and wistful qualities, written in the language of a connoisseur. He wrote simply, graciously, and often in an understated way. There were moments when, despite his disappointment and ire, he sustained a youthful enthusiasm for all kinds of literature and art, relishing the discovery of something new every day.

CHAPTER 3

Marcel Proust and René Blum

An Uncommon Friendship

arcel Proust's charm and unique brilliance gave him an entrée into upperclass Parisian society that fed his extraordinary imagination in the writing of *Remembrance of Things Past*. The odd, everyday peccadillos taking place in people's dining rooms, summer gardens, and private haunts formed the settings for his deep analysis of human emotions. Proust's sensitivity to the shifting moods and colorations of the psychology of salon life, writer Emily Eells tells us, "contributed to the inauguration of modernism by turning around the mirror of nineteenth-century objective realism, and re-positioning it in the privacy of the bedroom."[1] Driven by forbidden homoerotic urges, he reflected the shadowy references to other sexualities among his friends and enemies. He thereby visualized a new reality, a new way of seeing human relationships. It has been largely forgotten that René Blum brought Proust's genius to light in the twentieth century.

"I want to write quickly to tell you how profoundly grateful I am to you . . . it is absolutely essential that you ask me for any sort of favor, as it will give me great pleasure. I thank you with all my heart and shake your hand very affectionately."[2] Proust wrote these words of gratitude to René Blum in 1913, after hearing that Blum had arranged for *Swann's Way* to be published. His affection for Blum grew as he came to appreciate the depth and quality of Blum's intellect and character.

In his short biography of René Blum, Frank Biancheri attested to René's long friendship with Proust, which began in the early twentieth century. "We discover René Blum in company with Proust as early as 1902, and then he is cited as being invited formally to the Proust home on the 16th of July, 1903. But we must wait until February 20, 1913 for the first letter from the great writer to this most extraordinary clairvoyant, and rare reader of Proust's debut writings"[3]

René, seven years younger, spent a great deal of time with Proust, who in 1902 began to take a liking to him. René socialized with the *Revue Blanche* crowd, a group of young gadabouts in Paris who were Proust's close friends: Comte Bertrand de Salignac-Fénelon, Armand Guiche, Georges de Lauris, and Antoine and Emmanuel Bibesco. In a letter to Antoine Bibesco, Proust described their meeting: "When dining out one evening, I glanced up to discover René Blum. I saw a reddish blond, smiling wavy-haired, intense Hippolytus, a living sculpture from the most glorious period of Ancient Greece."[4] In a teasing tone, Proust noted that Blum's cheeks were flushed, and that when they began a conversation, Blum confided that his face was red because he was often constipated.

Proust immediately analyzed this statement: "The redness is symbolic of his difficulty in producing."[5] In addition, Proust wrote about Blum's "bizarre mania" for telling people that he (René) was devilishly embarrassed for not visiting them and for not writing to them, and that this behavior was inexcusable. Proust remembered that Blum spoke about his sadness, because he missed the company of his friends whom he did not visit. Proust criticized the zealously polite Blum for not knowing how his words affected people. One wonders whether these observations tell us more about Proust than Blum, but he ended the letter to Bibesco saying, "Blum is very charming and has a deep affection for you"[6]

A year later, on July 16, 1903, Proust asked a friend to invite Blum to a formal dinner at Proust's home. The friendship and mutual respect matured and as early as 1906, Proust contemplated giving Blum some of his writings. In a letter to Emmanuel Bibesco, three years later, Proust declared that he wanted to send Blum some material to review and asked for Blum's address.[7] On April 8, 1907, after reading an article in *Gil Blas* by Léon Radziwill, Proust wrote his friend "Loche" or Léon, chastising him for his lapses in style. He suggested to Léon that he consult René Blum, "as he is your friend, and Blum is rather skilled in writing."[8] Several years later, on March 24, 1912, Proust wrote Georges de Lauris that he planned to deliver some short stories to Blum.

Proust's and Blum's real relationship began in 1913, when Proust was desperate to find a publisher for *Swann's Way*, the first volume of his remarkable novel *A la Recherche du Temps perdu* (Remembrance of Things Past, or In Search of Lost Time). Previously, the manuscript had been rejected by the publishers of *Nouvelle Revue Française*, by Ollendorff, and also by Fasquelle. Through the Bibescos, Proust discovered that Blum was close to the distinguished publisher Bernard Grasset. Writing to his close friend Louis de Robert on February 19, 1913, Proust said he had heard that Blum would like to publish some extracts of his book in *Gil Blas*, but that he (Proust) had rejected this idea. However, Proust confided, "I will ask Blum to talk to Grasset about publishing the book at my expense, and about the fact that I will also pay for publicity."[9] In concluding his letter, Proust described Blum as a very kind and charming person, and also commended his capacity to win the trust and confidence of many people.

After World War II, in the book of homages dedicated to Blum, Antoine Bibesco recounted the circumstances of Blum's next meeting with Proust:

> At a moment when Proust had been deeply humiliated by the editors who refused to publish his first novel, *Swann's Way*, I thought it wise to reintroduce Proust to René Blum. At the same time, my brother Emmanuel read to René a few extracts from the same book. René was startled by the genius of Proust's writing. He wanted immediately to rectify the errors of those undiscerning editors. With an amazing and obstinate energy that Blum rarely used for his own interests, he sought out Bernard Grasset and pleaded Proust's cause. Grasset began work on its publication, and I recall Proust's satisfaction when he heard the news. René's joy was no less; the pleasure he brought Proust became his own recompense.[10]

In the late nineteenth and early twentieth centuries, there was much gossip surrounding Proust's relationship with Léon Blum and the *Revue Blanche*. Proust was an ardent critic of the Symbolist movement; however, its poetry was heartily praised by the editors of *Revue Blanche*, especially by Léon Blum. Animosity arose between Proust and Léon because Proust believed that the Symbolist poets suffered from a lack of clarity.

When Proust began publishing his own works, more troubles began to emerge. *Les Plaisirs et les Jours* appeared on June 13, 1896. It received good reviews in *Le Figaro, Le Gaulois,* and *Le Temps.*[11] However his *Banquet* colleagues[12] regarded him as a traitor to literature; in their criticism, they mingled sarcasm with reluctant admiration for his brilliant writing. Léon Blum, in *Revue Blanche*, rebuked him for "affectation and prettiness—his gifts ought not to be wasted."[13]

It is a great irony that the most talented French writer of the twentieth century, the one who best understood and described the abject morality, anti-Semitism, and petty prejudices of the French upper class, was Marcel Proust, the son of a Catholic physician and a Jewish mother.

In his letter to René Blum on February 20, 1913, Proust warned him to save his address, as letters tended to go astray. The author was unusually suspicious; throughout their correspondence, Proust worried that people would find out about his personal letters and use them against him. His letter of February 20 was meant to follow up his phone call to Blum at the offices of *Gil Blas*. Proust's first galleys comprised 800 pages, but Grasset advised him to cut 300. They reached a compromise length of 600 pages. In addition, Proust requested an interval of ten months between each volume.

Then, in a quite sincere tone, he asked politely if it would embarrass Blum to contact Grasset. Proust went on to explain or rationalize that he had been working on this book for a long time, and that Blum would be doing him an enormous favor if he could persuade Grasset to publish *Swann's Way*.

In the same letter, Proust turned to another obsession, his health, bemoaning his sickness, and the fact that he needed rest and comfort. Referring to his book, he requested that Blum speak for him as Blum could provide "an intelligible presentation of my work." And in a harsher tone, he added: "What I want for you to be able to say to me in a week is that this affair is concluded!"[14]

Proust strategized percentages of sales in this long epistle, but asked Blum to keep the letter confidential, especially the possible connection to Grasset. Impugning several of his trusted friends, he suggested that it was better not to tell anyone about their dealings (e.g., Antoine Bibesco). This is odd since Antoine introduced Proust to Blum. Proust's forceful personality colors the rest of the letter. His confidence stemmed from the fact that he was financing the book's publication and that he therefore had total control over the entire enterprise, a situation rarely experienced by novelists with their publishers. Proust offered the services of his musician friend Reynaldo Hahn, who also would be willing to visit Grasset.

Proust acknowledged that writing this crucial letter to Blum had exhausted him, yet he begged René not to telephone his valet de chambre, and only to call him when absolutely necessary. Always the obsessive, Proust proposed that Blum speak to M. Grasset about the publication date and, in a note, also suggested that Blum seal his letters with wax. In a brief explication of the novel's composition, he added that "as for this book, it is, on the contrary, a deliberately formed whole, although the composition is so complex that I am afraid no one will grasp it and that it will appear to be a series of digressions. It is quite the opposite. See if you can do this favor for me; it is tremendous; but only if it is complete, definitive and assured. Your wholly devoted, Marcel Proust."[15]

René Blum was able to convince Grasset to agree to Proust's terms for the publication of *Swann's Way*. Proust's next letter to René, on February 24, 1913, indicated that he would communicate with Grasset by telephone when he felt well, which only happened once a week for an hour or two. The reader can only imagine the illness and neurosis that plagued the writer. Yet, in an accommodating tone, Proust offered to visit Blum at the offices of *Gil Blas*.

In his correspondence, Proust tried to surround this negotiation in mystery. He confided to Reynaldo Hahn that Blum helped arbitrate the publication of the book with Grasset, but he did not want anyone else to know about Blum's generosity. He also told Blum to encourage Grasset: "Since I have published nothing for a long time, I think that the friends of my writings will make this book profit by the sympathy they have for my ideas." He then hinted unabashedly that he could "submit it for some Goncourt prize or other."[16] Proust knew decidedly his own value, as he did receive the Prix Goncourt five years later in 1919.

In his final paragraphs, Proust began a fascinating discourse on the ambiguity of the book's form. He recounted that "it is a novel, or not quite," elucidating the fact that the main character, Monsieur, who narrates the story, used the nominative "I." He continued this testimony by acknowledging the book's surprises, saying that there were protagonists in the second volume who behaved in a way that the reader would never suspect after reading the first volume. "The composition is so complex," Proust affirmed, "that it will not be clear until much later, when all the 'themes,' have fused and begun to be combined."[17] The letter ended with a brief but striking picture of Proust's sad obsessions when he confessed that "my illness is taking the form of holding me up for months on some one word I am incapable of changing."[18] Though it was known that he died of asthma, it is intriguing to wonder what other ailments so troubled Proust throughout his youth; many opinions have been expressed. Did he suffer from a form of health anxiety, or chronic fatigue syndrome, or fibromyalgia, or was it asthma, as he thought, or perhaps a very neurotic disposition?

During the period, the French who could afford it often traveled to spas or a sanatorium for a "rest cure." When Proust decided to visit Florence on short notice, René Blum had already left for a stay at Dr. Widmer's sanatorium at Valmont in Normandy. Proust had thought of accompanying Blum, knowing that he had to change his hours in order to visit Florence by daylight. In a letter dated March 15, 1913, Proust asked René if he were feeling better and if the cure were helping him.

Months later, in November 1913, Proust wrote very briefly to Blum "because I am very ill. First because I have been worse I have not been able to undertake the condensation of a part of the novel into a short story for you."[19] No doubt Blum wanted to place such a short summary in the journal *Gil Blas* in order to publicize the book. However, Proust asserted that he would be satisfied if Blum added an announcement about the book in his journal as well as a few words about its author. In a bewildered tone, Proust admitted his discomfort: "It embarrasses me very much to ask this of you.— And if it annoys you, oppose it as energetically as you did Maurass's malevolences." Proust confessed that he spent most of his life pestering people not to gossip behind his back, but now he wanted the world to know about his works. In the same letter, he pondered the titles of the various volumes of his oeuvre, saying that "the whole series will be *A La Recherche du Temps Perdu*, or *Remembrance of Time Past*, and perhaps the novel following

Swann's Way would be *A l'Ombre des Jeunes filles* (*In the Shadow of Young Maidens*), or *Les Intermittences du Coeur*, (*Murmurs of the Heart* or *Fickle Affections*), or perhaps *L'Adoration perpétuelle*, (*Perpetual love*) or perhaps *Les Colombes poignardées* (*The Stabbed or Mutilated Doves*)."[20]

Proust recognized that his book contained "the best of my thoughts and even my life" and worried that it might be considered a series of articles, rather than a complete work. He offered a long meditation about the book and his praxis:

> It is an extremely real book, but supported after a fashion by a peduncle [or cluster] of reminiscences to imitate involuntary memory which in my opinion, although Bergson does not make this distinction, is the only valid one; intellectual and visual memory give us only inexact facsimiles of the past, which no more resemble it than pictures of spring by bad painters.[21]

Thus, for lack of remembering, we miss many of the sad and beautiful reminiscences of our past. However, in an encouraging impulse, Proust wrote that with a sudden whiff of perfume, memory is renewed. This sensory perception is especially strong when we see an object that belonged to a departed loved one. The forgotten fullness of our lives returns as Proust reaches back to the past:

> Immediately my whole life at that period is revived and, as I say in the book, like the Japanese game in which little pieces of paper dipped in a bowl of water become people, flowers etc., all the people and gardens of that period of my life arise out of a cup of tea.[22]

Proust stressed the unique nature of memory. Writer Evelyne Ender saw this revelation as "extraordinary," because "this sudden convulsive resurgence of the past, to which he gives the name *mémoire involontaire* creates a scene whose existence had remained, until then, unknown to the rememberer."[23] With those striking moments of sensibility, Proust confirmed the discovery of the unconscious and the power of memory that Sigmund Freud and Henri Bergson were simultaneously describing.

With Proust mindful of the teachings of the renowned philosopher Henri Bergson, his education included Bergson's lectures at the Sorbonne. In addition, he relished encounters with him at his home, as Bergson was a beloved cousin of his mother, Madame Weil Proust. Bergson's importance as a psychologist and philosopher impressed Proust, and many have suggested that Proust's work is bathed in Bergson's strategies of the unconscious and the circularity of time.

Proust continued this enthralling commentary from the November 1913 letter by admitting that he knew his work was often described as "delicate" and "sensitive," attributions he deplored. He wished to counter this impression by reminding us more importantly that his work was "living" and "true," not "the truth."

In one of the most concise and telling statements about his work, Proust revealed, "My book is a history of life. From my childhood until today, I find my characters across a whole world of people, their loves, and their pleasures until their demise when I enclose them in my creation."[24] Proust continued this focus on his characters: "My book is a painting of several layers of society, taken from different epochs, salons at the end of the nineteenth century, and both before and after the revolution that was termed the Dreyfus Affair. In my work the people of the world appear broken and crushed even by the grandeur of their names, that they are not worthy of owning."[25]

History and critical social commentary converged in Proust's painterly memories. As Ender described:

> Each successful retrieval of an involuntary memory follows the same carefully delineated pattern: an initial mood of quiescence, the sensory trigger, the sudden and renewed sense of identity that accompanies the recollection, and finally the gradual unfolding of memory that grows incrementally through associations into an intricate, reticular, structure of images.[26]

The literary critic Pierre-Quint also penetrated Proust's personal thoughts on his writing and identity by emphasizing the importance of Proust's consideration of the role of unconscious memory and his search for the "real" reality buried within each individual. Our recognition of the heart of our being through involuntary memory reveals what Pierre-Quint noted were these "instant privileges, these extraordinary resurrections, the source for all profound reality."[27]

Blum remained close to Proust during the whole process of publication. He arranged for "echoes" or brief notes that announced the release of *Swann's Way;* they were short, tantalizing descriptions to attract the reading public. Proust thanked Blum "with all his heart" for the valuable comments by Jacques-Émile Blanche, a critic for *Gil Blas.* In the April 14, 1913, *Gil Blas* issue, Blanche wrote:

> *Du Côté de chez Swann* (read it and you will see how well chosen this intriguing title is), carries in it the most irresistible and magical moments. It evokes a Paris that no longer exists; without being a roman à clef, I do indeed recognize two or three true models for each personage; it has the savor of an autobiography, and also of a work overflowing with sensibility and intelligence.[28]

Proust knew that Blum savored the innovative qualities in his writing. But in order for Blum to enter its hermetic universe, he had to spend quiet moments with Proust, immersing himself in Proust's glorious prose and questioning Proust about his praxis.[29] This occurred when Proust invited Blum to his home to read aloud from *Swann's Way*. When Proust became fatigued, he summoned Blum to recite the portion about Combray, the garden and its inhabitants, and the famous madeleine cake taken with a cup of tea. That same evening, Blum was apparently stunned by the brilliance not only of Proust's eloquence, but also of his insight into the construction of memory and the meaning of time. Proust's understanding of the nature of memory, taken from his own reflection on the connection of smell and taste to lost memories, appeared to have shocked René into recognizing that his seemingly precious friend was a genius. It was after this encounter that Blum made an all-out effort to persuade Grasset to publish the book.

The encounter also stirred Proust's recognition of Blum's literary sensibility and critical intelligence. In an afterthought to a subsequent letter to René on November 13, Proust mentioned several lines from *Swann's Way* that had impressed Blum, those that "you adored when you read out loud to me the other evening. And because you read them to me, the words retained, enveloped as though by dark and delicate silken scarves, the sonorous sounds so rough, yet so sweet of your voice, harsh and tender, the voice of both critic and friend."[30]

Proust sent many short, directorial missives to Blum, and tried constantly to control events surrounding *Swann's* publication. In the November 23 issue of *Gil Blas*, Blum wrote his column "Le Livre du Jour":

> Tomorrow will appear the very first volume of the highly anticipated, *Swann's Way*; it is the youthful masterwork of a literary series by Marcel Proust. . . . *Remembrance of Things Past* marks a remarkable evolution of this amazing new and enlarged talent. Take a look at this short piece that shows Proust's exquisite delicacy and the richest stylistic ingenuity.[31]

Finally, a book arrived in Blum's office, with this dedication:

> Dear René:
> I want you to have this rather elegant first edition that Grasset sent me. In this way you get back the book that you brought forth with such a noble gesture and consecrated by a great artist who carried forth the head of Orpheus.
> Your grateful friend, Marcel Proust[32]

In what might seem like a betrayal of all that Blum tried to do, three years later, on May 31, 1916, Proust told Blum to break off ties with Grasset. Blum had considered it himself, since *Nouvelle Revue Française* (or *NRF*) had recently asked Proust if it could publish his work. And Proust did lose a great deal of money on the first editions. Grasset could not produce

Proust's next book right away because the publisher had been mobilized for the war effort, and his publishing house shut down temporarily. Impatient, Proust wanted to be released from his contract with Grasset and to reclaim the first volume, since he had paid for the publication. Apparently, the *Nouvelle Revue Française* was already working on the proofs of four volumes that Proust had arranged for the simultaneous publication of.

One year after the original publication in 1913, Grasset was drafted; he fell ill from typhoid in the summer of 1915, was hospitalized, and then sent to a Swiss sanatorium. It was in the midst of the war, when René Blum was in the army, that Proust asked him to find Grasset. This was a sensitive and awkward situation, as "Grasset had incurred large expenses since the whole of the second volume was already in print; in the proofs he had received in June, and the final pages were typed."[33] The writer Painter revealed that Grasset "had given Proust an excellent contract, with twenty percent royalties for this and the rest of the work; and now he was expected to relinquish not only the future volumes but the already successful *Du Côté de Chez Swann* without compensation, to sign away one of his most promising authors without protest, almost as an atonement for injury."[34]

An interesting aside to these negotiations was the importance of André Gide, who founded the NRF along with Jacques Copeau, Jean Schlumberger, Eugène Montfort, and others. When the first issue appeared in 1908, a quarrel with Montfort ensued and he was let go. The NRF strongly reflected the influence of Gide until 1940. Gide had rejected Marcel Proust's initial entreaties to publish *Swann*, as he found Proust an extremely demanding and unreasonable author. In his biography of Gide, Alan Sheridan pointed out that "what was known of Proust was not encouraging. He was clearly a social climbing snob, who moved in a quite different world from the rather serious-minded NRF group."[35] Also, Proust irritatingly laid out many conditions for publication, and what tipped the decision against it was that the work was "extremely indecent and dealt, among other things, with homosexuality."[36]

After reading the Grasset publication, Gide realized his great mistake and agreed to publish the volumes that followed. Gide was a practicing homosexual (or invert, as the Victorians said) and extremely interested in problems surrounding his sexuality. In those days, when homosexuality was considered a psychiatric disorder and sinful, its discussion was most often hidden. Sheridan recounted that Gide and Proust became quite good friends in Proust's final years, and that shortly before Proust's death, he sent a car to fetch Gide; they spoke in a stiflingly warm room, while his host was shivering with cold. Proust longed to discuss homosexuality with Gide. Gide objected to the stigmatization of homosexuals in Proust's *Sodome et Gomorrhe*, but Proust denied this allegation and mentioned that he did not long for youthful beauty in men as did Gide, but rather was fascinated by the nature and complexity of homosexual desire.[37]

Proust implored Blum once again, in the May 30, 1916, letter, to initiate the "divorce," but like a guilty husband, he cautioned Blum not to hurt Grasset. This was a difficult time for Blum, as he was in the military and stationed in Amiens. When on leave, he was able to travel to Paris, probably to see family, but on the way he visited Proust. Proust's health had not improved and he was deeply concerned about his friends in the war. He admitted that one of his medications was adversely affecting his memory. Life was distressing. He spoke about several of his friends who were fighting the Germans—Jacques Rivière, Jacques Copeau, and others. But what was most crushing was that his friend Bertrand Fénelon had fallen in battle. He bemoaned his plight: "So cruel is my anguish for me to stay in bed without quantities of veronal, so cruel is my anguish that I cannot expect to see Fénelon again." Proust divulged that he loved Bertrand and the time they spent together. He regretted his loss: "Now I never speak of him. But I know with what affection he loved you, loved us." In his last sentence he cried, "It is a great sorrow, but a great compensation to talk to you about him."[38] And with this last sigh, the letter ends.

In July 1916, Proust thanked Blum for smoothing over the rupture with Grasset. Then he spoke about Blum's mobilization: "I know my dear, that I cannot speak about the one thing about which everyone is talking, of the one thing that I am thinking about, like everyone else, and a bit 'cruelle-ment,' because all that is very close to us, and we know that you wish to be going there. But I know that such things are forbidden to write about. So let me say that though your courage is most alarming, it also strengthens my affection for you."[39] This mysterious, self-censored paragraph is about the misfortune of Blum being sent to the Somme, where a great battle of the war raged, and where many men had died. At the Somme, Blum would be cited for bravery and given the Croix de Guerre.

Proust did not forget Blum's role in guiding his relationship with Gras-set. In his next letter to Blum on July 17, Proust told Blum that he thought about him a great deal, and realized that he had misjudged his qualities: "My dear René, I am very touched by your words, those that remind me that you think of me a great deal, even though we have not seen each other, and that you have a place where an interior Marcel Proust resides." Perhaps the war brought out these deep feelings. Proust added that "though you do not know it, you too live in me." In some ways Proust was a cynic, in others a trusting friend. He told Blum he was "the only person with whom I can be totally sincere."[40] Proust was a flatterer. He repeated Blum's name several times—"in any case, we return to the misunderstood René Blum, to René Blum who is punctual and conversational and gifted with qualities that do not insist on his talents—this René Blum with whom I have the pleasure of sharing your esprit and your heart."[41]

Despite the daily miseries of war, Blum participated in the odd and triangular correspondence between Grasset, Proust, and himself. Due to Blum's subtle persuasion, Proust succeeded in annulling his contract with Grasset, who acceded to most of Proust's wishes, even though Grasset had his own serious financial problems and a debilitating illness from the war. In these last letters, we imagine Proust as a war hero, suffering and alone, and pressuring everyone to print his works before his death. In an August 14, 1916 letter, Proust described to Blum the torments of his illness, noting that an intense and pounding fever was weakening him terribly.[42] A month later, on September 25, 1916, Proust wrote that he could no longer write Grasset because his eyes were failing and this malady was exhausting him.[43]

One of the last times René Blum's name appeared in Proust's correspondence was in a letter written to Jacques Hebertot, a critic for *Gil Blas*, on January 31, 1917. "I would be very grateful if you sent my most tender thoughts to René Blum. I haven't written him because I suffer so much from my eye problems, but I think a great deal about him."[44]

However, in a gesture of appreciation in December 1919, Proust sent Blum copies of his *Pastiches et Mélanges* with a brief note explaining that he intended to send him first editions, and that he had someone searching all the bookshops, but could not recover any of them. Proust complained that he had to leave his home, and "that nearly killed me. How happy I would be to see you."[45]

Proust died four years later in 1922. A sad casualty of the aftermath of his death was the loss of most of René Blum's personal letters to him. Perhaps Proust did not save them; only a few letters from Blum to Proust were recovered in the archives of the publisher Gallimard.

In Proust's multivolume *Remembrance of Things Past*, he painted many portraits of those individuals who populated the elegant salons of his era. Both Philip Kolb[46] and Ilan Greilsammer[47] suggest that the fascinating figure Albert Bloch is modeled on the personality of René Blum. Naturally, many qualities of this stunningly crafted person exceed Blum's makeup. For example, Bloch at times pushes people around and imposes his ideas on others; overly emotional, he overwhelms the Victorian and aristocratic French. At one point, he drags the hero of these volumes to a brothel. Some of these events reflect poorly on Blum's nature. But in many ways, Proust fashions a Blum-like picture of the enigmatic Bloch. For example, he is a young, very good-looking Jew who frequents the fanciest of salons in Paris; he is widely considered deep, philosophical, and informed, although opinionated. In *Within a Budding Grove*, Proust defined him as "capable of being extremely nice."[48] In Bloch's relationship with the hero, "He understands him, cherishes him, and grows sentimental to the point of tears."[49] The main character, a sickly youth, reaches out to the world for exotic experiences and knowledge, and turns to his friend Bloch for rich conversations about literature, especially about de Musset and Leconte de Lisle. In a sense, Bloch is the ultimate aesthete, judging all aspects of words and nature with an eye to perfection. But Bloch's Judaism, however hidden, prevented him from being accepted and welcomed by the parents of the protagonist, as if Bloch's presence might infect the hero. Bloch also takes a fiercely positive view of the contemporary writer Bergotte, who has not as yet succeeded in convincing others of his great talent. Bergotte fills the hero with a joy "without comparison, with his taste for uncommon phrases, the same musical outpouring, the same idealist philosophy."[50] Could Bergotte represent the young Proust whose writing and career Blum helped to launch?

The intriguing story of the Proust/Blum correspondence ended in 1924, when the literary historian and editor Léon Pierre-Quint wrote René about collaborating on a book that included Proust's letters to Blum: "These letters from Proust to Blum seem to me to be of a major historical and literary interest. They tell the story of a fickle, seemingly superficial man who became a great creator of literature."[51] On December 2, 1924, René Blum wrote to Pierre-Quint that Proust was "great and well known," but that he saw little of him, especially in recent years, because Blum's life had changed and Proust kept company with new friends. Blum recollected those years: "I loved him very much, and also, I believe that he felt a certain friendship for me. It was I who made the connection between Proust and Grasset, who received the honor of publishing his first novel."[52] Pierre-Quint and Blum arranged to meet on December 12, but Blum indicated that he was very busy editing seven plays in rehearsal in Monte Carlo for January performances.

Probably Pierre-Quint and Blum did meet in Paris as they made plans to collaborate on this book. Pierre-Quint wrote Blum on May 2, 1925, that Doctor Proust, Marcel's father, had suggested that he and Blum prepare an article on the revelation of place and the importance of the senses in Proust's letters, organizing the letters for publication in a revue that would bear the signatures of both Pierre-Quint and René Blum.

Subsequently, Pierre-Quint sent Blum proofs of his book, which he asked Blum to read. On November 27, 1925, he restated his wish to create a book with Blum that would include the letters Proust wrote to Blum, as well as Proust's letters to the publisher of the *Revue de Paris*. Pierre-Quint asked Blum to write a "petite introduction" to the book.

On December 1, Blum responded, saying that he had no time to find the letters from Proust as they were locked in a box in his apartment and that the key was in Monte Carlo. The following year, on April 15, 1926, Pierre-Quint suggested that the book be titled *"Marcel Proust: Correspondance relative à A la Recherche du Temps Perdu*, d'un Éditeur avec une introduction et des notes par Léon Pierre-Quint and René Blum."

The last related letter in the Bibliothèque Nationale's Département des Manuscrits is one that Pierre-Quint sent to Blum on April 19, 1926. The letter contained a contract "relatif à la correspondance de Marcel Proust et René Blum" and asked Blum to sign it. Unfortunately, such a co-edited book was never published, although Pierre-Quint did publish his own, *Comment parut "Du Côté de chez Swann": Lettres de Marcel Proust.*[53]

CHAPTER 4

The Great War and René Blum

The First World War was unexpected, as most Europeans thought free trade made war a practical impossibility. Technological innovations of the nineteenth century had brought railroads and steam ships, the telegraph, anesthesia, the telephone, great improvements in health care including antisepsis and the X-ray, and widespread and growing international commerce. Who would want to destroy the worldwide prosperity that forty years of peace and nineteenth-century finance had created? For France and the French, la Belle Époque seemed to dull the public's appreciation for the tensions that existed between Serbia and the Austro-Hungarian Empire. It was also difficult to take seriously the bellicose obtuseness of Kaiser Wilhelm or to take into account certain strains in Russian society.

The war came, almost by accident, after the assassination in Sarajevo of the Austrian Archduke Franz Ferdinand and his wife by Serbian nationalists on June 28, 1914. This led Austria to declare war on Serbia on July 24, and Russia to respond with a general mobilization of its forces in support of Serbia, its ally. Germany then mobilized its army in response to Russia and on July 31 demanded that France declare itself neutral. Events accelerated; on August 1, Germany declared war on Russia, which was allied with France, and France in turn mobilized its forces. On August 3, Germany declared war on France and invaded neutral Belgium in order to outflank and bypass French defenses. The next day Britain declared war on Germany in support of its alliance with Belgium, and Europe found itself in a general war.

A mood of nationalistic euphoria swept through Germany, France, and England, summoning all patriots to enlist to defend their homelands. The Blum brothers, imbued with a great love of France and French culture, were swept up in the same events, and all five brothers volunteered, as did many of René's literary and artistic friends.

René Blum received the Croix de Guerre for his service in World War I in 1918.[1] He was lucky to have survived; the loss of 1,300,000 French lives was catastrophic. The following is a direct translation of the commendation that he received:

To René Blum:

Interpreter in the 19th Squadron of the Railway Supply Trains [the French version of the Quartermaster Corps]

For his auxiliary service in meeting the needs of the Allies, he did not cease in the course of the evacuation of Amiens and from the first advances of the other Allies, to show proof of his great courage, his complete dedication to his country, offering spontaneously during perilous missions to evacuate great historic objects in the localities situated in immediate proximity of the front line. He particularly distinguished himself in the course of reconnaissance operations to save works of art in Corbie and in Péronne during the bombardments by heavy cannon and at St. Quentin at the time of the bombing with asphyxiating gas. He gave proof of his perfect sangfroid and complete disdain for danger. Signed, Laguiche.[2]

Blum was 36 years old in 1914, yet he enlisted at the very beginning of the war, soon after August 4. Since he was too old for regular duty, he was seconded as a translator to an English division.

Reading about Blum's life and his devotion to artistic pursuits, one would never imagine that he might stand out as a brave war hero, as he did in World War I and toward the end of his life when he courageously spoke out

Figure 4.1
René Blum at war. Courtesy of Francine Hyafil.

to guards against horrific conditions in the French concentration camps at Compiègne and at Drancy. Who knows what he might have said to the German guards who led him to his death at Auschwitz?

Like René, his brothers (except for Léon, who was forty and had very poor eyesight) all served heroically in World War I. Georges Blum was sent to the front with the rank of aide-major; he was decorated with the Croix de Guerre and made a chevalier of the Legion of Honor. Georges Blum had been denied an internship after medical school because he was a Jew, but according to his daughter Françoise Nordmann, at the front he served as a physician/medic, taking care of the sick and wounded. The eldest Lucien also served bravely as a soldier. During 1915, in the battle of the Argonne, Marcel Blum was captured and remained a prisoner of war until 1918. During his captivity in Germany, he wrote heart-wrenching letters back home.[3] René was also taken to a prison with his British brigade in 1918; his great-niece, Francine Hyafil, provided this author with a photo of him in the prison camp. In sum, the Blum brothers made great sacrifices for the France they loved.

Many of René's friends from his early days in the Proust circle also served with honor. The whole of French society joined to fight, bore the brunt of the casualties, and essentially won the war for the Allies. The suffering of the French explains their insistence on German reparations after the war, which in turn would make German/French reconciliation impossible and contribute to the later rise of Hitler.

Comte Bertrand de Salignac-Fénelon, the anticlerical Dreyfusard, died on the battlefield in Mametz on December 17, 1914, at the very beginning of the war. Marcel's brother, the physician Robert Proust, was in constant danger. His field hospital in Étain near Verdun was bombarded and shell fragments fell regularly on the operating table, nearly killing him. Despite the hardship, Proust continued to place himself in harm's way and was promoted to captain.

Proust's close friend, the musician Reynaldo Hahn, was posted with the writers Fernand Gregh and Robert Dreyfus to a safe regimental depot at Albi in Provence. But he demanded to be sent to the front and arrived there in November 1914. Hahn was a very talented young man, the favorite pupil of Jules Massenet at the Conservatoire and a gifted singer, pianist, and composer. Not French, he was born in Caracas, Venezuela, of Jewish parents and lived in Paris with his mother and several sisters. Proust met him at Mme. Lemaire's Tuesday salons on the Rue Monceau, where he sang at her musical evenings for twenty years. Proust and he maintained a passionate affair from 1894 to 1896, and afterward they remained good friends until Proust died. Reynaldo saw and risked death every day, yet he composed a joyful regimental march that the soldiers in his regiment, the Thirty-First, would whistle.

Cocteau, wearing a beautiful uniform designed by the famous couturier Paul Poiret (1879–1944), joined an ambulance unit organized by Misia Edwards and her third husband to be, Jose Maria Sert. According to Painter, Cocteau "became the mascot of a marine unit, then was recommended for a croix de guerre, arrested as a spy, and rescued in the car of a general who happened to be a friend of his father. Jacques Bizet served for a while at the Hôpital Saint Martin and later ran a munitions factory during the war."[4]

Georges de Lauris joined André Gide at the Foyer Franco-Belge, a relief center for Belgian refugees, while the Duc Albufera served as Maréchal Joffre's chauffeur. By the end of the war, Joffre was the commander in chief of all French forces. Loche Radziwill organized a Polish brigade with "privates," as everyone wanted to be an officer. The surrealist poet Guillaume Apollinaire died as a result of brain injuries. Proust, of course, could not fight, but the war became part of his life.

At the outbreak of the fighting, publisher Bernard Grasset, along with his editors and printers, had been called up to the army, and the publication of Proust's second volume, originally planned for October 1914, was postponed for the duration of the hostilities. As mentioned before, Grasset fell ill from typhoid in the summer of 1915 and remained in a military hospital until he was transferred to a Swiss sanatorium.

The outrageous Robert de Montesquiou, hoping to show his allegiance to France in some way during the war, arranged in 1915 to read the first volume of his war poems *Les Offrandes Blessées* to a group of friends at the Palais Rose in Vesinet. He created 188 elegies on the war.

A series of letters René wrote during the war to various literary figures is housed in the Bibliothèque Nationale's Département des Manuscrits. In a postcard to Robert de Montesquiou dated October 26, 1914, Blum acknowledged that his isolation on the front was more formidable than any solitude one could imagine. He recalled spending pleasant hours in Montesquiou's garden in Vesinet near Paris; since then, he lamented, "I cannot communicate the chagrin and the pain of mourning, bereavement and loss that I am experiencing."[5] With his journal echoing his miserable condition, he wandered from town to town, from station to station "without force, without refinement, and without the consolation of imagining a beautiful death" ("sans esprit, sans délicatesse, n'ayant pas même la consolation d'imaginer une belle mort").[6] "Please pity me," he asked, "and hope that I will finish this sad year for those who are going to begin their vows of happiness and please try to recall a memory of me that is warm and friendly." René received a copy of Montesquiou's *Les Offrandes Blessées* while at the front. In a letter dated May 24, 1916, he apologized to Montesquiou for not writing sooner. He confessed to thinking of him and their cordial meeting in Montesquiou's garden often, and remembering nostalgically the happiness he felt in being alive at that time and how he would have liked to respond to Montesquiou's affectionate words, but "did not dare."[7]

It is difficult to imagine Blum caring about this odd and flamboyant personality. Further on in the same letter, Blum meditated on his tormented sensibility, apologizing for not having thanked Montesquiou for the poems. He explained, though, that he had read the poems to his "camarades" blinded in the war, and that while traveling in ambulances, they listened intently and applauded the sonorous elegies. Blum revealed to Montesquiou that he was at the Somme in the 4e English Army, and hoped that Montesquiou would not revile him for his "trop long" silence. He signed the letter from Le Service de Ponts et Chaussées (Military Engineers), at Amiens.

In other letters from the trenches—or as the French called them, the Zone des Tranchées—he intimated how frightening the war was there. He also wrote Porto-Riche, the playwright, in 1917 about how his brother suffered gravely in a prison camp in Germany. He asked Porto-Riche for help in securing Marcel's freedom and possibly securing Marcel's promotion as well.

Blum kept a brief wartime journal, fragmentary and missing some pages. It offers a close narrative on his war, the tedium and crashing boredom of daily chores, the mindless traveling by train back and forth, and the waiting.[8] The journal spans just eleven days at the war's outset, from August 27 to September 6, 1914. It is possible that he wrote additional entries that are now lost; however, it is fortunate that this little booklet survived.

The early pages describe the constant thunder of distant cannon, and how the sounds called forth historical memories of the war of 1870 against the Prussians. He thought many of his countrymen must also have remembered seeing or hearing about the enemy and wondered why the officers in this new war could not make up their minds to attack. In a conversation with himself, he asked, "Are we leaving? Must we stay and fight? This would be the greatest desire of our Colonel. However, all my comrades do not share his impatience. They prefer their vagabond existence, a bit jolting but leisurely for the past two weeks. Once again we are on the march at night toward the station this time." The French soldiers finally learned that their destiny was Rouen. Time passed and they tried to keep warm; the wagon trains arrived late with Belgians who were poorly paid and inhabited circles of squalor compared to the French accommodations. There was a constant movement of trains filled with ammunition and men. Although only one hour from Paris, Blum felt infinitely far away.

When he arrived in Rouen, René wrote, "We realized that the only other soldiers are English and Belgian. The English live in superb accommodations, sanitary and clean. But the Belgians are frightening to observe, poorly equipped, without guns, without proper equipment or uniforms. Their faces suffer from misery and dirt; their country has lost, or been compromised and they seem very discouraged. . . . As we march through the city, we are impeded by constant streams of cars and supply vehicles driven by the English. They seem carefree and living in prestigious luxury, not at all like us. Their supplies come from London, including London taxis; it is a curious spectacle." Blum's company made its way to a village outside of Rouen, arriving at a school where they were bivouacked. He continued to bemoan the plight of the Belgian army: "The Belgians have left behind a disgusting mess, despite the fact that they behaved like heroes during the war, they ignore the most elemental rules of hygiene. In vain do we clean and disinfect; we try to eliminate the strong odors. I am unable to sleep here and must find other accommodations." In both the first and second world wars the British, and later the Americans, were treated better and paid more than the French, although it seems that conditions for the Belgians were even worse.

Blum mentioned that he spent some happy times in Rouen with a fellow soldier, M. Durand. They walked to the center of town where they encountered a lighthearted, merrymaking mood. This was preferable to staying in their bunks and waiting for disaster. Thousands of men in uniform enjoyed the outdoor cafés and balconies. In a huge restaurant, he chanced upon an old friend, André Nital from Brussels. He wrote that it was difficult to sleep due to Durand's snoring, so off he went to town again to eat. Rouen was filled with the English and with wounded Belgian soldiers. Blum drifted to the Hôtel Angleterre where he was disappointed not to find mail from his friends or family. On the way, he stopped a drunken Englishman from running his lance through another unsuspecting Englishman.

As in all wars, he reported that there was always the same boring idleness—it was merely a question of passing the time. After a languishing morning, he and Durand looked for another friend, Wagner, and then ambled to lunch close to headquarters. It pained Blum to think about his brothers, especially Georges, when he passed the military doctors. "I cannot stop thinking about my brother 'Jo,' Georges, from whom I've received no news for a long time."

Blum was concerned about the young and thoughtless soldiers, no older than children. "There is a threat of punishment for the absent ones, as we leave tomorrow with the English and the Belgians. We are forming the defense of Rouen, and finally are becoming useful. The administration is very severe but so ineffective."

On the tramway to Rouen, he met another old friend, Jean Levêque, who dined briefly with them, as Jean had to return to his post. Blum wrote about the dinner:

Next to us a soldier described some very moving events of the war. He told us how an English officer did not respond to the summons of a sentinel who then killed two of his own men and for some reason, cut off their fingers. He simply got up on his horse and smoked a cigarette. The weather was horrible and rain drenched everything. Allied soldiers kill one another and cannot stop unless an interpreter becomes aware of this contemptible act and warns them. Many other stories are so simple and sad. Another diner told us that he was made prisoner, surprisingly near Valenciennes; happily he was able to escape at night, without his uniform. But he held on to his money hidden beneath his undershirt.

Near the battlefield at a small station, Blum narrated some mundane events as the war and the enemy drew closer: "It's the last train. The station chief and his wife line up all the travelers on the staircase and on roofs, as the enemy is near. Everyone is accounted for. A heavy package falls at the feet of the wife; it is a shell that doesn't explode. She climbs the staircase, her husband follows, a bullet is heard; the train takes off. We arrive in Rouen, full with trucks and soldiers." Assurance is supplanted by fear that quickly dissipates. Blum describes meeting his friend Wagner: "We rejoin an auto that carries my friend Wagner who is distributing a quantity of letters from Paris. We cross a little quiet village, a solemn church surrounded by small shops with trifles and gifts from Germany for their tourists." He is relieved to discover a letter from his father: "Watching the doling out of letters, for the first time I notice my father's handwriting and this is enough to engender warm feelings for this place. We are lodged in a girl's school whose brave directors try to distribute bedclothes and covers. But I refused their straw pallet and looked for another refuge."

Blum sought more comfortable accommodations:

I find my way to a tombstone factory, but suffering from a kind of superstition, I move on. On the advice of my friend Durand I display my badges. This brings on a welcome from a peasant household. They offer their bed; they have no less than nine children who are astonished to see me. Their mother has told them that, "here is a soldier with a crown—a heroic soldier." The youngest child imagining that he is going to see some majestic apparition, seems disappointed to meet another soldier like all the others.

There were brighter moments, such as when Blum awoke in Rouen to find a glorious day of perfect tranquility, with the gardens in bloom; he was able to sit down and write in the "charming simplicity." But his tone changed when he learned that his regiment must push on to Angers at 11 a.m. He was heartened by the groups of women who generously handed out drinks and food along the march. When the troop's train arrived, its destination changed from Angers to Le Havre. There the soldiers were told that they would receive bottles of wine. Unfortunately, others spotted the "potable delicacies" and made off with them. Thus there was no wine, but somehow everyone collapsed into laughter and general hilarity.

A decided hierarchy existed among those serving in the war; a few were privileged and lived well, while others were deprived. Blum suffered from insomnia and being in the war only exacerbated this condition. On the trains most soldiers were forced to sleep on hard benches. "The war is not a soft, plushy place to work," Blum noted. "On one side of great hangars the soldiers are volunteers, on the other side they are 'dockers' in charge of transportation services; they wear impeccable military uniforms and are perfectly groomed and elegant, while the others are dirty and unkempt."

When the soldiers arrived in Le Havre, they found a bustling city crammed with trucks, trains, and storage areas packed with coal. Housing was only partially built, but there were several dance halls where train employees might grab a meal. The dining hall was drafty and uncomfortable, with hundreds of English soldiers everywhere, "most half drunk," to Blum's horror. Blum described the ridiculous attempts of his soldier companions to make themselves understood by the English. "It is a ludicrous pantomime." Blum made a great effort to practice his "erudition" in the English language, but he quickly admitted that the listeners were puzzled by his refined speech.

Finding himself ascending and descending from one end of France to the other, Blum eschewed any criticism of the zigzag routes the troops followed. For example, military officials dispatched them from Rouen far south to Le Mans, and then immediately to the northwest coast to Le Havre, where they collected many English soldiers and then moved on once again to Ponthène near Le Mans. The reasons for these and many more such journeys were never clear, but then war is never clear.

In Le Mans the soldiers were transported in a very heavy English wagon to an electric tramway. The mood there was lighthearted and buoyant, with the streets overflowing with French and English soldiers. The stores were full and the cafés overwhelmed with people. Newspaper vendors were everywhere, and most people were engaged in conversations about the war and the news of battles that seemed more and more depressing. All the animation centered in the Place de la République, but there were no more rooms in the Hôtel de France where they were supposed to stay. Once again, Blum lacked a decent place to sleep. Finally, he discovered an unoccupied building where, in a corner, a big box of hay stood. There he slept. Protecting himself from the freezing cold with a thick cotton hat, he wrote, "This must have been laughable to behold!" The narrative leaves off suddenly just as he was deposited in new lodgings without any chance for exercise, where he and his men did much sulking and grinding of teeth and were left limp and depressed. The final pages of the journal include a schedule of their train travels and times of arrival.

Blum wrote this intriguing chronicle before the true horror and carnage of trench warfare had begun. We participate in his Candide-like entry into a topsy-turvy and somewhat chaotic world. As a sophisticated young man, he loses his bearings and experiences a sense of helplessness and exhaustion. He is startled by the senseless and gratuitous decisions of officers who play a Simon Says game and change their strategies midstream. All these things caused Blum consternation and a feeling of unending boredom, until he was actually involved on the battlefield.

The First World War left France exhausted. It had held back the German advance, and finally, with the help of Britain and America, defeated Germany. In so doing, though, France lost 1,300,000 men and had to provide for 1,000,000 wounded. Its industrial base in the north was in shambles and the French franc had lost much of its value.[9]

The French army that in consort with its allies had defeated Germany remained the strongest army in the world. Yet it would succumb, as would all of France, to renewed German aggression in 1940. The tumultuous events of the interwar decades could not but have affected René.

In the United States, despite President Woodrow Wilson's enthusiasm for the new League of Nations, the Senate refused to ratify the Treaty of Versailles, which might have protected Europe and France from another world war. In France too many factors militated against this. After the Armistice, the split between the working classes and the middle and upper classes soon reemerged. From the end of World War I, the French left could only see the war as a capitalist battle over land and resources that would not benefit the working classes. Horne writes:

> For the French Left the Russian Revolution of October 1917 touched a deep-rooted historical memory that would influence socialist thinking until the advent and even after World War II. An important schism reemerged between the working class heirs of 1789–93, the revolution of 1848 and the Commune of 1871 and the middle classes of France.[10]

The First World War caused lasting damage to the French financial system. In 1914 the exchange rate for the French franc was 5 to the dollar. In 1918 one British pound sterling bought five U.S. dollars, while the French franc was 26 to the pound. By 1919 one pound was worth 51 French francs. In May 1926, that value had plummeted to 178 French francs to the pound and by August 1926, to 220 French francs to the pound.[11] With rapid inflation, these wide fluctuations in the value of the franc mirrored the difficulties that all currencies were experiencing in the 1920s and 1930s. Yet in 1937 the value of the franc fell to 175 francs to the pound sterling, a fall that caused René Blum considerable grief. By 1945, one dollar would purchase 45 French francs.[12]

Despite the crisis in its financial system after World War I, France rapidly recovered and repaired its industrial and agricultural base, and by 1926 it was again economically productive. The war had brought together the French people in a national purpose to defeat Germany, but the postwar years exposed deep schisms in French political life between the working classes—who saw themselves as the heirs of the revolutions of 1789 and 1848, and the Commune of 1870—and the middle class of shopkeepers, professionals, and farmers. Further divisions existed among those who adhered to conservative Catholic beliefs, monarchists, the military class still angry over the Dreyfus affair, and the broad majority of the people who considered themselves conservative republicans.[13]

As the consensus that had helped France and its allies defeat Germany broke down after 1919, political chaos ensued. France was to have innumerable governments, including seven different finance ministers in the 1920s. There were five new governments alone between 1929 and 1931. Despite Germany's weakness in the 1920s, the French felt obligated to maintain the largest standing army in Europe and to build a series of alliances to surround Germany. In France the left remained alienated from the government; indeed, government and industry had little regard for the needs of workers. But the workers did not present a coherent front, split into Socialist, Communist, and Catholic blocs, although the Socialists held 107 seats in parliament by 1928.[14]

The inflation that bedeviled the monetary system was in part due to the increasing demands of French workers for higher wages and improved working conditions. The French also expected that the United States and Britain would forgive France its debts, but they did not. When Germany defaulted on its reparations, France occupied the Ruhr, which angered Germany and contributed to the rise of Hitler and the Nazi Party. A lack of leadership prevented France from extending a hand to or reconciliation with Germany, which might have turned the tide of anger and recrimination between the two countries.

Perhaps more than anything else, as Alistair Horne pointed out, "By the end of the 1920s it was painfully apparent that the Third Republic was suffering from a deficit of great men as much as it was of great ideas." Further, "With the return of Alsace-Lorraine, the supreme motivating and uniting ideal had been removed from French Politics."[15]

Of all the educated professional men mobilized to the army, 23 percent were killed, including a number of René Blum's friends. Perhaps that accounts in part for his silence in the years immediately after the war. France had lost a whole generation of future leaders. Blum would have to build his remarkably successful theatrical career in a financially and politically unstable world that in the end would undo his best efforts.

With his appointment as the director of the Théâtre de Monte-Carlo in 1924, René Blum's career flourished, reaching a new high with his assumption of the leadership of the Ballets of the Opéra of Monte Carlo in 1929, and finally directorship of the renewed Ballets Russes in 1932. That Blum was able to succeed with these three ventures, despite the political and financial turmoil in France between the wars, speaks to his remarkable abilities. Perhaps Monte Carlo provided a financial and political stability not found in France during those tumultuous decades between the world wars.

CHAPTER 5

René Blum and the Théâtre de Monte-Carlo (1924–1931)

In late 1924, René Blum was hired as artistic director of the Théâtre de Monte-Carlo, charged with creating a rich and exciting repertoire of new musical plays and comedies from December 19 through January 11. He did not hire dance companies in his debut year, but the number of productions and performances, including dance, increased dramatically as Blum's reputation for assembling innovative seasons spread.

Like many of the cities on the Côte d'Azur, Monte Carlo spills serenely down a hill overlooking the sparkling, sapphire Mediterranean Sea. The Genoese Grimaldi brothers, ferocious pirates, captured Monte Carlo in the thirteenth century, hoping to gain advantage from its well-situated port. Eventually, the Rainiers, another side of the family, achieved control through their military prowess and clever dealings with France. The tiny spot of land, only 1.9 kilometers square, began to prosper in the nineteenth century from the beauty of its seacoast and mountains, as well as from the money that could be made from gambling and the general profligacy of the world's leading playboys and girls. Secrets of the city were murmured everywhere, from suicides to bankruptcies, love affairs, broken romances—all the makings of soap opera.

Gambling caused the Grimaldi-Rainiers much torment, as well as profit. They were haunted by scandalous tales of losses and rejections. But during Blum's tenure, the casino's winnings contributed 95 percent of Monaco's total revenues and were the mainstay of the city's many sites of performance and amusement. Today, surprisingly, gambling only contributes between 5 and 10 percent to Monte Carlo's economy, having been replaced by international banking and commerce.

Figure 5.1
View of Théâtre de Monte-Carlo, 1911. Courtesy of Archives Monte-Carlo, SBM.

Monte Carlo has long been the subject of imaginative press reports, as well as the source of popular gossip and envy. One rogue was said to have faked his own death, smothered himself in tomato sauce, and then walked off with a fat wallet before the police arrived to claim the corpse. Parisian journalists hired to investigate Monte Carlo's monopoly on gambling reported that a small, secret cemetery in French territory, some miles from Monaco, was reserved for people who lost their fortunes at the gambling tables and then committed suicide. They were carted off surreptitiously in the dead of night.[1]

A visit to the principality was not a foreign journey for the French, who considered Monte Carlo a tiny municipality of France. The railroad from Paris and its luxurious "train bleu" banked dramatically along the Mediterranean, carrying passengers from all the major cities in Europe, America, and the rest of the world.

In 1924, Bronislava Nijinska's ballet *Le Train bleu*, created for the Diaghilev Ballets Russes de Monte-Carlo, parodied the fashionable and often frivolous characters who rode from Paris to the Riviera. With costumes by Chanel, a stage curtain by Pablo Picasso, music by Darius Milhaud, and a libretto by Jean Cocteau, it was the quintessence of chic so adored in Paris. According to Vladimir Fédorovski, the actual train was constructed in 1921, in "bleu roi" or royal blue, and began its first journey in 1922. The chief designer built the sleeping cars of metal, rather than the traditional wood, and decided to paint the trains blue as a sentimental reminder of the decorations on the uniform he wore as a young Alpine guide.[2]

In the late nineteenth century, Princess Alice, who married the great oceanographer Albert I of Monaco, was a widow with a large coterie of aristocratic gossips and art lovers. She was the daughter of Michel Heine, the

Figure 5.2
Le Train Bleu. From left: Lydia Sokolova, Anton Dolin, Jean Cocteau, Léon Woizikovsky, and Bronislava Nijinska. Photo by Sasha, courtesy of Getty Images.

poet's nephew, and, oddly enough, a native of New Orleans. Her Jewish background nettled Monaco's subjects, who wanted a princess of royal blood. Albert, who sailed frequently in the Mediterranean and the Atlantic to study ocean life, was rarely home. (Eventually, Albert's collection became the famed Oceanographic Museum in Monte Carlo.) Alice lost interest in Albert and soon found another lover, Isidore de Lara, a Sephardic Jew and conductor of the Monte Carlo orchestra.

In 1892, with the help of the opera's first director, Jules Cohen, Princess Alice hired Raoul Gunsbourg to take over the full-time direction of the new Salle Garnier, named after its architect, Charles Garnier, who also designed the Paris Opéra's Salle Garnier in 1874. The Salle Garnier in Monte Carlo was inaugurated in 1879 with Sarah Bernhardt dressed as a nymph and reading poetry. With nearly six hundred theatre seats to fill, it was essential to attract the thousands of visitors who came each year for the opulence and sweetness of life in Monte Carlo.

Gunsbourg's regime lasted for sixty years; he was responsible for hiring René Blum as artistic director of the Salle Garnier in 1924.[3] An exceptionally witty and exciting personality, Gunsbourg preferred the artistic flair of the designers for the Ballets Russes, Léon Bakst, and Alexandre Benois; most importantly, he had a genius for handling star performers who trusted him. According to Stanley Jackson, "He captured the loyalty of his orchestras by offering handsome salaries with pensions for long-term service, but he insisted on the highest standards."[4] It was not long before brilliant singers such as Melba and Caruso performed in Monte Carlo, where only 20 francs (worth one dollar in the 1920s) were charged for theatre seats. The population of Monaco rose from 1,200 in 1861 to over 20,000 at the end of the nineteenth century, though very few people were Monégasque citizens. Today, there are approximately 32,000 permanent residents in the entire country; only about 5,000 of them are Monégasque citizens. In the 15 years between 1924 and 1939, there were close to 100,000 visitors, or approximately 6,000 people each year.[5] These figures offer an idea of how many people came to gamble; to watch the automobile, aviation, and boat rallies; and to attend the theatre. The aristocratic upper crust may have diminished after World War I, but the "beau monde" of industrial and bank magnates and movie stars increased a great deal.[6]

Monte Carlo became the perfect destination for foreign opera, theatre, and dance troupes, largely because France, and especially Paris, suffered severe economic problems between the wars. Taxes were very high in France, and only a few Parisian theatres could accommodate the large scenery that major productions required. Also, orchestras that claimed exorbitant fees could be afforded in Monte Carlo, contributing to the popularity of both Monte Carlo and London as destinations for dance companies.[7]

Figure 5.3
Profile of Raoul Gunsbourg. Photo by DuGuy, courtesy of Arts du Spectacle, Bibliothèque Nationale.

Prior to World War I, many members of the Russian nobility vacationed on the Mediterranean or nearby in Monte Carlo for two or three months every winter. The Romanov family dominated the social scene and Tsar Nicolas II, a fan of Caruso in St. Petersburg, was delighted that Gunsbourg had arranged for him to sing in Monte Carlo. The patronage of the tsar and his family could make any restaurant an instant success, and the fashionable and luxurious Hôtel Hermitage, where they stayed, was immensely popular, as it still is. In those prerevolutionary days, a Russian entourage would arrive by wagon-lits or sleeping cars with retinues of mistresses, valets, and even soothsayers to assist in their gambling forays.

The Société des Bains de Mer or SBM (Society of Sea Baths, or spas), an overarching organization of financiers and administrators, controlled the Casino de Monte-Carlo and its games, spas, and theatres. One of the most successful of the SBM businessmen was Basil Zaharoff, a clever upstart who made a lot of money during World War I selling munitions and land at cheap prices. He became rich and powerful, owning a majority of shares in the SBM along with Prince Léon Radziwill.

René Blum, who was aligned with Prince Radziwill, also held stocks in the SBM. At the Préfecture de la Police in Paris, archives containing documents concerning Léon Blum included a few pages regarding René Blum's affairs. On May 2, 1931, it was reported that:

> In the past 6 months, Prince Louis of Monaco has tried to obtain a majority of SBM stock in order to oust M. René Blum who represents the interests of Prince Radziwill's heirs. Blum's brother Léon is the Deputy for Narbonne. With a majority of the shares, and speaking for his group, René Blum offered Prince Louis the majority, but at double their value. The Prince refused the offer and told Blum that he would go to the press and reveal this story, especially to embarrass his brother Léon.[8]

René Blum was financially astute, especially in his loyalty to Radziwill, with whose family he spent a great deal of time in Paris. Having powerful allies ingratiated René with his superiors Alfred Delpierre, the president of the SBM, and René Léon, a brilliant manager with an interest in science and mathematics. They both promoted the Oceanographic Museum in Monte Carlo as a major tourist attraction, as well as a place for experimentation and research. Along with Gunsbourg, they recognized the importance of having a first-rate theatre with distinguished opera, ballet, and theatre stars.

Of all prewar attractions, and second only in tourist appeal to the casino itself, the Ballets Russes won Monte Carlo great prestige and fame. The creation of Diaghilev's independent company, with Monte Carlo as its headquarters, came about almost by chance and for the silliest of reasons. Gunsbourg owed his most spectacular artistic triumph to a pair of Nijinsky's too-revealing silk tights.

In 1910, Gunsbourg had attended the season of the Ballets Russes in Paris and found the dancer Tamara Karsavina gorgeous and graceful, while Nijinsky astonished him with his "electrifying entrechats."[9] Gunsbourg offered Diaghilev a contract for 8,000 gold francs to which Diaghilev agreed. At the Maryinsky

Figure 5.4
Interior of Théâtre de Monte-Carlo. Courtesy of Archives Monte-Carlo, SBM.

Theatre in St. Petersburg, trouble was brewing. *Giselle*, an established ballet favorite, was chosen for a gala performance for the imperial court. Nijinsky went on stage in a black velvet vest and the close-fitting white silk tights, but without the small slip obligatory for all male dancers. The dowager empress took one scandalized look and fled from her box, followed by the tsar's young daughters. Monte Carlo, on the other hand, embraced such scandal.

Blum knew and admired Serge Diaghilev. In an article in *Comoedia*, April 2, 1936, by P. M. (Pierre Mortier), Blum elucidated:

> I must tell you that during those seven years that I knew Diaghilev intimately, I found him a master, a great artist, a creator to whom we owe the resurrection of dance in this theatre in Monte Carlo. First of all, he showed me the immense resources of modern ballet as an eclectic art, how it synthesizes harmoniously dance, music, poetry, architecture and painting. One day Diaghilev made an offer that I collaborate with him, which made me terribly proud.[10]

In an earlier letter dated June 12, 1926, René Léon wrote Diaghilev that he was surprised to receive a letter from him, and that he thought Diaghilev no longer wished to play in Monte Carlo since he had not heard from him in a while. "If you are planning to have a January season in Monte Carlo," Léon said, "then you must contact René Blum for further discussion."[11]

Blum and Diaghilev were watchful witnesses to each other's endeavors in Monte Carlo, especially when Blum took over as artistic director of comedies and operettas in 1924. As a young man in Paris, Blum reveled in the excitement of the Ballets Russes. It may well have been an important reason for him to accept the job of producing in Monte Carlo. In 1924 Diaghilev found himself happily courted by the new Prince Louis's daughter and husband, Pierre de Polignac. Sjen Scheijen commented: "Pierre, who cultivated a reputation as a lover of culture, took

Figure 5.5
Serge Diaghilev. Courtesy of Arts du Spectacle, Bibliothèque Nationale.

up the role of Diaghilev's guardian angel. Monaco would become the Ballets Russes' base of operations, and during the winter months would play the principality's theatre."[12]

During the five years that Blum worked with Diaghilev, they were cordial but often at odds. In early 1925, Diaghilev asked for six machinist stagehands to help in his productions and a dress rehearsal. Unfortunately, Blum's productions were performing concurrently at the traditional Théâtre de l'Opéra and needed all available machinists, while Diaghilev's company played in the smaller Nouvelle Salle de Musique. Diaghilev's request was denied, which only made him more jealous of the power and quality of the publicity for Blum's theatrical season. He inquired who had done such a professional job organizing the productions and was told that Blum himself had designed and arranged for everything in his budget.[13]

In a letter written on January 24, 1928, to his superior, René Léon, Blum complained in precise detail about a particular incident concerning the costumes for the opera *Le Mariage de Figaro* that Blum had brought to Monte Carlo. To allow Diaghilev free reign in all areas of the theatre except the valuable *Figaro* costumes, Blum locked them up in a particular loge and gave the key to his costumer in charge. Diaghilev's costume person proceeded to make nasty remarks about Blum, his personnel, and his productions, in order to recoup the key to the loge, which was refused. However, another key was found that opened the costume area, and when its door was left ajar, one of the costumes disappeared. Greatly upset and insulted, Blum felt personally attacked by Diaghilev, who certainly knew everything about the item's disappearance. Blum asked Léon to "make an inquiry into the incident," and to "sanction the costume woman who disobeyed Blum's instructions about those opera costumes."[14] Despite such incidents, so typical in theatre life, Blum and Diaghilev developed a mutual respect and an amicable relationship.

It is interesting to compare the ways in which Blum and Diaghilev appeared to the critical press, and responded to questions concerning their artistic choices. In an essay by dance historian Lynn Garafola concerning Diaghilev's interviews with critics and writers, his strong modernist tastes supersede any polite conversation. We know from both history and legend that Diaghilev took charge of everything in the ballets, from ribbons and wigs to choreography and movement ideas. Blum, on the other hand, tended to stay within his musical, artistic, and editorial expertise, offering advice about the flow of a story, hiring designers whom he knew in Monte Carlo and Paris, and making suggestions about scores for ballets and plays. He did not insist that a choreographer follow his counsel on how the balletic steps

Figure 5.6
Stamp from Monaco, 1966. Photo by David Bennahum, courtesy of Francine Hyafil.

should be formed. Blum's amenable personality allowed him to work with and better tolerate those with whom he might disagree.

Diaghilev never recovered from the loss of his "Mother Russia" to the Communist regime, a situation he blamed in part on Germany's aggression in World War I. His blatant hatred for Bolshevik propaganda art and German music underscored many conversations with journalists. Blum, on the other hand, rarely alluded to politically sensitive issues in the newspapers, especially because his brother's career might be harmed by an offhand or thoughtless remark about governments working with France, and also because he seemed to embrace a variety of musical compositions from many countries.

Diaghilev's passionate love for Russian music reflected his émigré status and his true appreciation for the modern ideas of Stravinsky and Prokofiev. Diaghilev spoke and wrote truthfully about his opinions. According to Garafola, "He unleashed a diatribe against German music and the English taste for it. His intemperate language with its repeated use of the derogatory term 'Boche' for German, gave a political and national dimension to what was, in effect, an artistic argument—the superiority of modern French and Russian music."[15] At one point in 1919, Diaghilev engaged in full battle with a music critic from the *Observer*, responding to the critic's comments with biting letters. Blum would likely have expressed his thoughts in a discreet and diplomatic manner.

Above all, Diaghilev was a creative genius, with impeccable insight into the potential of ballet choreography when fused with art and music. His ability to court and mentor potentially brilliant artists served him very well in the twenty years he ran his company. Though Blum wore many hats, his major concern was his job as a producer, like Sol Hurok, who fundamentally relied on his business acumen and the strategies of booking theatres to which audiences would flock. Blum's talents included bringing artists together, but his knowledge of ballet was much more modest than Diaghilev's. It is important to remember that Blum was a critic; his attitude toward the press was thus progressive, as he understood its role in the politics of art.

As Blum became more accustomed to his authority in Monte Carlo, he must have enjoyed a warm fellowship with his aristocratic audiences and through his newly found relationships with the powerful Grimaldi/Rainier families. The friendships of his early years on the Paris art scene continued, and he hired these artists for his seasonal productions. His lack of narcissism and self-aggrandizing behavior appear to have been much appreciated, although in his later struggles with the Colonel de Basil, he was often trumped by the colonel's powerful ego.

As a Jewish boy born to a father of modest Alsatian heritage, he did not take the luxury of his new social class for granted. His contacts in Paris during the time he visited the salons of Geneviève Straus and Arman de Caillavet must have impressed and spoiled him to some extent, but in Monte Carlo, far from the scrutiny of "tout Paris," he found his place. Young Marcel Proust wrote to a friend, "I would like to indulge myself in the fantasies of a great nobleman."[16] Certainly, René shared his friend Proust's sentiment, and by all accounts, he achieved that status in Monte Carlo.

In one of the tributes compiled in *René Blum (1878–1942)*, a book edited by Marcelle Tristan Bernard in 1950, Georges Huisman spoke about Blum's importance as a producer and how his far-reaching knowledge of the arts stood him in good stead:

> He had read everything, seen everything, and heard everything. He would know exactly what play, opera or ballet could be produced by any French house as he had a deep understanding of the inside workings of companies and producing. . . . He was born to make discoveries; he was the first to make public the comic powers of Marcel Pagnol as well as the analytic genius of Marcel Proust.[17]

Antoine Bibesco also lauded Blum's theatrical flair, reminding us that many great French artists such as Jacques Deval and Marcel Pagnol owed their celebrity to him.[18]

Antoine's cousin, the author Marthe Bibesco, was in Blum's debt as well; Blum had encouraged her in her writings, as he had many other young writers. Marthe admired Blum's magical gifts: "His career followed an enchanted path in literature, music and dance. He consecrated his life to all the things that went into a ballet—writing, color, music, rhythm, harmony and movement."[19] She added that after Diaghilev's death, René brought back the genius of the Ballets Russes de Monte-Carlo to the world.

One of the many artists who worked with Blum in Monte Carlo, Jacques Chabannes, recalled their close partnership: "When he was asked in 1924 to direct a season in Monte Carlo, I became his closest collaborator with his friend Henri Gautrin. We saw Madeleine Renaud in *La Beauté du Diable*, a piece by Jaques Deval, with a talented young comic Michel Simon."[20] Both Renaud and Simon became great stars of French theatre and film. Chabannes stopped working with him in 1928, but their friendship never ended.

The great author Colette also characterized Blum as an astute producer. She recalled him in Monte Carlo as someone who brought the same "good grace to any situation."[21] Blum convinced her to perform the role of Lea in her play *The Last of Chéri* along with Léopold Marchand as the boxing teacher, in December 1924. At dinner after a late rehearsal, Marchand was experimenting with different shades of makeup. When asked if one of them was more suitable, Blum responded ironically, "But of course you now look like a sportsman with an attack of Scarlet Fever."[22] Colette spoke arrestingly about her "amateurishness" as an actress, and she liked it when Blum encouraged her to be outrageous. Colette's experience as an actress had begun at a very young age, and during the 1920s, she toured in her play *The Last of Chéri*.[23] So perhaps her claim to amateur status was designed to protect her from the critics.

In an impassioned homage addressed to René Blum, the writer Romain Coolus wrote: "Of all the intellectual activities that captivated you, it was particularly the theatre."[24] He knew how much Blum respected men of theatre like Antoine and Lugné Poe, and how closely he followed their careers. Coolus mentioned the beauty of Blum's dramatic work *Les Amours du Poète*, which received a very warm welcome in Monte Carlo and elsewhere.

Yet how difficult it is to find traces of René Blum. The elusive quality of his life story may be due in part to his modesty. Coolus also praised Blum's self-abnegation and the fact that he served others with little attention to himself. This went beyond the theatre, as was noted in his last days at the concentration camp at Drancy. In the same collection of essays, Georges de Lauris echoed Coolus: "He never put himself before others,"[25] and he loved socializing with theatrical personalities such as Tristan Bernard, Georges de Porto-Riche, and others. There are many vibrant photographs of Blum with the dancers, actors, and other artists in Monte Carlo in the 1930s. He seemed so happy to be in their company.

Writer Roland Dorgelès was one of the young artists Blum discovered and encouraged after World War I. He remembered, "You were an indefatigable dilettante, capable of counseling a director, a painter or a ballerina or musician. And at your office on the rue Taitbout, there was always a parade of people waiting for you."[26] He speaks of a time when a dilettante was not a trivial person, but rather one with many interests and talents.

By 1938, as World War II loomed and the French franc plunged in value, Blum was fired by the authorities of SBM, but not before he had achieved the influential artistic aegis that he merited after sixteen years in Monte Carlo (far from his brother's political career). As the historian Frank Biancheri noted:

> During his sixteen years as producer for the universally known stages in Monte Carlo, René Blum deployed his taste for perfection, and his passion for the discovery of new talent. This gave to the theatre an extraordinary vitality, an effusion of performances, of creations, a parade in the principality of authors and actors known and less known throughout the seasons of theatre, opera and ballet under his direction.[27]

From 1924 to 1935, Blum produced 140 different works for the annual winter seasons each December and January in Monte Carlo. For the Anglo-Saxon patrons, there were forty new English productions.[28] Forty brand-new productions in eleven years is a major theatrical accomplishment that gives us a measure of the man.

To illustrate the complexity of Blum's work, in one of his many of letters to Société des Bains de Mer Director René Léon, dated October 5, 1924, Blum's lucid commentary on three projects offers an idea of the myriad difficulties he encountered before each season was set on the calendar. One dealt with his meeting with a theatrical company manager/owner, M. Alexandre, who requested 30,000 francs for his troupe to pay for travel, costumes, etc. Alexandre wished to perform a play by Raoul Charbonnel, "*La Grande Machine* in verse, distinguished, honorable and rather boring," but Blum wrote confidently that this was the sort of drama that would play well in Monte Carlo. He made three requests of René Léon: to change the dates for the Alexandre group, to rethink the cost of bringing the company for 30,000 francs,[29] and to question whether the actor Maurice Rostand's talents were suitable for the female role, La Gloire. Such was the mundane, yet essential, everyday business of the director of the Théâtre de Monte-Carlo.

In December 1924, Blum produced *La Corinthienne* by Charbonnel with actors from the Comédie Française, *La Beauté du Diable* with Madeleine Reynaud and the great comic Michel Simon, *Les Bulles de Savon* by Jager-Schmidt with the clown Harry Baur, and in January 1925 Pirandello's *Henry IV*, in a performance that astounded the audience. Despite the diverse and often philistine nature of the Monte Carlo public, Blum did not hesitate to produce complex and challenging theatrical works.

For example, Alain Corneau in the *Journal de Monaco*, in January 1925, commented on René Blum's production of Pirandello: "This amazing dramatic writer of such distinguished reputation, a philosopher and a poet as well, put on stage with remarkable intelligence a subject so complex, so troubling, and of such a dramatic intensity, and of such a remarkable elevation of thoughts and ideas. . . . This man is a masterful artist, and we must discover his worth with profound respect and admiration."[30]

The Pitoëff Company offered Alexandre Dumas's celebrated *La Dame aux Camélias*, with the admirable actress Marguerite Gautier performing the role for the first time in France, on January 7, 1925. Blum closed the 1924–1925 season, on January 11, with superb acting by Lucien Guitry in Émile Augier's *Le Gendre de M. Poirier*. On January 6 Guitry also appeared in *La Griffe* by Henri Bernstein, a distinguished playwright who had numerous stage successes. Guitry was among the greatest actors of his time; these were his last acting roles, as he died in 1925.

Others, like the famous Antoine of Paris' Théâtre Antoine, spoke glowingly of Blum's first two seasons in Monte Carlo.[31] In 1924, after experimenting with the film *Le Miracle des Loups* by Raymond Bernard, a cinematic triumph, Blum staged *Je suis trop grand pour moi* by Jean Sarment, followed by *Le Prince Charmant* by the incorrigible Tristan Bernard, after triumphant performances in Paris at the Théâtre Michel. Blum sought a balanced and interesting array of titles, each with its own theatrical luster, knowing that Paris welcomed plays that had a successful run in Monte Carlo.

After mounting such interesting projects his first year, Blum believed his situation to be more secure. On October 19, 1925, he wrote René Léon about how invigorated he felt, but that in making arrangements for future productions in Monte Carlo, he needed certain assurances from the Council of Administrators at SBM, as he felt inhibited by his "transitory position." He added that he did not enjoy speaking about himself and reassured Léon that his "friendship and good faith" empowered Blum to request that his position as director be confirmed for the forseeable future.

Opening a month earlier, in November 1925, and running through January 1926, the second season also radiated excitement. Blum added operettas such as Romain Coolus's *Les Bleus de l'Amour*. As we noticed with Tristan Bernard, Henry Bernstein, and Coolus, Blum's Jewish heritage often led him to collaborate with authors and composers of Jewish descent.[32]

In early 1926, *Le Roi des Schnorrers* (a Yiddish term meaning "someone who takes advantage of others") by Israel Zangwill was staged. The comedy season also featured Jean-Jacques Bernard's *L'Âme en peine* and British plays like Oscar Wilde's *The Ideal Husband* and George Bernard Shaw's *L'Homme du Destin*, a daring move as the predominantly French audiences were generally repelled, as Michel Pharand stated, "by Shaw's insistence that intellectual passion transcends any physical passion."[33] But Blum calculated that he must also appeal to his English visitors who, after World War I, were increasingly attracted to Monte Carlo as a beautiful and exciting playground.

Raoul Charbonnel's *Bertrand de Born* was part of the season, as was a new piece by François Curel (of the Académie Française), *La Viveuse et le Moribond*. Blum added some repertory as well: *Peer Gynt* by Ibsen (with music by Grieg), for which Blum wrote, not surprisingly, a learned introduction on Ibsen's prodigious importance as a playwright. Another presentation was the eighteenth-century comedy, Marivaux's *On ne badine pas avec l'amour* with M. André Brûlé, Mary Bell, and Josette France, who became Blum's great love and the mother of their child Claude-René. Another risky production, Shaw's *Sainte Jeanne* was presented on January 1, 1926. Seven plays by Shaw were produced in Paris before *Sainte Jeanne*, and none were successful. What made the difference was the extraordinary performance of Ludmilla Pitoëff as the young warrior. She and her husband Georges were Russian émigrés whose company had acted in *La Dame aux Camélias* in Monte Carlo the year before. Ludmilla created a resounding success in Paris on April 28, 1925. Pharand wrote, "Ludmilla was the very Jeanne that Shaw would have despised: tearful, frail, vulnerable, sentimental, melodramatic and saintly. The French loved her."[34] As a result of the play's success in Paris, Blum was able to attract French audiences to this production.

For the Comédies/Operettes 1925–1926 season, Georges Courteline wrote a brief introduction to the souvenir program. He spoke of his long, close relationship with Blum, whom he called a "most charming and clear-minded person." He praised him for his ardor in bringing to life new and exciting ideas that Georges espoused. Courteline lauded the season to come as a threshold that would bring Blum great renown; finally, he embraced him as a brother, a friend, and an artist.

One of the pleasures René's travels to Monte Carlo provided was the opportunity to visit with and observe the formidable Diaghilev, whose company was in Monte Carlo for its seasonal performances. The sophisticated followers of the Ballets Russes who promulgated, in a sense, the famed modern art agenda—Jean Cocteau, Misia Natanson Sert, Clive Bell, and the designer and wealthy patron of modern art Comte Étienne de Beaumont—brought the salon-promoted modernism from Paris to Monte Carlo. Since its inception, the Ballets Russes had introduced audiences to exotic fare, challenging their aesthetic values with innovative productions, first under the guidance of Diaghilev and after 1929 under René Blum.

For example, in 1924 Ballets Russes performed *Les Tentations de la Bergère ou L'Amour Vanqueur* with choreography by Nijinska and scenery and costumes by Juan Gris. Nijinska was the sister of the extraordinary dancer and choreographer Vaslav Nijinsky, who became mentally ill and unable to continue dancing. Francis Poulenc composed the music and Marie Laurencin designed the scenery and costumes for *Les Biches*, a charming romp by Nijinska about the rich and *très chic* denizens of the Côte d'Azur.

The following year in 1925, Diaghilev presented spectacular if less innovative performances to Monte Carlo. Looking to attract the more traditional ballet audiences, Diaghilev returned to Petipa and Tchaikovsky's *Sleeping Beauty*. A one-act suite of dances, *Les Contes de Fées*, brought together Nijinska and Gontcharova in the hope that a splendid production might lure larger audiences. A shortened version of Act III of *Swan Lake* was also staged, while Massine choreographed *Zéphir et Flore* with music by the renowned Russian/American contemporary composer Vladimir Dukelsky, a.k.a. Vernon Duke.[35] For Blum, the opportunity to observe the rich Diaghilev tradition determined the choices he would make with his own ballet company.

The popularity and success in the 1920s of films from both the United States and France were not lost on Blum. His office on the Chaussée d'Antin, located in the middle of the Right Bank, was several blocks from the Paris Opéra, and one block from the Mogador Theatre, which played spectacular operettas when not showing films. The Mogador, originally called the Palace, opened in 1919, and was considered "le premier théâtre d'operette de Paris."[36]

The value of film as both expression and memory gradually became important to performance. Though Massine was a fan of new technology and bought a camera to record dances he was researching, Blum actually encouraged Massine to film his rehearsals, so as not to forget the day's new choreography, and to create a history of the ballets on which he was working. In *Ballet Annual*, Pierre Michaut reiterated:

> Everyone in the ballet world knows that Léonide Massine had made records of his ballets on 16mm film, and that he makes use of these films when reviving works of his own repertory. He first began this series of films at Monte Carlo, the idea being originally that of René Blum, founder and director of the Compagnie des Ballets de Monte Carlo. In 1936, René Blum, who had been in the twenties one of the leading members of the Cinema Club movement, was still interested in the problems and possibilities of the cinema; he it was who gave the order that the repertory should be filmed.[37]

A headline in the London *Daily Telegraph* of April 22, 1925, announced that the Casino de Monte-Carlo was being transformed into a movie studio. The article, written by Alder Anderson, touted the panache and excitement of the groundbreaking film being produced at the casino in Monte Carlo.

Although no mention is made of René Blum's name, there can be little doubt that he was responsible for this turn of events.

The British Gaumont Company and the Phoca Film Company of Paris teamed to create *Monte Carlo*, a brilliant presentation of the city's opera house as transformed into a banquet and ballroom. Lights blazed everywhere to illuminate the hundreds of guests from Friday evening to dawn the next day. Anderson spoke sarcastically about how the bright film lights varied the colors of the crowd to what he called a "dully grayish purple" and "the faces to a sickly yellowish green hue propitious for shooting."[38] The scene, however, was extremely animated, with cameras set up in every possible corner to catch the lively events and celebrities, especially those of English heritage. Flowers and balloons were strewn and tossed from the heights of the galleries, while Betty Balfour, the "star" of the film, and other cast members, including Colonel English and Carlyle Blackwell, were busy acting out their roles under the prodding of director Louis Mercanton.

René Blum's passion for cinema found further expression in his programming for the Monte Carlo theatre. A list of the films shown from 1925 to 1927, all with orchestra, included: November 28, 1925, *Destinée*, by film author Henri Roussel; February 12, 1926, *Carmen*, based on Mérimée's story; January 13, 1927, *Le Chevalier et la Rose* (Grand Film), created after Hoffmansthal; and December 20, 1927, *La Valse d'Adieu*. The heartbreaking scenarios of these passionate films appealed to the romantic bent and escapism of visitors to Monte Carlo.

Blum's approach to dance was no different from his ongoing interest in whatever was new in art; all styles of dance excited him. In 1925, Blum contracted the services of Loie Fuller and her company, the remarkable dancer and pioneer in modern dance, if only for one performance. Her company's use of movement in *Ballets Fantastiques* was minimal compared to their startling manipulations of hundreds of yards of silk and other materials illuminated by dramatic lighting. Casting attention on the body, extended and ornamented in a way never before seen, Fuller's dancers enthralled audiences. Her eloquent and diverse choice of composers, from Debussy to Schubert and Berlioz, enhanced the depth and quality of her company's performance.

In another area of innovation, Art Deco, René Blum also made a lasting contribution. In 1925 he was one of the organizers of the annual spring International Exhibition of Decorative Arts in Paris, where his name figured prominently on the program. This was the luminescent site for the origin of the Art Deco style to which he contributed through his acute taste in art books as well as his highly developed sense of what was new and exciting in all the visual arts.

The decorative arts were not considered minor arts during this period. John Ruskin, the celebrated philosopher of art highly respected by the writers of his generation, announced that there was not an existing art higher than the decorative arts, and they were not just the privilege of the rich.[39] Ruskin's insights enhanced the popularization of commercial home design. One only has to think of Ralph Lauren and Martha Stewart at Dillard's and Kmart today to appreciate the democratization of interior design, and theatre and film entrepreneurs such as René Blum helped establish modern taste and style. Programs for the 1925 Decorative Arts event recalled the universal exhibition of 1900 on the Esplanade des Invalides, which spread over the river to the Champs Elysées and the Grand Palais.

Decorative arts comprised such crafts as furniture, textiles, silversmithing, art books, architecture, fancy housewares, pottery, stained glass, and carpets. This first international enterprise was inaugurated on April 28, 1925, with millions of francs dedicated to the various national exhibits of twenty countries, including Italy, France, Switzerland, Austria, England, Japan, Turkey, Czechosolovakia, and Belgium, with its palace built in a massive cubist style. With a touch of irony verging on ridicule, a critic wrote that "Soviet Russia has put up a bizarre structure something like a greenhouse, all the walls, apart from the glass, being painted an aggressive blood red."[40]

Britain was allotted four times more space than any other foreign country, probably because it was still a great industrial power and asked for more space to display its brilliant products. Since large numbers of visitors from all over the world attended this fair, exhibiting fine specialties enhanced national reputations. There was definitely a competitive edge to the proceedings. All the most important French dignitaries and politicians, including the president of France, participated in opening ceremonies that attracted thousands of people and were broadcast throughout Europe.

The couturier Paul Poiret appeared with a showing of his many creations on four separate houseboats. Several pavilions were built by the great department stores to house their displays. (Unfortunately, we do not know if the Blum brothers, who were in the clothing trade, participated in these displays.) Not only adults were enchanted; children also reveled in the special enclosure known as the "Village of the Toys," where all the structures were built in the form of toys with a toy windmill at the center.

A Scandinavian reporter for *Apollo, a Journal of the Arts*, Bengt de Törne, wrote several enlightened articles on the Decorative Arts Exhibition. He asked a key question, "What is an international exhibition meant to express"?[41] He replied that "the nineteenth century created many changes, more than any other in the history of mankind and was optimistic about the new abilities in the decorative arts to find a simpler, less ornate or detailed aesthetic." He praised Cubism for its clarity and Platonic vision, and predicted that "modern aesthetic ideas were in opposition to the nineteenth century.... Visitors will see the strong northern influence on buildings. The charm and attraction of mysticism is profound in our days."[42]

In another article, Törne discussed, somewhat ingenuously, a remarkable talent in Cézanne's canvases: "He just builds up his design with rocks that look tangibly solid. But if the objects have solidity, and if his painting reproduces distance, it is not that of nature. . . . Cézanne's paintings create an illusion of nature, 'a chaos of forms' which it was his business as a painter to translate into a cosmos."[43]

Törne also described the theatre of the exposition, wryly criticizing Parisian producers for placing too much emphasis on Luigi Pirandello. However, he felt he had to summarize the narrative of one of Pirandello's more fascinating plays, *Così è (se vi pare)*, in which the characters all seemed to be imagining their own realities. "The philosophy of this play," according to Törne, "is a derivation of the idea of Schopenhauer."[44]

After this stimulating exposition to which René Blum contributed his taste and organizational skills, he embarked on a new summer season to produce the Boris Kniaseff Ballet Company, booking the troupe at the theatres where he was artistic director. Having learned from Diaghilev about exceptional production values, a compelling libretto, and a fine score, he hired the talented Kniaseff to appear at the groundbreaking Théâtre de l'Exposition Internationale des Arts Décoratifs in Paris from July 22 to 29, 1925. The programs consisted of *Étude d'après Verlaine*, with music by Chopin; *Le Feu sacré*, with music by Gabriel Dupont and Spendiarov; *Obsession*, with music by Sibelius, and *La Soif*, with music by Glazounov.

Born in St Petersburg in 1900, Boris Kniaseff studied with the renowned teachers Michael Mordkin and Kasyan Goleizovsky; he left Russia for Constantinople and worked there with stage designer Pavel Tchelitchev and several Russian dancers before moving to Sofia, where he became ballet master at the National Theatre of Bulgaria. He married and partnered the famed prima ballerina Olga Spessivtzeva, and later settled in Paris in 1932, where he ran the ballet at the Opéra Comique.

Kniaseff's attention to careful training inspired him to create what is known as floor barre, or "barre par terre," which many dancers learn to this day in order to protect their bodies from overuse and overwork. Kniaseff's company stirred great interest in Monte Carlo in 1930, and Blum invited him back for the 1931 season.[45] Over the years, Kniaseff built an experienced and talented company; many of the dancers eventually performed with Blum's Ballets Russes.

Monte Carlo still adored watching Diaghilev's sumptuous new works. On May 4, 1926, Diaghilev's Ballets Russes presented *Romeo and Juliet*,

Figure 5.7
Boris Kniaseff in *Aux Temps des Tartares*. Photo by Waléry, Paris, courtesy of Jerome Robbins
Dance Division, the New York Public Library for the Performing Arts, Astor, Lenox, and Tilden
Foundations.

designed by the modern artists Max Ernst and Joan Miró, and choreo-
graphed by Nijinska with an entr'acte by Balanchine. And in 1927,
Balanchine created *La Chatte* starring Spessivtzeva and the eloquent
Serge Lifar.

During the 1926–1927 season, Blum made an ineluctable contribution to French theatre when he engaged Marcel Pagnol, a relatively
unknown Provençal writer, to stage in Monte Carlo what would become
his very popular *Jazz*. The play had attracted some attention in Paris,
and consequently Blum brought it to Monte Carlo on December 6,
1926. In a later program, from the 1929–1930 Saison de Comédie et
Operette, Marcel Pagnol offered a charming and detailed description of
his first encounter at René Blum's apartment on the rue de Tocqueville
in Paris:

The walls were covered with books, and what books they were! While I was waiting for him, I glanced at the titles and handled the leather books reverently. There were there all the poets, all the romantic writers, all the dramatic authors. And in what editions! But in the middle of the book case, on a special stand, stood the most beautiful Marcel Proust in the world, attached were the letters of Proust to his friend René Blum.[46]

Pagnol continued his narrative about Blum, "He entered the room, tall, thin, blond with a short, wide moustache. He sat at his desk and began to read *Jazz*, he seemed to know it better than I." Blum, like most French people, spoke with his hands, but in large slow gestures, and he went on about the whole production with the keen awareness of a production manager confident in his choices for his theatre.

Apparently, Blum impressed Pagnol with his lively imagination: "What he constructed before me was a kind of dream about my play, and I listened with a calm joy not at all thinking that this could all take place in two months." Pagnol's *Jazz* centered on a brilliant man who dedicated his entire life to his work and, realizing too late the uselessness of this sacrifice, vainly tried to recover his youth. The production achieved a great success for Pagnol. One of his friends, the playwright Henry Bernstein, wrote a brief introduction to the production of *Jazz*, predicting that "Pagnol will become a great dramatist, 'a man of the theatre,' and that this is his true vocation and his greatest destiny."[47]

Some time later, Pagnol recalled opening night at the theatre of the casino in Monte Carlo, when he was so nervous that he was unable to watch from the audience. Backstage, he encountered René Blum, who took him by the arm, saying that it would be better to stay away until the end of the first act. Blum handed him 5 chips worth 500 francs, and told him to gamble prudently. He did, and when someone came to reassure him of the laughter and success of *Jazz*, he cashed in his chips only to discover that they were worth 6,200 francs ($270 at 23 French francs to the dollar at the time).

Gambling was not necessarily the most important pastime in Monte Carlo, as the city offered a vast network of marvelous entertainments. During the day, there were sailing, swimming, and competitive sailing regattas; motorboats, planes, and automobile racing also amused visitors. Baron Henri de Rothschild, Henry Ford, and John D. Rockefeller all gambled and played in Monte Carlo, living in luxury on their gorgeous yachts.

During the 1920s, René Léon tried to attract other American visitors to nearby Cap d'Antibes for evenings in Monte Carlo and Le Sporting Club with its top cabaret entertainment such as "Les Girls," a troupe of leggy Broadway lovelies that included a former Ziegfeld Follies dancer. Prohibition in the United States made Monte Carlo an even more attractive destination; by the early 1920s, Monte Carlo welcomed a diverse if fickle group of English-speaking visitors. These included the F. Scott Fitzgeralds; the Dolly Sisters, inveterate gamblers; Gerald Murphy, an American who painted sets in Gontcharova's studio; Elsa Maxwell, Cole Porter, Noel Coward, and the Ali Khan, who became one of "Elsa's ninety nine most intimate friends."[48]

With Blum directing the theatre at the casino, the quality of the productions greatly improved. During the 1926 season, the acting company of the famous Louis Jouvet put on an odd play, *Outward Bound*, by the English playwright Sutton Vane and received a kind of "succès de curiosité." The existential play appealed to audiences horrified by the relentless deaths during the fighting in World War I. It told the story of eight passengers on board an ocean liner who discover that they have no idea where they are going, or why they are onboard. It becomes apparent to the passengers that they are dead and they must go before an Examiner to determine whether their fate lies in heaven or hell. Perhaps this play presaged the later paralysis of Europeans before the emerging Fascist menace.

The more traditional dramas, *Lorenzaccio* by de Musset and *Le Bourgeois Gentilhomme* by Molière, garnered better reviews and pleased larger audiences, as they were performed by the celebrated troupe of the Comédie Française. Appealing to those who appreciated drawing room comedies, Blum also put on the musical comedy *Qui Êtes Vous?* by Paul Gavault and Georges Berr, and *Le Marchand de Lunettes* by his future co-writer George Delaquys, starring his partner Josette France. The film *Carmen*, written by Jacques Feyder, was played with a live orchestra, as were the plays *Demetrios* by Jules Romains and *La Grande Cathérine* by George Bernard Shaw, with music by Rimsky-Korsakov and Mussorgsky.

In 1927, Blum produced six new plays, including *Le Chevalier à la Rose* by Hugo Hoffmanstal, and once again he hired Clothilde and Alexandre Sakaroff. Earlier in the year, they had performed a *Gala de Danses*. The Sakharoffs fused a breadth of movement styles with a strong musical sensibility, offering scenic vignettes exploring different musical and choreographic forms such as the gavotte and the minuet.

They established an interesting niche for themselves in the world of show business. Like Loie Fuller, who radicalized dance performance with her eloquent lighting and scarf manipulations, they too found their own special kind of performance. Alexandre, born Alexandre Zuckerman in what is now Ukraine, trained in acting, modern dance, ballet, and acrobatics, and then coalesced these forms into what he termed "abstract pantomime." He married Clothilde von Derp in 1919, and their plasticity and elegance attracted audiences across the globe.

Alexandre's painterly talents inspired gorgeous, highly ornamental costumes that were the rage in theatres, variety houses, vaudeville, and grand casinos. Many important performers played in vacation spots, often attached to casinos where the well-to-do, or aspiring well-to-do, went to enjoy themselves and spend their fortunes. Occasionally, the critics were put off by the Sakharoffs' strange mélange of movement genres. Some years later, the *Journal de Monaco* on January 11, 1934, rebuked the company for not really performing ballet. It reported that "they were more like pantomimists than dancers. In addition their dances were cut off by entreactes of boring music, despite all the thunderous applause and bravos." On the other hand, the article continued, "Never have we seen such a gorgeous use of arm movements."[49] It concluded in a profusion of superlatives paradoxically contradicted by criticisms that questioned Alexandre Sakaroff's creative abilities.

Figure 5.8
Alexandre and Clothilde Sakharoff. Courtesy of Jerome Robbins Dance Division, the New York Public Library for the Performing Arts, Astor, Lenox, and Tilden Foundations.

The season brochure for 1927–1928 featured an essay by Georges Lecomte, a writer and member of the Académie Française. With great warmth, he described the qualities that distinguished Blum and his innovative work at Monte Carlo. Energy, optimism, youthful personality, and his intellectual curiosity were the sources of Blum's wonderful accomplishments. Lecomte referred to the thirty years that Blum had spent in both critical and creative writing, when as an adolescent, he emerged refined, sensitive, and fervent in his debuts in literature. He adulated Blum's career and the fact that he became a well-known personality in the Paris literary and art world, as well as backstage. Lecomte said of Blum, "All are unanimous in their opinions about his refined intelligence, his character, his taste and his graceful behavior. And this is especially remarkable for a man of the theatre."

Lecomte then launched into a discussion about another kind of successful artist, the egotistical and self-important writer. He insinuated that we know about such people who, the moment they reach a certain point in their lives, begin to act arrogantly and, for no good reason, create much fanfare about themselves. But, Lecomte noted, "Blum is discreet and speaks softly, and thoughtfully. He avoids the word 'moi,' and instead of vanity, he has the sense to know how to listen and the courtesy to appear pleased by what he hears."

Lecomte recalled Blum's years as an art critic when he wrote with discernment and taste concerning paintings, sculpture, and engraved works. He recognized that Blum was a pioneer in his support of beautiful art books as a new craft, by then much sought after. Furthermore, Blum's literary studies were penetrating and refined. Lecomte commented judiciously, "What few people knew was that Blum, in a quite original move, organized a union of writers, a kind of federation of intellectuals."[50]

The seasons continued to flow, with Blum pursuing his eclectic tastes and creating a canvas of sensitive performances of exceptional diversity. Small dance companies and even solo concerts seemed to play well at the Théâtre de Monte-Carlo. On January 1 and 3, 1928, Carina Ari appeared in *Scènes dansées* and followed with more performances that month. Born in Sweden, she had studied with Fokine in Copenhagen, and was a ballerina with the Ballets Suédois between 1920 and 1925. In a mildly ecstatic description of Carina Ari's dances, the writer Henry Malherbe painted a poetic picture of her eight dance scenes, describing for the reader how refined and agile her movements were, how supple and vital her plastic body sculptures were, and how she became a heroine worthy of Paul Valéry's magical poetry. Malherbe admired the sensitivity of her artistic taste, and the beauty of her costume and scene designs, writing that "there is no doubt that Carina Ari's stunning and innovative performance captivated the Monte Carlo audiences."[51]

To bring to a climax the 1928 theatre season, Blum scheduled *Les Ballets Fantastiques de Loie Fuller*. Unfortunately, Fuller could not perform, as she became ill and died suddenly of cancer. A brief obituary and review appeared in the *Journal de Monaco* on Thursday, January 26, 1928. For this performance, her company was able to carry on despite their loss. According to the critic, "The light exhibits lost none of their originality or their powerful impressionistic values." The critic briefly described each of the "delectable" scenes in very flattering and almost obsequious terms: "The exquisite sketches of streaming colors give infinite pleasure to the spectators, with their unprecedented brilliance. Here is where legend, poetry, the fantastic, and immaterial meet in the mysteries of scenic magnificence."[52]

One of the highlights of the 1928–1929 year was the appearances of the extraordinary Ida Rubinstein and her company. Blum had met Rubinstein years earlier when he tried to arrange a meeting between her and the composers Gabriel Fauré, Georges de Porto-Riche, and Jacques Rouché.[53] In Monte Carlo on January 10, Rubinstein, using the talents of the very best choreographers, combined several dramatically different ideas that were meant to explore the myths of diverse cultures, including a Greek mythological tale based on Cupid and Psyche, the biblical story of David, and the

Figure 5.9
Loie Fuller. Courtesy of Jerome Robbins Division, the New York Public Library for the Performing Arts, Astor, Lenox, and Tilden Foundations.

Figure 5.10
Ida Rubinstein. Photo by Drouet, courtesy of Jerome Robbins Dance Division, the New York Public Library for the Performing Arts, Astor, Lenox, and Tilden Foundations.

Russian fable *The Swan Princess*, among other themes. She also presented the passionately rhythmic piece *Boléro*, by Maurice Ravel. Perhaps the exotic forays of the American modern dancer Ruth St. Denis influenced Rubinstein or perhaps they influenced each other.

Rubinstein was born into an extremely wealthy Russian Jewish family from Kharkov, with a vast fortune in multifaceted commercial activities in the Ukraine. Both her parents died when she was a child; she was sent to her cultivated Aunt Madame Horwitz in St. Petersburg where, surrounded by innumerable cousins, she grew up in a very sophisticated environment. Traveling widely, Rubinstein wanted to see the land of her ancestors, and arrived in 1908 at age twenty-two in Palestine. Before World War I, the Middle East was an important destination for painters seeking new sources for their creative work. Thus, Rubinstein's worldly-wise youthful experiences prepared her to work with Fokine, Debussy, and D'Annunzio on *Le Martyre de Saint Sébastien*, produced in 1911.

A complex, narcissistic, and spoiled "star," Rubinstein was determined to create a company to rival Diaghilev's. She worked with great composers such as Ravel, Stravinsky, and Debussy, as well as the brilliant choreographer Bronislava Nijinska. After World War I, she acted in plays, danced at the Paris Opéra, and formed a company that Blum brought to Monte Carlo to great acclaim in 1928.

Her personal life was more outrageous than her professional one; today she might well have been a rock star. Her lifestyle shocked and intrigued everyone who knew her, due to her affairs with women artists such as Romaine Brooks as well as her ardent flirtations with several men, including the Italian poet Gabriel D'Annunzio, and a long-term relationship with Walter Guinness of the Guinness family of brewing fame. One of her most devoted admirers and friends was Robert de Montesquiou, the close friend of Proust and René Blum. Proust noted that Rubinstein was sensual, exotic, and had the most sublime legs.

In another attention-getting move, Rubinstein owned a panther with which she strutted about Paris. On one occasion, the panther jumped at Diaghilev when he visited her, forcing him to take refuge on top of a table. Several days later, probably on Diaghilev's initiative, the panther was removed from Rubinstein's household as a danger to human life.[54]

Before Diaghilev's premature death in August 1929, his company presented one new ballet in Monte Carlo in May: Balanchine's *Le Bal* to music by Vittorio Rieti, with costumes by Giorgio de Chirico, as well as a few lovely and provocative older works by Fokine, Balanchine, and Massine. Blum would successfully reconstitute these talents that dispersed after Diaghilev's death.

The luxury of an ocean liner did not escape Blum when he traveled on business to New York. In 1929, the sumptuous *Ile de France* gave him a much-needed rest from the stress of his career. He wrote on February 21, 1929, encouraging his brother Léon to plan a trip to America to offer lectures, something that René was trying to arrange. When René traveled to America, he presented himself as Léon's intermediary and publicist. The most important contact, it seemed from this letter, was to be the editor of *The New York Times;* however, the lectures did not occur. It is intriguing to consider, as the brothers grew older and lived far from one another, how close René remained to Léon, whom he admired profoundly. Unfortunately, the loss of many of their letters and the manuscript of René's autobiography leaves us without an intimate knowledge of their relationship. It is not clear how often Léon visited René in Monte Carlo. One or two letters indicate that when Léon represented Narbonne, west of Marseille on the Mediterranean coast, as a deputé, he visited Monte Carlo, where he undoubtedly enjoyed the sea air and the theatre productions.

In 1929 Blum's career took great strides forward. His contract as artistic director of the Théâtre de Monte-Carlo was renegotiated for the next three years and signed in April. With his other responsibilities, he also became the artistic director of Les Ballets de l'Opéra de Monte-Carlo, charged with the organization of theatre performances. He was additionally responsible for the grand celebrations of art for the Société des Bains de Mer, six festival evenings with ballroom dances and other festivities. For his services, Blum would receive 30,000 francs each year for three years. He alone was to choose the plays, the designers, and the actors. In addition, he was to arrange contractual payments with outside companies. But all of these "pourparlers" or negotiations, especially financial loans and disbursements, had to be approved by René Léon, the director of SBM who agreed that Blum was to receive a credit of 17,000 francs for each presentation, between November 15 and January 24. The contract further required that Blum produce at least thirty-five shows, with René receiving 50 percent of the receipts for each performance.

In August 1929, in Venice, Diaghilev died unexpectedly of sepsis as a complication of his diabetes, leaving the future of his company at risk. The eminent ballet historian Cyril Beaumont wrote reverently of Diaghilev's reign: "When Diaghilev died in 1929, his famous company, the product of twenty years activity, melted away like an army seized with doubt and misgiving at the loss of a tried and trusted leader. During that period, the art of ballet, once regarded in this country as an exotic form of entertainment, became an established cult with an ever-increasing band of worshippers drawn from all classes of society."[55]

Wanting continuity, Blum again employed Serge Grigoriev, Diaghilev's ballet master, along with thirty dancers from Diaghilev's troupe. Grigoriev was to mount the ballets in the operas of Monte Carlo and was promised 234,000 francs for the next three years. Most of the dancers for the future Ballets Russes company came from this core group. By the time Blum created the new Blum/de Basil Company, he was being paid nearly 700,000 francs a year. Evidently, Blum was gradually accruing more and more administrative authority as the successes of the plays and presentations he chose grew in importance and scope.

Having secured the dancers, Blum began to inquire about the company's sets, costumes, and dancers. In an October 7, 1929, letter, complicated dealings with the Ballets Russes taken over by Walter Nouvel and Serge Lifar continued.[56] Lifar and Nouvel were planning a season in April 1930, but nothing had been decided, which was frustrating for Blum and his colleagues.

Preceded by an agricultural depression in the 1920s, the Great Depression had begun in the United States with the stock market crash of 1929. The French economy, always more agricultural and less industrial than those of Great Britain and Germany, had recovered remarkably from the ravages of World War I, and for a few years remained somewhat insulated, protected by high tariffs from the economic difficulties that the United States and Europe experienced. Although France's economic and political troubles escalated rapidly after 1931, the brief hiatus allowed Blum to revive the Ballets Russes in the first years of the decade.

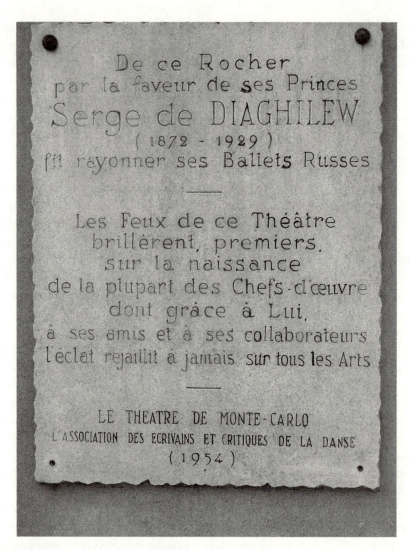

Figure 5.11
Plaque honoring Serge Diaghilev in Monte Carlo. Photo by David Bennahum.

While working to bring back Diaghilev's ballet company, Blum confided to René Léon in the October 7 letter that there were what he considered, "very few good ballet companies to engage, worthy of the Monte Carlo theatre, and that difficulties extended not only to a lack of time before the season was to begin, but also a lack of funds."[57] Blum's more thoughtful letters depict a sincere, but rather emotional character: "Yesterday I was in despair about the ballet, but today, I am able to recover my confidence."[58] He was hoping for what he said were "a series of operatic performances, and then a season when the Ballets Russes de Nemtchinova would perform,

René Blum and the Ballets Russes

much like Diaghilev's group, which had had a successful run at the Théâtre des Champs-Elysées in Paris."[59]

Nemtchinova, a former Diaghilev ballerina, insured her legs for 50,000 pounds in the 1920s. Her beauty and brilliant pointe work were legendary and she also had a talent for administration. It was she who pulled together the dancers from Diaghilev's company to perform in Monte Carlo. This helped Blum to build a longer season of ballets and assign the ballets their own evenings on Monday, Wednesday, Friday, and Sunday.

Though Nemtchinova's company dominated the 1930 spring season of dance, along with a short visit by the Sakharoffs, the Ballets du Théâtre National de l'Opéra debuted on April 10 with *Soir de Fête, Les Deux Pigeons,* and *La Nuit Ensorcellé.* Its performances included *La Tragédie de Salomé, Impressions de Music Hall,* and the ever-dependable *Coppélia.* The Paris Opéra ballet thrived after World War I under Jacques Rouché's consummate leadership and modernist ideas. Sets and designs were opulent and the training of the company became much more refined and demanding under Carlotta Zambelli; however, the Russian influence suffused all areas of production. Rouché brought on the incomparable Olga Spessitstseva to perform principal roles, although she soon left for Diaghilev's company in 1926.

In addition to the comedies and operettas, dance companies well known to Monte Carlo made visits in 1931, including Boris Kniaseff, Uday Shankar and Simkie, the highly respected Ballets du Théâtre National of the Paris Opéra, and Vicente Escudero. These diversified and provocative dance presentations were the prelude to Blum's serious intention to have Monte Carlo once again become a center for superb ballet dancing and choreography.

During the next months, many brilliant dancers were featured in operas as well in their own concerts. For example, on February 8, *Manon* was performed with ballet; March 28 saw a gala with *Samson et Delilah* and *Schéhérazade* with Alexandra Danilova, Lubov Tchernicheva, Ludmilla Schollar, Natalie Branitska, and Anatole Vilzak; on March 29, Blum and his administrators presented *La Traviata* with ballet; on April 2, they offered *Salomé* and *Schéhérazade,* and on April 4, they presented *Carmen* with ballet.

When the legendary Anna Pavlova saw Uday Shankar, she was stunned by his breathtaking sinuosity and grace. She invited him to create *Radha Krishna,* a ballet in which they both appeared. Blum brought Shankar and Simkie, his partner, along with his Hindou Orchestra, to perform in Monte Carlo on April 6 and 8, 1931. Shankar, born in 1900, had studied with his father; together they performed stories from the Hindu religious canon. Touring widely as a solo dancer, Shankar introduced the Western world to the intricacies and beauty of Indian dance, and also established a school in India. The dances of Shankar and Simkie included

> the innumerable ragas that constituted their heritage, with some melodies, and themes that represented the essence of each hour of the day, and of each season with every moment from the spirituality of one's soul. They contain tonalities with appropriate colours; they offer certain poems as well as certain legendary tales and they are represented here as symbolic human beings.[60]

Figure 5.12
Uday Shakar and his partner Simkie. Photo by Gordon Anthony, courtesy of V&A Images/Victoria and Albert Museum, London.

In a clear effort to establish the highest standards, Blum invited one of the best classical ballet companies in Europe, the Paris Opéra Ballet (or Les Ballets du Théâtre National de l'Opéra) led by Serge Lifar, to perform on April 19, 1931. After Diaghilev's death, Rouché hired Lifar, whose exotic looks and charisma enchanted audiences. Initiating some interesting reforms such as preperformance rehearsals with the male dancers in the Foyer de la Danse, Lifar consolidated his tentative control over the company.[61] The troupe presented *Prélude dominical, Les Créatures de Prométhée*, and *Soir de Fête*. One of the more popular ballets during its engagement in Monte Carlo proved to be *Les Créatures de Prométhée* (1929). In this spring season performance, Olga Spessitzeva graced the stage opposite Lifar in *Les Créatures de Promethée*. Ivor Guest recounted the ballet's interesting genesis. Jacques Rouché decided to plan a new ballet to Beethoven's score, suggesting that Lifar dance in the work and choreograph it. Lifar, in a rare moment of modesty, realizing his lack of experience, declined to choreograph and he suggested that "Balanchine be engaged as the choreographer."[62] Unfortunately, Balanchine became quite ill with pneumonia and was unable to accomplish the task. Rouché then returned to Lifar, who created a libretto based on the central role of a dancing Prometheus. Bernard Taper recounts a different story, emphasizing that Balanchine did indeed begin choreographing a not inconsiderable part of the ballet but was unable to continue owing to his illness, thus giving Lifar the opportunity to take it on. However, Balanchine received enough money from Rouché to pay for his medical expenses, while Lifar was amply paid for his dancing.[63] The success of Lifar as dancer and choreographer was undeniable; Rouché risked the animosity of many people and hired Lifar as ballet master and principal artist to revitalize the Paris Opéra. The Italian element in the Paris Opéra training diminished and transformed into the more lyrical Russian school, which, as Guest surmised, "had itself developed out of the old French school."[64]

As the spring season drew to an end, Blum brought in the renowned flamenco artist Vicente Escudero to perform his *Danses* on April 21 and 23, 1931. The appetite for flamenco dance and music began with the great dancer La Argentina, who was well known as a purveyor of Andalusian culture.[65] Escudero's abilities resided in his elegant bearing and impeccable footwork, which had designated him the aristocrat of Spanish dance. He toured with Pavlova in 1931, and in 1934, performed around the globe with La Argentina.

In Monte Carlo, Escudero danced with his longtime partners Carmita Garcia and Almeria, accompanied by his pianist and guitarist. Part of the new fascination with flamenco lay in the early twentieth-century passion for the

Figure 5.13
Vicente Escudero. Photo by Edouard Beaudu, courtesy of Bibliothèque du Musée de l'Opéra.

exotic and the primitive, and Escudero emphasized the flamboyant Gypsy background of this Andalucian art form. In the program, Escudero fancifully imagined the history of flamenco, surmising that it was "transmitted from generation to generation among the Spanish gypsies, their origins must be placed very probably at the origins of the Chaldo-Assyriens, although the secrecy of their religious codes causes us to think that these people were the heirs to the Egyptians; their dancers seem to create similar poses."[66] Despite the exotic charm of Escudero's proposal, modern scholarship situates the origins of the Gypsies in Rajasthan, from where they began their migration in the ninth century CE following the Islamic invasions of India.

When the Ballet de l'Opéra Russe à Paris came to Monte Carlo in April 1931, Blum had the opportunity to meet Colonel de Basil and his ballet master Boris Romanov. Nijinska was also a ballet master in 1931 with the Opéra Russe. Though Blum and de Basil had surely met in Paris, this intense and potentially fortuitous encounter provided the occasion for planning the next year's rebirth of the Ballets Russes. Blum, de Basil, and Romanov became close allies. De Basil, neither a dancer nor a choreographer, was shrewd and ambitious. He had an unfailing flair for leadership, and his ballet career began when he married a stage dancer. He initiated a small dance group that toured and eventually started an artists' agency, where he teamed with Alexis Zereteli and Michael Kachouk; together they inaugurated l'Opéra Russe à Paris. Unfortunately, de Basil's tendency toward self-promotion would create an incompatibility between René and de Basil in the years to come.

Blum's old contract of April 1929 was soon to expire, and in 1931 he requested further funding and new modifications to suit the varied popular fare he proposed. He requested the monies and authority to hire a ballet company with a ballet master and thirty dancers from the Diaghilev's former company. The contract was to last for the 1932–1934 seasons, and involved sixteen performances to run between April 1 and May 15 each year. In addition, the dancers had to participate in the gala spectacles for the benefit of SBM, not exceeding two galas a year. Blum also requested that the word "Russes" be omitted from any company name, but such was not to happen.

Monte Carlo was the ideal site for René Blum to create the very best in exciting concepts of performance—always with an eye for his audiences who loved the new, the curious, the funny, the upside-down world that followed the horrors of World War I. After all, this was the jazz age. Blum had been preparing for this job his entire life, especially during his years in the offices of *Revue Blanche* absorbing knowledge of the worlds of literature, poetry, theatre, and art, and holding the important position as editor for *Gil Blas*, where he became friends with prodigious personalities. All of this contributed to his successes in Monte Carlo. His service as a soldier in World War I, former prisoner-of-war status, and Croix de Guerre for heroism certainly did not hurt his reputation. Perhaps it was the suffering and the experience of others' pain that matured him and gave him a sense of his own mortality as well as the authority that he carried so gracefully. He was now ready to offer his future partner de Basil the Théâtre de Monte-Carlo as the headquarters for his "cherished scheme of forming a Russian Ballet at Monte Carlo."[67]

CHAPTER 6
René and Josette

René Blum fell madly in love with Josette France, an actress who performed in his Théâtre de Monte-Carlo in 1924. Born Madeleine Augustine Louise Frèrebeau in 1900, she long outlived Blum, dying in 1988 in Picardie. Their story is preserved in a series of sixty-two letters from René to Josette, written over several decades and housed in the Arts du Spectacle of the Bibliothèque Nationale in Paris.[1] Though there are many chronological gaps, René wrote to Josette until shortly before he died. They shared a son, Claude-René Blum, born out of wedlock on February 7, 1925.

Members of the Blum family disliked Josette. They knew René tried to help her obtain a divorce from her husband so that they could marry. They suggested that her many affairs meant that she lacked an enduring love for him. However, their age difference, their inability to marry, their many separations, and an emotionally ill child may all have played a role.

Few letters in the collection were written by Josette, so we are unable to experience the depth of the problems and frustrations that she faced. Many of René's letters refer to her pleas, her pouting, and her many demands. She was the collector and protector of René's letters, and it is assumed that Josette may not have saved her own correspondence.

Unfortunately, many of René's private letters have also been lost, and fewer personal materials have survived. Many postcards from distinguished authors written to René when he was editor at *Gil Blas* remain intact. These postcards reached René's older brother Marcel, and were subsequently given to a great-great-grandchild, Sophie LaVigne. Josette also saved one of his passports, his brief journal from World War I, and dozens of scores from various musicals, operas, and ballets with extensive notations from Monte Carlo, as well as programs and hundreds of photographs. Two of his traveling trunks were discovered, but were empty. His famous autobiography continues to elude researchers, as well as the letters sent to him by other friends and family. Several letters from René to his brother Léon were recouped and are included in the Léon Blum collection at the Centre d'histoire de Sciences Po. Letters to Françoise Nordmann, his niece, are in her possession in Paris. Correspondence from Marcel Proust to René was printed long before the Second World War, and, thankfully, it was protected.

Since few of the letters from Blum to Josette are dated, it is difficult to know when they were sent, unless references to a play or particular event suggest a recognizable time. They wrote letters several times a week, so some indicate a Wednesday or Saturday, rather than a month or year. Reading them provides a textured glimpse of their lives, and creates a picture of their shifting moods. Many of the letters dealt with the mundane details of their everyday life, such as buying a piano or hiring a chauffeur; some of the correspondence speaks with a visceral, emotional energy, often compassionate although sometimes piqued.

René met Josette when he began to produce theatre and operettas at the Casino de Monte-Carlo in 1924. Undeniably, he was attracted by her glorious smile, her easy-going and flirtatious way, and her convivial manner. As an actress, she had the perfect doll-like looks for situation comedy, whether she was the ingenue, the damsel in distress, or the naughty "other" woman. Born in 1900, she was twenty-two years younger than he and this disparity seemed to underline many of their letters, becoming a true source of dissension as time passed.

Their professional relationship underscored the early years of their kinship. He cared deeply for her as an actress and oversaw her career by arranging auditions for her and asking playwrights to cast her in their comedies. When Josette was chosen for one of her roles, René wrote in a slightly condescending tone, saying that the role was quite good for her, charming and much more lighthearted than profound. Rather paternalistically, he assured her that "it'll be enough for you to bring some substance, and a certain tender gravity that you can deliver, when you wish to work at it. But especially take care to enjoy this victory, and don't pout!" Josette took advantage of René's singular position as producer. At one point, he encouraged her, saying that she would receive better opportunities with more than a few lines, and that he would arrange it with the author. When there was a question about her salary, he convinced her that she would be paid.

René worked in her favor as much as he could. He spoke of the playwright Marcel Simon, "who has a lovely role for you if you are able to sing" for an operetta in the spring. In the middle of his discussions about acting and plays, he asked Josette if 5,000 francs would suffice for the moment, and wrote that if she needed more, he would scratch the bottom of his savings to find it.

The source of René's passion for Josette seemed to have no bounds:

Tonight I will be ecstatic to have you, as it's been six days without you. I will experience such joy and gladness when we meet at the station and when we are together tonight and when I hold you in my arms. I will feel the delight of your caresses which become more sure with every passing day. Au revoir, Doudou, I kiss you as you like, and I embrace you, simply embrace you!

In time, these ecstatic expressions were felt more keenly. "All day," he longingly told her, "I have wanted to write to you, and I began at least ten letters, but I am so busy, constantly interrupted it was impossible. Saturday evening was sad, and I am now so used to spending the night with you that I automatically reach out for your body, only to be surprised by my aloneness."

Early on, Josette began to lose some interest in René. He recounted a crushing experience that he had after he read one of her letters. He sat in his office with a colleague and suddenly began to cry as he recalled her "reproaches." In response, he wrote her that he was no longer very young, although still in his forties, but "my heart is not decrepit," and "I have great manias, those which push me forward—ambitions, cares, occupations, duties, artistic tastes which I cannot renounce, and friends whom I adore."

Each time he heard from her, he forgot the travails of everyday existence because he said, "Your letters are a delightful diversion at night from my cares during the day." But another letter had the opposite effect. The time passed quickly when the day's activities were so absorbing and the evenings seemed to bring sadness. René confided that "I sense a melancholy in the evening and my solitude weighs heavily that moment when I return to my home."

When he left her, he treasured the fact that Josette needed him physically and loved him, and in a tender voice said, "It is a sudden stroke of pain that I felt when I left you yesterday, and how deeply was I touched by the care, so delicate and so sympathetic that you felt for me, and for all my worries about our home that seemed so disorganized at the moment of my departure."

At almost every point in their relationship, René spoke about his desperation to have news from Josette. He confided that he had his faults, and that he could not always choose one thing or another, because he was driven by a powerful force inside him. "You cannot understand," he wrote, "this kind of modesty or self-abnegation, and timidity that afflicts me." Was he unable to hug her or to kiss her at some point? He knew that she accused him of not being tender enough, but added that his poor heart was overflowing with affection, and that he thought of her all the time. He often repeated that her denunciations were no doubt justified, that like all men, he was essentially unhappy, and that he was somewhat split between his desires and his experiences.

Surprisingly, when Josette became pregnant with their child, her feelings changed and she seems to have rejected Blum, leaving him heartbroken. The relationship became quite different and in some ways more alluring for René. According to Françoise Nordmann, his niece and the daughter of Georges with whom René was very close, René tried desperately to marry Josette, but she wanted only his money and did not want to be legally bound to him. Several pictures of her in a wedding dress with other men exist, and it is possible that she was married several times to others. Since Blum was a man of particular probity, this relationship caused him a great deal of pain.

In one letter, we glimpse René's confusion when Josette told him that she was pregnant. He exclaimed, "My dearest, dearest, you don't understand, you cannot understand. This child, I never expected and to be truthful and sincere, I did not welcome its arrival." Although he did not expect this child, he made it clear that he never deceived her, or tried to deny that it was his child. He wrote, "Immediately I accepted the fact that this would be my child."

René announced that he would take care of the child and that nothing could separate them, stating firmly, "Let me be the one who recognizes him and gives him my name." Some thought that he did not trust Josette to take care of the child, and that he would assume such responsibility. But he also warned her that if she separated him from the child, he would be very unhappy. His tone was rigid and somewhat threatening. Indeed, his next words reveal the problem. He feared that Josette did not love him and declared that "the lover has disappointed you, but the father will not! He will be worthy of your respect and admiration."

René criticized Josette for wanting too much from life: "Please do not aspire to this sort of idealistic happiness as you believe others to have and which in truth does not exist." He told her not to drown herself in illusions and implied that she should stay with him and try to love him. Once she wrote him that she did not have happy memories, that she recalled only the sad ones. He reassured her that her souvenirs and kind thoughts would provide the basis for a wondrous future for them. He cautioned her not to make hasty decisions, to be courageous, and reminded her that once she returned to him, his embraces would erase all her bleak thoughts. In an eloquent flourish, he said goodbye and told her "I embrace all the subtle qualities [jeux] of your body that I adore."

When their son was born, their troubles multiplied, as René was traveling and working ever more intensely. He knew that she was lonely and told her to please let him know if she needed him, as he would fly home for a day. Different irritants continued. René installed Josette in a comfortable apartment in Paris with her mother, Madame Marsoulam, who took care of the child, Claude-René. René chastised Josette for inviting too many of his friends to their apartment, because it was not large enough for many visitors. He also cautioned her about money. "Please don't argue," he implored her. "The painters are going to ruin me, and we have quite a sufficient number of marvels for our home to look like a Chinese museum."

Figure 6.1
Josette France, baby Claude-René, and René Blum. Courtesy of Arts du Spectacle, Bibliothèque Nationale, Paris.

Each time that he wrote Josette, René expressed his love for her, but this adoration did not appear to be shared. Years after they met, in a letter written in 1932, he disclosed that she had deeply hurt him, ruined his happiness at all turns, and spoke with a blatant lack of awareness of his feelings. "If you want a simple and good life, as you claim," he wondered, "why can't you stay with our son?" He reminded her that he sacrificed a great deal for the child, without hesitation and complaints. He eventually became furious and said, "For the past seven years, I held back my bitterness, my misery, and I supported with resignation the sickening torture of your capricious and bitter distrust. Last winter you caused me such an atrocious time by keeping him from me." He commented that this could only have happened because her mother adored the child, and in turn, the boy loved his grandmother. At that point, it would seem that the mother turned her son against his father.

In the Arts du Spectacle archives, a short biography of Josette France revealed that she suffered from an illness in 1932, and was obliged to spend time in a "rest home."[2] This suggests the reason why she was away from her son. In 1936 she was the victim of an automobile accident and struggled with circulatory problems for at least a year.

The letters about his son Claude-René depict René's boundless concern and affection for him. As Claude-René grew, he increasingly dismayed and distressed his parents. René, the true guardian of the child, took him on tours to England and France. On a ship to South Africa in 1936, René tried to look on the brighter side:

He is much more calm than I had hoped: he eats, he sleeps, and functions quite well. He is loved by everyone, in spite of his brashness. I think that I was absolutely correct in taking him with me and this voyage will certainly be good for him. For the moment, he is very content and I shall try to see that he keeps calm, especially as it's becoming hotter as we reach the Equator.

Claude-René, nicknamed Minou or Minouchou, was not emotionally well. His doctor administered some sort of medicine for his seeming hyperactivity. René explained that "unfortunately it is very difficult to put him to sleep at night as he never wants to leave my side." Evidently, René took his son to various physicians, and a "cure" for the boy was recommended. René resigned himself and wrote, "I have habituated myself to the idea that this treatment is indeed necessary, and Minou accepts this in principle."

When he spent time in Monte Carlo with him, René offered comforting words to Josette: "He is sleeping well, and is in a very good mood, happy to be living, not too nervous, with some special humorous moments, none of his nervous crises that gave me so much heartache before. The treatment, I believe, is working."

Figure 6.2
Claude-René (Minichou) and René Blum. Courtesy of Arts du Spectacle, Bibliothèque Nationale, Paris.

Perhaps one of the most anguished letters René sent to Josette contained his handwritten will, dated at midnight on May 26, 1932, in which he confessed an "odious presentiment," and, unable to sleep, decided to write these lines. He wanted, above all, to be honest with her and let her know that his greatest desire was to help his son as he grew up, until he could help himself. René hoped for his son's support and said, "I want him to keep a memory of a tender and debonaire father who loves him more than anyone in the world and ardently wants him to be happy." René wished that Claude-René would love his own son, as he loved him, and cautioned that "if he is tempted to judge him too severely, let him try to be indulgent, as I have."

In this improvised testament, René did not forget the boy's mother and grandmother. Then, he launched into a Polonius-like speech advising his son "to learn to love his mother," and to always have an affectionate gratitude for Mamy who brought him up with devotion from the very first day of his life. René feared that Minou's outbursts would damage him, and warned him to avoid distrust and disgust for others, as it would make him very unhappy, as well as unjust.

He offered Minou some informal advice, knowing that the boy disliked the Blum family. René asked him to try to love his family—his uncles and cousins whom Minou had treated badly. He then awarded his son almost everything he owned, with the proviso that his brother Georges would oversee his property. René listed all the people who deserved something that he owned, some souvenir of his being. The will goes on for several pages, and at the very end he confirmed: "I embrace with all my heart this beloved son whom I think about all the time, and whom I will love till the day I die."

The letters often made references to the Blum brothers, their friendly dinners, the various cousins and aunts who embodied the warmth and meaning of family, and his many rendezvous with Léon whose name was strangely absent; he was simply "mon frère." In one of the letters, René thanked Josette for making an effort to see his family: "I am happy and not surprised by their angelic and wonderful welcome to you when you visited. And I feel a great joy in your having such a perfect relationship with my brothers."

The Blum relatives with whom this author has spoken all reviled Josette France for her selfishness and her many liaisons, but in the end she had a magnanimous heart. She wrote to René in prison, helped him with arrangements, and most importantly, she sent him food packages. René responded in a letter to Josette dated five and a half months into his detention, toward the end of May 1942.

The writing in this last letter lacked his usual formalities and stylistic flourishes; it was virtually stream of consciousness. He spoke about his despair, entrapment, and the monotony. "We pass the days by counting them." However, he cherished his marvelous ability to retain his sense of humor, and optimistic belief that he would return to his "berceil," or home. During this waiting period, he tried to care for and rid himself of the terrible effects of his stay in Compiègne, before being sent to Auschwitz where he feared his life might end.

Josette sent a "chancelière," a foot muff, which helped him through the cold weather in his last two weeks at Compiègne. He described his weak condition, "that he walked slowly and dragged his swollen feet in slippers that were too tight." He was at his wits' end, predicting that there would remain no trace of this miserable past. He desperately missed their son, but was consoled when he thought of him. He told Josette that his friends and relatives sent him occasional packages with food that even she might not find in Paris. René wrote, "I am a bit ashamed of such luxuries." He was happy to recognize her handwriting and to feel a return of his love for her. Although their relationship soured very quickly after the birth of Claude-René, in the midst of war and captivity, a revival of their love seems to have occurred.

René thanked Josette for the gift of a ham that he shared with his friends, and that would certainly last five days along with the other canned alimentation. He confided that he knew nothing about her present life, but that he was delighted that she had rediscovered Henri Gautrin, a lost friend and close associate throughout Blum's life. He revealed that "it was wonderful to see that she was content, having taken great pains to achieve satisfaction in her life in the last two years." Please, René implored her, "write to me about your health," but knowing the danger of their situation, he asked, "How can you do that?" He added that he had been thinking about a certain plan if several friends could help to make some business arrangements, and he referred to a notary. In his last paragraph, he expressed a desire to make contact with an administrator from les Éditions Choumine, a business that he owned or ran. He forgot the name of a theatrical person in the office of Eschig. He asked her to find out the names of these people so that he could transfer some of his money and hopefully see his son. He sent regards to Gautrin. All of his rambling and unfocused thoughts were perhaps a reflection of his starvation and misery.

The correspondence ended with this letter, and we sense not only his despair, but hers as well. In Josette's ongoing relationship with René, opportunities were provided for her, as he introduced her to many people in the world of theatre, film, and the arts. In the 1930s, she began acting in movies, playing little parts in the films *L'Assommoir* (1933) and *Les Misérables* (1934). Fortunately, she was able to continue working during the Occupation, and even after the war, as her mother and son needed financial support once René had been arrested, deported, and killed.

CHAPTER 7

The Resurrection of the Ballets Russes de Monte-Carlo

Despite the turbulence in René Blum's new life with Josette France and their child Claude-René, Blum proceeded in October 1931 with his plans for the renaissance of the Ballets Russes de Monte-Carlo, on which he hoped to imprint his aesthetic. Having studied art in all its forms and attended to audience tastes, he knew it was crucial to foster young and talented artists for the new company. His original contract with the SBM and de Basil bore the name Ballets Russes de Monte-Carlo, as well as that of the Ballets de Monte-Carlo.

For the 1932–1933 season, Blum was responsible for weaving together a complex tapestry of operetta and dramatic presentations, with ballet companies that danced in operas as well as full dance evenings. The schedule was quite hectic as the following outline shows: (1) plays and operettas had a five-week season of twenty performances with four shows each week from December 10 to January 30; (2) ballets in the operas had thirty-five performances in a season that lasted from November 15 through January 24; and (3) the ballet company had sixteen performances between April 1 and May 15 and participated in two galas organized by SBM. Those dates were subject to change and often did.

Blum had formed a partnership with the White Russian émigré, Colonel de Basil, that he would later regret. The contract for the Société des Ballets Russes et Ballets de Monte-Carlo between Blum and de Basil dated April 20, 1932, indicated that they formed a company whose shares were capitalized with 2 million francs, which included the larger contribution by Blum. It stipulated that 2 milllion francs would be divided into 400 shares of 5,000 francs each: 240 apportioned to Blum and 160 to de Basil, subscribed to cash. Blum and de Basil were each elected at the general meeting of shareholders to hold the position of director for ten years. Remuneration for Blum and de Basil was

120 shares of 5,000 francs each, and 500 founders' shares. Individual contracts were given to Balanchine and Massine that ended with their first season, and Boris Kochno was hired as a "conseiller artistique" for the sum of 3,000 francs a month. Thirty dancers started with the company. Although Bronislava Nijinska was invited to contribute ballets to the opening season, she declined, explaining that she preferred to lead her own ballet company with her name at the helm. Several years later Nijinska returned to choreograph in Monte Carlo when de Basil failed to fulfill his contract with Blum.

As part of the "dowry" contributed by de Basil, according to historian Garcia-Marquez, a contract was signed in January 1932 between de Basil's Opéra Russe and the Société des Bains de Mer stipulating that the Opéra Russe would donate all its ballet scenery, costumes, and props to the Ballets de Monte-Carlo.[1]

Figure 7.1
Colonel de Basil. Photo by Gordon Anthony, courtesy of V&A Images/Victoria and Albert Museum, London.

No one believed that the fledgling company should reinvent Diaghilev's vision, but many thought it should reflect the taste and sensibility of the experienced producer René Blum. Garcia-Marquez noted: "The new Ballets Russes was by no means meant to imitate the seminal modern works of Diaghilev's period. Blum never presumed to repeat Diaghilev's remarkable reign. Rather he saw himself as a Maecenas, a wealthy patron of the arts, an astute reader of the artistic moment. Blum envisioned another avant-garde, another beginning."[2]

When the Ballets Russes de Monte-Carlo made its debut in the spring of 1932, hope for the continuity of ballet in Europe was resurrected. The years that ushered in economic chaos (although initially the Depression had scarcely affected the principality of Monaco) had witnessed the loss of two individuals who had established international touring companies: Serge Diaghilev, who died August 19, 1929, and Anna Pavlova, who died January 23, 1931. The dancers in their defunct companies had to struggle to find work, and Blum's social conscience impelled him to hire many of these dancers who were without means or proper passports.[3]

Most of the reviews of the company's first season in Monte Carlo and on tour confirmed Blum's highest hopes. According to Charles Richter in *Le Figaro* of February 16, 1932, "It is to his great merit that René Blum sensed the necessity of reconstituting Diaghilev's Ballets Russes that played in Monte Carlo, its brilliant home for 15 years."[4] The season was dominated by excitement caused by the unexpected appearance of three young ballerinas aged nearly fifteen years, true child stars brought up in good Russian studios in Paris. Writer Pierre Michaut remarked that few people but Blum could have achieved this accomplishment.[5] And in *Comoedia* of May 4, 1932, Richter exclaimed: "René Blum has telegraphed to the world that The Ballet Russe is not dead!"[6]

On June 15, 1932, in the *Feuilleton du Temps*, Henry Malherbe attested to the brilliance of the new company's Parisian tour: "The revelation of an entirely new and brilliant means of expression introduced by Diaghilev was given to us at the Théâtre des Champs-Elysées, thanks to the dedicated attention of MM Blum and de Basil. The artfulness of the Diaghilev model was rediscovered and elevated with a generous zeal."[7]

However, in a cranky article on July 2, 1932, Henry Prunières lectured readers on the new Ballets Russes, and berated the project. He said that no one should attempt to follow Diaghilev and that it was futile to reorganize his ensemble as it was doomed "to failure." Yet he praised René Blum for

bringing us a troupe and a conception equally new with the Russian Ballet of Monte Carlo. René Blum does not offer the stimulus of Diaghilev yesteryear. Rather the spectacle is in good taste, charming and amusing. He diverted us and that's it. His dancers are excellent as is Balanchine as the Maître de Ballet, with Grigoriev as the regisseur and Voisikovsky while Toumanova dances with technical mastery.[8]

Figure 7.2
Seated from left: Boris Kochno, René Blum, de Basil, and George Balanchine, standing from left: Christian Bérard and Serge Grigoriev. Courtesy of Archives Monte-Carlo, SBM.

The critics pleased Blum and de Basil, but the two men heeded their warnings to be wary of "imitating" Diaghilev and to move on to something new with which they could find distinction. That was the idea Balanchine proposed and that Massine would reenact.

Serge Lifar as well found fault with the idea that Blum and de Basil might audaciously try to perpetuate the Diaghilev tradition. He wrote in his *Histoire du Ballet Russe:*

> The great citadel for the Russian ballet was the Ballets Russes de Monte Carlo, directed by René Blum and Colonel de Basil. All the directors were former collaborators of Diaghilev, forcing themselves to perpetuate the tradition. However, they would be epigones or poor imitators, because it is impossible to continue the legacy of Diaghilev.[9]

In a pique of jealousy, Lifar could not resist criticizing Balanchine through Diaghilev's eyes. He said that before Diaghilev died, he had become tired of Balanchine's "ballet acrobatique" and wanted to look for other choreographers more in tune with his concept of ballet, like Lifar himself.[10]

The programming for this first season in 1932 could not have been more brilliantly conceived; it offered a broad spectrum of artistic strategies, both musically and in movement.[11] For its debut, Blum/de Basil centered ballets on theatrical illusion and strong characterizations rather than on expanding ballet technique, although the baby ballerinas in their company were phenomenal technicians.

During the "maiden voyage" of the Ballets Russes, three outstanding Fokine works were revived: *Petrouchka, Danses Polovtsiennes du Prince Igor*, and *Les Sylphides*. These pieces represented the continuation of the initial triumphs of Diaghilev. Boris Romanov further enlarged the repertoire with his *Chout* or *Le Bouffon, Pulcinella*, and *L'Amour Sorcier*.

Balanchine, who had staged some of Diaghilev's last ballets, became the first choreographer for the new company and created three new works for the Monte Carlo premiere. He brought two of the soon-to-become "baby ballerinas" from Paris: Irina Baronova and Tamara Toumanova, along with Tamara Tchinarova, all from the studio of Olga Preobrajenska. Balanchine rehearsed and presented Offenbach's hilarious *Orphée Aux Enfers* in December 1931 at the Mogador Theatre, which was located only one block from René Blum's office on the Chaussée d'Antin, and five blocks from the Paris Opéra. Since Blum continually traveled back and forth to Paris—not only for his family, but also for artistic and business reasons—there is no doubt that Blum had met Balanchine and saw the lovely young ballerinas in *Orphée* at the Mogador studio. The reviews for Balanchine's ballets in *Orphée* were excellent, and the whole production was a tremendous success. He loved to work with young ballerinas, as he felt that he could mold them to meet the demands of his choreography. Tamara Tchinarova Finch, in the March 1988 issue of the *Dancing Times*, wrote eloquently of her experiences in the corps of the Offenbach ballet.[12] Later she reinforced some of these reflections in a letter to the author. She noted that "Balanchine had selected six girls from the studio of Olga Preobrajenska. We could all, more or less, turn well. For example, Baronova had a solo piece in the 'nymphs' ballet, where she came forward and did 32 fouettés that brought the house down."[13] At the time, Balanchine lived with Danilova in an apartment in Paris, and when she asked if he would take her into the Ballets Russes company, Balanchine told her that she was too old.[14] She was then only twenty-seven. Later, she was invited by de Basil and became the centerpiece of the company for years.[15] With Balanchine as ballet master, auditions for the new Ballets Russes were held at the Mogador Theatre's studio.[16]

In the opening season, Balanchine's four new works stunned and excited the ballet world: *Suite de Danses* (only performed three times); *Le Bourgeois Gentilhomme; La Concurrence;* and *Cotillon*, a remarkable contribution to the panoply of works that included several by Fokine, and some older ones by Balanchine such as *Aubade*, which he had created originally for Mme. Nemtchinova in 1930.

Although *Cotillon* had been given a special preview at the celebration of Prince Louis II of Monaco, for the Fête Nationale de la Principauté de

Figure 7.3
Le Bourgeois Gentilhomme. Curtain, scenery, and costumes by Alexandre Benois. Photo by G. Detaille, courtesy of Archives Monte-Carlo, SBM.

Monaco on January 17, 1932, it opened officially on April 12, 1932, with Balanchine in one of his rare appearances in the lead male role, later assumed by David Lichine. It featured a stunning marbleized décor, trimmed in red, white, and gold by designer Christian Bérard with costumes executed by the young Karinska and a fascinating libretto by Boris Kochno. In his biography of Bérard, Kochno revealed the excitement of the January opening night: "*Cotillon* was a great hit. When the ballet was over, the audience left the theatre reluctantly, as if they were leaving the end of a wonderful party. . . . And I heard Balanchine say with feeling, 'I think we have really accomplished something tonight.'"[17]

The story of *Cotillion* takes place amid a scintillating program of festivities; Fate appears in the guise of a mysterious woman wearing black gloves. A young girl telling fortunes is rebuffed by the Mistress of Ceremonies and runs off, but reappears later to lead the Grand Ronde in which she pirouettes around the ballroom by herself, until the guests join her, spinning with fouettés, until the curtain falls. According to ballet critic and afficionado Irving Deakin in *Ballet Profile*, "It is, in a way, a little masterpiece of sophistication, with a youthfulness about it, and a nostalgia that alternates with gaiety, all in the mood of the brittle brilliant music."[18] Arnold Haskell suggested that there is about it that vagueness of the dream, of a dream we have tried to put down on paper when we have sleepily and partially waked and on completely waking in the morning to read what we have written, have found it tortuous and uncertain; yet it was so clear and vivid when we dreamed it, that the remaining impression is still disturbing. ... Something has happened but who can tell what?[19]

Dance critic A. V. Coton admired Balanchine's keen ability to choreograph a poetic vision, "As a creation of atmosphere—in the absolute sense, not an atmosphere of a time or place—nothing else in ballet compares with *Cotillon* . . . a revelation of a ghostly assembly going about its ghostly business, away from the comprehension of men."[20] The gorgeous central pas de deux "The Hand of Fate" was the subject of much discussion, not only because of its exquisite expression, but also because of its mystery. Manchester recalled that

in the pas de deux, the girl is as though she's everything that night ever is. Enormous mystery. And the wonderful final gesture where they both have hands above their heads and then they turn their heads and as the last note comes, their hand goes too. It's terribly simple but you never forget it.[21]

Tamara Toumanova remembered excitedly: "The rehearsals for *Cotillon* started immediately in Paris, not Monte Carlo. From the beginning I had the leading role."[22] She recalled that Balanchine gave charming rewards to his dancers: "If I had done a very good rehearsal or performance, he would go to Pasquier's, a wonderful patisserie in Monte Carlo, and buy me a magnificent chocolate that I could never afford."[23]

Another delightful work by Balanchine, *La Concurrence*, also premiered April 12, 1932. The setting for *La Concurrence* is a 1900 French provincial burlesque scene, with music composed by Georges Auric (commissioned by Blum), and scenery and costumes by André Derain. Reduced to its essence, *La Concurrence* was an acid commentary on life, in which impossibly incongruous things happened but always in an ordered and logical sequence. It moves as in the dream of a young girl who seemed to have no place in the "story" of the ballet, but who was the raison d'être of the ballet itself.[24]

Two rival tailors, both selling fashionable apparel, vie for the attention of eager shoppers. The tailors begin to quarrel and the customers are drawn into the commotion. Citizens of the town intervene and disperse the crowd; the two tailors find themselves alone and, pleased with their profits, become reconciled. Manchester commented on the ballet's singularity for Balanchine, as it was a character ballet, with a narrative, however slim. According to Sorley Walker, "The highlight of the ballet was Woizikovsky's brilliant

Figure 7.4
Cotillon, Valentin Froman and Lubov Rostova. Scenery and costumes by Christian Bérard. Photos by G. Detaille, courtesy of Archives Monte-Carlo, SBM.

solo as a flea-bitten hobo."[25] Manchester added that Balanchine often cunningly included unpredictable events: "At the end it introduced a totally different mood for no reason at all. A girl came on and sort of drifted around the stage, and she hadn't anything to do with the rest of it. It was a strange sort of Balanchine-esque sort of thing."[26]

Figure 7.5
René Blum with Tamara Toumanova, Georges Reymond, and Doris Sonne. Photo by Erlanger de Rosen, courtesy of Bibliothèque du Musée de l'Opéra.

Pierre Michaut in his *Histoire du Ballet* reiterated that "one finds at the end of *La Concurrence* and in certain episodes of *Cotillon* a kind of profound vision with a true poetry, a mysterious appeal that offers the keen impressions of a dream."[27] He was surprised by the clever use of pantomime and gesture in Balanchine's *Cotillon* and *Concurrence* and praised Balanchine's esprit: "The wit is not at all forced and the irony is alert and light with a trace of gaiety."[28]

Dancer Toumanova remembered working on *La Concurrence:* "During rehearsals, Balanchine would not only demonstrate the steps, he would explain the idea. For example, every time he did a choreography for me, even a brio choreography, there was always a nostalgia, a sort of tristesse."[29] She recounted that she first appeared in a long blue dress with a large bow on the left shoulder. "There was a competition of fouettés, and on each side of me there was a dancer competing to see who could do the most turns."[30] There was no question of Toumanova's turning abilities. Sixteen double fouettés were like breathing for her.

Even as a very young girl, Toumanova was touched by the sorrowful end of the ballet: "*Concurrence* ends very sadly, because I go to sleep in my memories of what has happened. . . . *Concurrence* is a comic competition, but as the evening comes I went on my toes across the whole stage, went to the side, went on my knees and became very sad."[31]

Audiences were astonished not only by the diverse spectrum of Balanchine's work but also by the speed and efficiency with which he made

Figure 7.6
La Concurrence. Center front: Toumanova. Photo by Raoul Barba, courtesy of Archives Monte-Carlo, SBM.

ballets for the season's eighteen operas.[32] However, these successes did not secure his future with the company. Balanchine argued with de Basil about the direction of the company. Irving Deakin remarked, "Balanchine was all for an entirely new and young company to guarantee independence from any Diaghileff inheritance, while de Basil wanted some older artists as well."[33] Both Balanchine and de Basil prevailed, for the company hired some of the finest dancers from the former Diaghilev company, along with a group of highly promising young dancers—the children of imperial émigrés, and products of Russian ballet schools in Paris who were brought in by Balanchine.

Occasionally, Monte Carlo's devil-may-care atmosphere could not ignore dire, adverse political or providential events that intruded into the aura of the casino and the theatre in Monte Carlo. In May 1932, the president of the French Republic, Paul Doumer, was assassinated by a mad Russian anarchist and most institutions closed out of respect for the office. Performances, as well, had to be suspended. In a letter from the Archives de la Société des Bains de Mer, Blum wrote that, of course, two Ballets Russes performances would be canceled, but that he would appreciate the SBM sharing in the loss of receipts (we recall his contract stipulated that he would receive 50 percent of the receipts for each show), as he had already hired and paid staff for those productions. The administration agreed to his request.

At the end of June 1932, after a tremendous success in Paris, rumors began to circulate about who would take over the direction of the company. Already the tensions between Blum and de Basil could be sensed. "It was said," recalled Baronova, "that Colonel de Basil had asked Massine to join the company as resident choreographer and leading dancer and that was not in Mr. Balanchine's plans"[34] Balanchine took umbrage as "his agreement had been with Blum."[35] In his biography of Balanchine, Bernard Taper makes it very clear that Balanchine liked Blum very much, but was very wary of de Basil. He simply did not trust him, as de Basil was known as a trickster. He often tried to get Balanchine to sign receipts as a ruse to ply more money from Blum.[36] Taper told an amusing, rather pathetic story about Blum, who owned a lovely new car, and de Basil. After a short amount of time, de Basil was seen riding in the car. Taper testified that de Basil "had persuaded Blum that the car should be considered part of their enterprise. Not long after that he got Blum to give him a bill of sale for it. 'You know what?' Blum said wistfully to Balanchine, 'de Basil has just bought my car from me with my own money.'"[37]

In October 1932, two large bus coaches were rented at a good price, and the scenery and costumes stacked on the roof and covered. They made their way from Paris to Brussels, then Holland, Germany, and finally Switzerland in a grand tour.

Figure 7.7
Group photo around dining table. Blum is fifth from left. Balanchine is opposite; de Basil is smiling, third right from Balanchine. Courtesy of Jerome Robbins Dance Division, the New York Public Library for the Performing Arts, Astor, Lenox, and Tilden Foundations.

The truth about Balanchine's quick departure is complicated. Some people said that he was ousted by de Basil; others accused Massine of working behind the scenes to undermine Balanchine's ambitions. Irving Deakin knew about a disagreement between de Basil and Balanchine.[38] And historian Garcia-Marquez was told that Blum and de Basil became "dictatorial about their decisions and said that the company's success was due to them."[39]

Blum would not have dismissed Balanchine; it was not in his nature to discharge such a talent, especially as they had become great friends. Balanchine probably left because he discovered that de Basil had chosen to work with Massine for the next season, a development that dishonored him. (This author is quite sure that it was de Basil's chicanery, not Blum's, because in 1935, when Blum "fired" de Basil, Blum wrote Balanchine to ask him to come back and run the company.) Indeed, it was not a question of Balanchine's dismissal, as his original contract ran through the "social season in Monte Carlo, May 4, 1932,"[40] and this contract was not renewed.

Coming from the same ballet company was no guarantee of friendship. There were ripples of discontent between Balanchine and Massine, who knew one another from the Diaghilev years when Balanchine's dislike for de Basil also erupted. Deakin knew that Balanchine and de Basil had quarreled and "there is every indication that it was a bitter quarrel. In the world of the dance, rows are possible at any moment of the night or day."[41] In 1932, the result of this argument between Balanchine and de Basil was that Balanchine left to form his own company, cleverly named Les Ballets 1933. Balanchine took Les Ballets 1933 to Paris to perform on June 7, the same day the de Basil/Blum company played at the Théâtre des Champs-Élysées, which only added to the fire. The Balanchine troupe "got across the Channel to London before de Basil, to draw that eagerly expectant public."[42] There is no documentation in the Monte Carlo archives from Blum or de Basil to further explain Balanchine's departure from the company.

When asked about René Blum's reign during the 1930s, writer Manchester replied that Blum was "historically much more important than anybody ever thought at the time." She referred to his autobiography that disappeared during the Holocaust, and asserted it would have given an accurate description of how Balanchine left the company as well as more insight into Colonel de Basil. "I think that Blum may have been the man who had all the taste of Diaghilev but didn't have Diaghilev's maniacal drive. And that's why he didn't achieve anything and was really sort of pushed around by people"[43] In retrospect, however, one sees that he quietly achieved a great deal.

Sorley Walker noted that adding Massine's name to the roster along with Balanchine's was inevitable, especially since Massine possessed costumes and decors from the Diaghilev ballets. Diaghilev's lawyer facilitated the acquisition of the materials by an American entrepreneur who wanted Massine to bring the Ballets Russes to the United States. But this plan was aborted in 1929 by the Wall Street crash. Sorley Walker added:

> Massine also possessed notated records of his choreography, and had an important name as a choreographer. He was a star performer, unlike Balanchine who because of a knee injury was no longer dancing. Certainly if Blum and de Basil wanted a widely-based repertoire which could draw on many Diaghilev revivals, Massine was the man for them.[44]

The mood changed in Monte Carlo when Massine took over. Sorley Walker perceived that the lighthearted, nostalgic environment when Balanchine was in control transformed into a colder and more regimented experience. "Nothing was easy-going any longer," she wrote.[45]

Before Massine returned to Europe, his career in New York vacillated. He fared well financially from 1928 to 1931, as he was hired to stage weekly ballet programs at the Roxy Theatre. These included choreographing a full-length *Schéhérazade* with four performances daily as the leading dancer.[46] Massine choreographed the League of Composers production of Stravinsky's *Le Sacre du Printemps* four times in Philadelphia and gave two shows at the Metropolitan Opera House in collaboration with conductor Leopold Stowkowski and the Philadelphia Orchestra; Martha Graham made one of her rare appearances, dancing the leading role in the ballet. However, despite his acclaim in America, when Blum invited Massine to join his company in 1932, he did not hesitate to return to Monte Carlo. There his success was based on drive and hard work, coupled with his marvelous dancing and his flair for comedy.

Massine's major contribution to the season was *Jeux d'Enfants*. Though Manchester labeled the ballet a mere "bluette" or "petit work," she was charmed by Bizet's music set to children's rhymes and Joan Miró's luminous décor, which she said looked so bright, "as if it were still a little bit wet from the fresh paint."[47] Since Boris Kochno, a close ally of Balanchine, also worked on the ballet, many people believed that it was choreographed by Balanchine. Massine's narrative lent itself easily to Miró's surrealistic designs, while the fluid integration of music and choreography carried on Fokine's seamless use of Chopin's score in *Les Sylphides*.

The story portrayed a child who is surrounded by toys that come to life. The choreography, with childlike movements for Riabouchinska, was quite simple. Two figures in white leotards, Eglevsky and Rostova, were the ardent spirits of the toys. Baronova, as the Top, wound up and all of a

Figure 7.8
Jeux d'Enfants. Set and costumes by Joan Miró. Photo by G. Detaille, courtesy of Archives Monte-Carlo, SBM.

sudden the fouetté popped out when a string was pulled. The fouetté, a whip-like turn, gave the impression of a constant swirl. The Child's "simple movements" reflected a gentle charm and innocence, while the whirling Top struck a virtuosic note. David Lichine, as the Traveler who went around the world, captivated and charmed the little girl in the nursery.[48]

The heart of the Blum/de Basil company resided in the talent, panache, energy, and solidarity of the dancers. They adored their new circumstances in Monte Carlo and were more than grateful for the exciting new beginnings. Baronova and Toumanova, as well as many of the dancers, were born in Russia during the revolution and grew up in émigré families that had lost their livelihoods, their status, and their way of life. Monte Carlo, not Paris, assuaged their inherent fear of loss as well as the memories of fierce Russian winters. Blum was sympathetic to their plight as refugees, and tried to ameliorate their distress. Some thought the life of the dancer glamorous and much has been written about this, but Blum witnessed the rigors of their daily lives and understood that the opposite was true.

During their stay in Monte Carlo, from the end of March to the end of May, the ballet dancers performed four times a week in the sumptuous Garnier Theatre before what André Eglevsky called "local tradesmen, casual tourists, and a sprinkling of balletomanes whose enthusiasm or curiosity brought them down from London and Paris."[49]

Despite its great reputation for dance following the Diaghilev years, Monte Carlo produced no great dancers, nor did it encourage its population to love ballet. At the time there were no schools of dance there. Yet it became the world's *foyer de la danse* and home for many of the Russian dancers. New works were constantly being shaped and rehearsed for world tours, and Monte Carlo audiences often decided the future of those works. The dancers in the "hothouse laboratory" worked hard to meet the demands of such brilliant choreographers as Balanchine, Massine, and Fokine, who experimented safely with new ideas.

An article by the youthful Eglevsky in the October 1938 issue of *Harper's Bazaar* described the daily routine of Blum's ballet company in Monte Carlo, a schedule without much respite or personal freedom. The dancer was the possession of those who made the artistic and financial decisions, and she performed exactly as she was told. If she were one of the "baby ballerinas," she also acquiesced to the wishes of her mother, who would be unfailingly by her side, if permitted, all the time. The tradition of mothers accompanying their performing children dates back hundreds of years, and, of course, their involvement in the children's lives was not without self-interest. They were banned from rehearsals along with the youngest and newest dancers, who sat outside the studio on a bench when not needed; on the benches the mothers gossiped and shared disappointments about who did or did not obtain certain roles. The producers and the mothers occasionally confronted each other over the grueling rehearsals and the frequent touring. The goal of every dancer and every mother was a full-time contract.

The older Russian teachers were nostalgic about their youthful lives on the famed Theatre Street in St. Petersburg. They were the custodians of the traditions, even in far-away Monaco. Monte Carlo thus became a central force, the place where dancers hoped for stardom and the stage where ballets were tested and painstakingly rehearsed before their seasons in London, Paris, or New York. Monte Carlo was therefore both a cynosure and a threshold.

In his article, Eglevsky narrated the dancers' daily routine: They began their days at nine in the morning with ballet class, where they displayed their mettle and proved whether they were worthy of solo parts. The casino theatre was perched on a hill, and dancers made their way into town to their favorite Russian restaurant by descending on a seaside road that still offers a magnificent panorama of the yacht-filled harbor. They then climbed back wearily for rehearsals, which often lasted well into the evening.[50]

The rehearsal studio was located under the opera theatre, with large windows open to the radiant beach and the Mediterranean Sea. If one looked to the left, Italy was far in the distance, while to the right was Cap Ferrat. At cocktail hour, the café tables at the Café de Paris opposite the casino were crowded with the designers, painters, composers, and teachers who worked for the ballet. Even when the tourist season was over, celebrities stayed for the excitement of the gambling tables.

But the enthusiasm and loyalty of the dancers did not diminish the difficulties inherent in the established administration of the company. From the very beginning of their relationship, de Basil boldly took advantage of Blum and ignored his position in their financial partnership. In an arrogant and perfidious move, de Basil ignored contractual arrangements with Blum and the Société des Bains de Mer, and purposely left their names off posters and programs, vital sources of publicity when away from Monte Carlo, beginning in late 1932. Many people in England and abroad had no idea of Blum's integral importance to the company. Almost immediately, Blum realized the mistake he had made in choosing to work with de Basil.

Colonel de Basil's original name was Vassili Grigorievich Voskresensky. He was born in Kaunas, in what is now Lithuania, in 1888 and died in Paris in 1951, and often bragged that as a youth he was a Cossack general and escaped to Paris as had so many of his countrymen. Although the title "colonel" worked in his favor, in the end most of those who did business with him discovered that he was not trustworthy, a character defect that led to frequent lawsuits.[51] When he worked with Prince Zeretelli at the Opéra

Figure 7.9
Dancers in Monte Carlo dressing room. Photo by G. Detaille, courtesy of Archives Monte-Carlo, SBM.

Russe à Paris, he gradually acquired a reputation for producing art. Martin Duberman, however, debunked de Basil's artistic portfolio, saying that he worked for fly-by-night companies and was "a genius of manipulation," which set him at odds with Balanchine and Balanchine's colleague Boris Kochno. In the opinion of some, de Basil gave "commercial success precedence over artistic experimentation."[52]

By December 1932, Blum knew that his original hopes for the ballet company in Monte Carlo had been dashed by de Basil, and resolved to end their partnership. The contract that he drew up on December 13 canceled the earlier contract from April and included a clause stipulating that de Basil owed Blum 500,000 francs. The contract indicated how and when de Basil would reimburse Blum: half of the money needed to be paid at the end of August 1934, the other half at the end of August 1935. The rest of the contract listed protections for Blum from any sort of mishap that might ensue, protections that unfortunately would not be enforced.

One reason for the failure of history to remember the contributions of René Blum may be seen in correspondence from the archives in Monte Carlo. There one finds a legal document dated July 7, 1933, sent by Blum, saying that "it is necessary to ask for the immediate cessation of their contract of December 1932 due to the wrong and grief that Monsieur de Basil has caused René Blum, concerning the fact that contrary to their agreement the name of René Blum, followed by Artistic Director was in no way mentioned in the publicity in either Paris or London, and by the London performances, M. de Basil had been warned and still did not accede to his contractual obligations."[53] Indeed, books and articles written about this new venture called the company the de Basil Ballets Russes, with only a brief mention of Blum's name.

Several weeks later, on July 25, 1933, this complex conversation continued between Blum and René Léon. Blum admitted that getting rid of de Basil was not a simple matter and that their contractual ties would probably endure for another miserable two years. He reassured Léon, however, that he would do everything in his power to smooth the troubled waters.[54]

The authorities in Monte Carlo had long predicted and feared that France would introduce gambling. Indeed, in an effort to raise funds, the French government did just that in 1933. This had an impact on Monte Carlo, as the French now competed with Monte Carlo for revenue, thus straining the situation with de Basil even more. Henri Guerin, a financial advisor, wrote Blum to help him sort out the future prospects of other ballet companies and to help plead his case with the powers at Monte Carlo, that is, the Conseil d'Administration. Guerin cautioned him to return to de Basil with a new contract insisting that all publicity include Blum's name and Monte Carlo's, and that de Basil step down as director and cede this position entirely to

Figure 7.10
René Blum watching rehearsal in Monte Carlo. Photo by G. Detaille, courtesy of Archives Monte-Carlo, SBM.

Blum. De Basil acceded to none of these terms and went about his business as usual.

Blum had to continue his contract with de Basil in order to recoup the 450,000 francs he had invested in the company in 1932. He acknowledged that he was a victim of his "confidence [in de Basil] and of his unselfishness."[55] Blum was in the process of arranging for another company to do the "saisons de ballet," perhaps the ballet of the Paris Opéra (the director of the Paris Opéra, Jacques Rouché, was willing to help) with Serge Lifar playing the role of intermediary. Unfortunately, this idea was rejected by the Société des Bains de Mer. In a letter on September 19, 1933, Blum asked reluctantly for an advance of 50,000 francs, to help him prepare for the following season. It seemed a desperate plea.

In 1977, with much hindsight, P. W. Manchester pondered de Basil's abilities:

> It became clear right away that de Basil did not have the "know how" of Diaghilev, and that he couldn't create anything. He couldn't bring out anything. He simply was a marvelous man for organizing, keeping together a lot of homeless dancers. The young dancers were supporting their parents from a very early age. You hear terrible stories about how he never paid them regular salaries. He would give them money for something and keep them tied to him.[56]

Despite the heavy demands of his fledgling ballet company and his perilous finances, Blum's contract also required him to provide ballets for the operas performed at the Théâtre de Monte-Carlo. In March 1933, he presented a rich season of such classics as *La Traviata, Boris Godunov*, and *Tales of Hoffman*. His responsibilities for plays and operettas were no less demanding.

Provocative and alluring ballet programs brought the kind of success that the Société des Bains de Mer had hoped for when they agreed to back Blum and de Basil. Albert Scotto, the financial accountant for the Société des Bains de Mer, reported on the 1933 spring ballet season. The required sixteen ballet performances given from April 13 through May 9 yielded a grand total of 91,320 francs, superseding the 1932 season by nearly 20,000 francs and ensuring that the de Basil/Blum operation had proven its present and potential value to SBM.

As if to startle his audiences and to impress Blum and de Basil, Massine became a veritable choreographic machine during the 1933 Monte Carlo season, turning out the following ballets: a new version of *le Beau Danube* (March 7), *Les Présages* (April 13), *Beach* (April 18), *Scuola di Ballo* (April 25), and *Choreartium* (at the Alhambra October 24). Blum, however, did not ignore the classics; he brought back the ever-popular *Les Sylphides* and *Petrouchka*, and added *Swan Lake*. Dance historian Lynn Garafola commented on Massine's brilliant output: "during the next five years, The Ballets Russes de Monte Carlo's most creative period, it served as a platform for Massine's work. There was nothing in those immensely prolific years that Massine seemingly could not do. He staged comic ballets, character ballets, ballets on period themes, contemporary themes, and American themes."[57]

The fresh musical conceptions, the dancers, choreographers, and designers associated with the Ballets Russes could not have happened without René Blum's creative imagination. Although he was hesitant about a ballet that Massine set to Tchaikovsky's Symphony No. 5, he trusted Massine's abilities, and was personally confident in the depth of his own knowledge of musical scores, his closeness to many composers and artists who were his contemporaries, and his catholic tastes in music.

Blum's intuition in hiring Massine was validated and a milestone achieved in Monte Carlo on April 13, 1933, when Massine presented *Les Présages*, set to Tchaikovsky's 1888 Symphony No. 5 in E minor, Opus 64. Without Toumanova, who followed Balanchine to Paris when he debuted his Ballets 1933, another brilliant performer, Irina Baronova, received the opportunity to dance with David Lichine in the pas de deux in which, Sorley Walker noted, she expressed "the deeply lyrical and loving nature of a passionate relationship."[58] After Massine's first use of the symphonic form in 1933,

Figure 7.11
Le Beau Danube. Décor and costumes by Wladimir Polunin after Constantin Guys. Photo by G. Detaille, courtesy of Archives Monte-Carlo, SBM.

he choreographed ten more ballets to symphonies. But he was not the first major choreographer to prove the exciting possibilities of dance and symphonic music. The astonishing Isadora Duncan hired full orchestras to accompany her performances, one of which was to excerpts from Tchaikovsky's Symphony No. 6.

A. V. Coton found *Les Présages* "a perfect fusion of Central European free arm and head movement, allied to the physical freedom of leg extension that ballet technique offers."[59] Youthful dancers were also the subject of attention as André Eglevsky, a mere fifteen years old, impressed audiences with his slow and controlled pirouettes and his double *tours en l'air.*

The program for *Les Présages* informed the spectator that the first part of Massine's scenario "represents human activity, often interrupted by distractions, such as desires and temptations." Suffused with Dantean warnings of good and evil, the second act tells of love and passion disturbed by a "mauvais sort," or evil destiny. The third part digresses, bringing some levity and frivolity to the dangerous fate of the protagonists. In the last scene, man's innate anger and need for conquest and heroism are awakened. The women experience a desire for powerful authority, and follow these new "heroes after a thousand dangers" who triumph and then dance in a vigorous celebration of their victory.[60]

Figure 7.12
Les Présages. Décor and costumes by André Masson. Photo by G. Detaille, courtesy of Archives Monte-Carlo, SBM.

Discussing a recent reconstruction of *Les Présages*, writer/critic Leigh Witchel compared the fourth movement's symbolism to the power of the railroad: "In 1933 the railroad was a symbol of power and transit; as the movement rumbles toward its climax, the massed corps moves in two lines like a locomotive."[61] He also sensed its militaristic ambiance: "There is a strong martial atmosphere, including how the dancers are moved around in block like squadrons . . . but what it inspired from Massine in the massed power of the dance design is still gripping."[62]

Massine's adventurous journey into the hitherto sacred symphonic musical form created quite a stir when *Les Présages* premiered. Music writers claimed that the dance could never reflect the complexities and organic meanings of musical compositions. However wonderfully danced, the ballet raised many eyebrows. The décor by André Masson caused a commotion; some absolutely hated it and others adored it. Theatre design critic G. E. Goodman found harmony in *Les Présages* and recounted its excitement: "Comets, flames, stars and waves surged stridently in a wild swirl of crude greens, garish reds and vivid purples—the whole gamut of a childlike delight in colour. From one high corner of the backcloth stared the huge symbol of an ever-watching eye, dominating the whole stage." Goodman found color everywhere, especially in the lush tints of the costumes and the dramatic entrance of the bat-like figure of M. Woizikowsky. "So finely balanced was the colour scheme that these usually mild and innocuous tints took to a decided sense of unpleasantness by virtue of their contrast with the surroundings."[63]

Almost immediately, an intense debate ensued over the melding of symphonic music and choreography. In the *Dancing Times*, The Sitter Out offered a lucid interpretation of the difficulties of choreographing a symphony and contended with another prominent ballet critic, James Monahan, about the need for suitable music for a ballet. He disagreed with the way a fugue was interpreted by a particular contemporary choreographer who, in his opinion, made movements so obviously mimicking the music that they seemed banal: "The entrance of each voice is personified by the appearance of a dancer who leaps from a hidden platform in the wings onto the stage, runs down stage, leaps again, and begins to do pirouettes alongside the other voices."[64]

In order to prove his point, The Sitter Out praised the young English choreographer Antony Tudor, who also used a fugue, apparently brilliantly, in his *Descent of Hebe*: "Mr. Tudor has followed the form of the music where possible, but ignored it where it suited his purpose, and thus he builds up a pattern of his own which forms a kind of counterpoint to the music."[65] The critic noted that many people found this approach to making ballets challenging, but that was how Massine worked—with "imagination and variety" in his symphonic ballets.

The Sitter Out's colleague, Mr. Monahan, differed with this point of view and agreed with the opinions of current music critics that symphonic music is so great and so complete in itself that it needs no accompanying ballet movement. To some, this meant that only a rather mediocre or limited music score worked best for ballet. These polemics cast new light on the ballet itself, its purpose and its possibilities. In conclusion, The Sitter Out pleaded for a "broader concept of ballet, one that acknowledged the beauty of changes in this art form, and one that incorporated innovation as a necessary development for its future."[66]

One of the highlights of the spring season, opening on April 19, 1933, was the ballet *Beach*, a tribute to the Principality of Monte Carlo and perhaps a gentle reminder of an earlier Nijinska ballet, *Le Train Bleu*. Massine wanted to honor his hosts with a pithy, jazzy, and charming representation. To a lighthearted score by the twenty-year-old Jean Francaix and witty, seascape designs by Raoul Dufy, the world of fashion came alive in the Monte Carlo characters who adored the open air of summer life.

Massine's *Scuola di Ballo*, which premiered on April 25, 1933, capitalized on the audience's natural affinity for and pleasure in watching a ballet class on stage. With a Baroque score by Luigi Boccherini orchestrated by

Figure 7.13
Beach. Decors by Raoul Dufy. Photo by G. Detaille, courtesy of Archives Monte-Carlo, SBM.

J. Francaix, set and costume designs by Étienne de Beaumont, and Massine's interpretation of the Carlo Goldoni play, its stereotypic comic characters charmed and delighted audiences. The ballet told the story of several greedy, deceitful, and uncompromising characters whose lives center on the activities of a dance studio. Professor Rigaudon (his name the title of a Renaissance dance form) watches closely over his class. One of his students, Lucrezia, an avid ballet mother, asks to speak to him confidentially, so he dismisses the other students, whereupon she urges the professor to give her daughter Rosina special attention. Rigaudon's friend Ridolfo then brings Don Fabrizio, a powerful impresario, into the room, and whispers to Rigaudon that for a sum of money, Don Fabrizio would like to meet a lovely dancer.

The story takes a comic turn when Don Fabrizio disguises himself and pretends to be a lowly ballroom amateur looking for a dancing partner. Rigaudon introduces him to Felicita, but first Don Fabrizio wants to see her dance. Rigaudon shows him a financial contract he must sign if he wishes to become Felicita's fiancé. Don Fabrizio returns with Felicita, whose dancing unfortunately is gauche and ungraceful. Fabrizio now wants to return her to Rigaudon, but Felicita begs him to recognize her talents as an actress, and they leave the stage together. Rosina and her mother enter in time for her lesson, while the discouraged and angry Don Fabrizio insists that he be allowed to watch all the students so that he might find the perfect partner. Soon he notices Rosina's beauty and agility, but Rigaudon refuses to give

Figure 7.14
Scuola di Ballo. Decors and costumes by Étienne de Beaumont. Photo by G. Detaille, courtesy of Archives Monte-Carlo, SBM.

her up. Finally, Don Fabrizio returns with a notary who claims that Don Fabrizio's contract has been broken. All the students taunt Rigaudon and profess that they will no longer continue to study with him, as they must find their way in life with their future friends and lovers so that they might marry. Rigaudon is left alone, desperate and miserable. Ballet teachers are notorious for their covetous relationships, especially with young students, and Massine exposes this tendency in his insightful work.

In the Paris *Daily Mail*, June 2, 1933, the critic praised the troupe's performance at the Châtelet: "These are the legitimate heirs of the original Serge de Diaghilev Ballets Russes, now under the direction of de Basil and René Blum."[67] Some critics recalled that the last ballets presented by Diaghilev's Ballets Russes displeased their audiences for varying reasons. In Paris's *New York Herald Tribune* of June 12, 1933, the often cynical Louis Schneider wrote:

> It must be admitted that the success of this presentation is due to an evident reaction against the ballets presented by the late Diaghilev from whose company this is an emancipation. There is no more aggressive music, or shrieking stage settings and costumes of another time. As for the choreography it is sane and in no way connected with acrobatics. . . . The dances seem to be part of the lightness of the music. In brief, the evening was a complete success.[68]

In *Paris Midi*, June 14, 1933, Louis Léon Martin wrote that the opening night of the Ballets Russes centered on Léonide Massine: "I entreat M. René Blum to continue to have the intelligence to give Massine the resources of which he is worthy."[69] In the 1933 Paris program, René Blum was credited with the "direction artistique" and W. de Basil was noted as "directeur."

L'Echo de Paris, June 19, 1933, announced the season of the Ballets Russes at the Théâtre du Châtelet: "Tonight a new season of the Ballets Russes proves once again that it is the true inheritor of the beautiful traditions of the old Ballets Russes; Blum and de Basil are at the head of this young company which so demonstrated last year its brilliant artistic value."[70]

The dispute between de Basil and Blum seemed relentless. Blum wrote René Léon on June 13, 1933, apologizing for the lack of publicity in Paris both for Monte Carlo and for Blum's name. Blum told Léon he was seeking legal counsel, and that he regretted this unpleasant affair. He confessed, "This must be the first time in my ten years working for you that you have a complaint against me."[71] Blum concluded by saying that he would make sure this did not happen again.

After the Paris tour, the Blum/de Basil company made its way to London and the Alhambra Theatre on July 4, 1933, for performances that took the city by storm. The troupe was supposed to stay for three weeks, but was rebooked and stayed four months. Manchester remembered seeing *Les Sylphides, Les Présages*, and *Beau Danube*, and called it an absolute knockout of an evening:

> Nobody had seen Baronova before, nor Riabouchinska, nor David Lichine. And there was Anton Dolin who had come back to do *Les Sylphides*. Here they were with Danilova, a great old favorite, and Massine who was still in his late 30s at his peak as a character dancer. There was incredible excitement. Something very special had arrived.[72]

While touring with the company in London, Blum wrote on July 4, 1933, to Georges Reymond, his secretary in Monte Carlo, in regard to several topics including Balanchine's Les Ballets 1933. The letter revealed a prickly side to Blum that seemed to increase as Blum continued to work with de Basil. He mentioned that a formidable publicity campaign praising the brilliance of Balanchine's talents had been mounted for Les Ballets 1933. Blum noted regrettably, though, that he found the ballets to be a failure, and that Balanchine's choreography had clearly regressed, "not because his ex-collaborator lost all his talent since he is no longer under the influence of Diaghilev, 'his genial great animator,'" but rather because he created too many ballets much too quickly. Blum found the only saving grace to be the very pretty costumes and splendid decors. Blum also discussed a problem that had been bothering him since he formed his joint venture with de Basil: he now found him unreliable. Indeed, Blum feared that Reymond might hire Balanchine's "Les Ballets 1933" company to replace the current de Basil/Blum company before Blum could find a new and equally talented ballet company for the next season.

At the beginning of this letter, Blum waxed poetic about the astounding success of his own ballet company, first in Paris and then at the Alhambra in London. He was excited especially by the response to *Les Sylphides, Les Présages*, and *Le Beau Danube*—a big victory. Naturally, he suggested a split with de Basil, but acknowledged that it was too early to discuss that possibility. Blum was exhausted and had come to realize that he had to defend himself from de Basil's ingratitude and the malevolence of his heartless behavior. In what was to become one of many emotional outbursts against de Basil, Blum lamented: "In any case, I can no longer continue to work with the wretch who has so compromised me. One of us must give in to the other. We will cry together if it is me, as that means that the ballets are finished [*les ballets sont morts*], these ballets that I so loved, and for which I sacrificed all that I possess, as well as the best of my thinking and my heart."[73]

Apropos the London debut of Les Ballets 1933, even Lincoln Kirstein, Balanchine's eventual champion, conceded that the Ballets Russes had the advantage of that season at the Châtelet: "Lincoln had obviously come to prefer Les Ballets Russes to Balanchine's Les Ballets 1933, as the Parisian critics and public gave de Basil's company far more acclaim, with the press commenting on how much it had improved over the previous year, when Balanchine had been ballet master."[74]

In an article titled "The Duel of the Ballets Russes Companies," the often bilious André Levinson also questioned the sad state of Balanchine's choreography for Les Ballets 1933 in *Candide*. Levinson referred back to the rollicking delight of Balanchine's dances in *Orphée aux Enfers* and the marvel of his perfect *pas de sept* in *Le Bourgeois Gentilhomme*, but "last night," he observed, "such fun only occurs in rare instances of the inexplicable torpor of certain passages in his Mozart and other pieces"[75]

After Les Ballets 1933, Blum had asked Balanchine to return to Monte Carlo and once again assume control of the company as he was intending "to separate from de Basil."[76] Blum would repeat this request again in 1935, after his break with de Basil actually occurred.

In the fall of 1933, when Serge Lifar was touring with a small ballet company, he found himself stranded in America. The tour was meant to attract audiences to the sets and costume designs commissioned by Serge Diaghilev for the Ballets Russes. Since Lifar was essentially broke, he sold the collection to Hartford's Wadsworth Atheneum.[77] With this tour, Lifar was also making an unspoken claim to Diaghilev's legacy that would insure Lifar's credibility as a European artistic force. The collection included spectacular designs by Bakst, Miró, Benois, Matisse, Rouault, and Ernst, which established the Atheneum as one of the world's greatest archives for early-twentieth-century stage art. Lifar wrote many volumes about his role in dance history, carefully protecting his reputation from negative reactions.

Consistent with his radical departure in the use of music, Massine premiered the formidable *Choreartium*, to Brahms' Symphony No. 4, on October 24, 1933, in London, with costumes by Tcherekovitch and Lourie, a curtain painting by Georges Annenkoff, and scenery by Elizabeth Polunin. In the foreground of painted scenery, there was a high-arched aqueduct, and in the distance, a rainbow.

The critic Baird Hastings, who appreciated the speed and spontaneity with which Massine moved large groups of dancers, observed that Massine explicitly positioned "his female dancers in the softer passages and featured male dancers in the loud passages."[78] The opening movement of *Choreartium* had a free-flowing style, whereas the second movement, in which Nina Verchinina led groups of eighteen dancers, was strident and somber. For the second movement, the stage was decorated in shades of yellow, beige, and gray, with Danilova, Shabelevsky, Riabouchinska, and Jasinski dancing in the foreground with a lighter, more folk-like style. In response to Brahms's music, the finale shifted to create a gray, stately feeling. At one point Massine had six male dancers executing "successively a series of tours en l'air, followed by an 'architectural' ensemble led by Paul Petroff with the other soloists and the corps de ballet."[79] It was a stunning, uplifting ending as Riabouchinska took over the flute theme and the whole stage breathed with a sense of "kinetic exhileration." Manchester also remembered that the men startled their audiences, although she increased their number: "Sixteen male dancers did double tours en l'air in the Fourth Movement and one of them, Borovansky, did a double tour en l'air to the knee."[80]

In a review dated June 1, 1934, Louis Schneider, writing for the *New York Herald Tribune* took a dim view of *Choreartium*, and at the same time revealed his startling lack of knowledge about dance:

> The novelty of the evening was *Choreartium*, a bizarre name under which Brahms' 4th Symphony is dissimulated. Can the great musician have composed that grave and severe work for dance? Brahms' directing thought seems to be somewhat floating, and capricious and does not descend to very clear signification. It is surprising that the dancing groups have been able to remember this choreography and to give it form. Let them be congratulated. But the costumes and the scenery were not beautiful.[81]

Critic Irving Schwerke saw beyond this naïve stance in the *Chicago Daily Tribune* of June 2, 1934: "The Ballets Russes gave a performance before a

Figure 7.15
Choreartium. Photo with Alexandra Danilova by Merlin, courtesy of Bibliothèque du Musée de l'Opéra.

Figure 7.16
Choreartium. Photo by Merlin, courtesy of Bibliothèque du Musée de l'Opéra.

dressy and capacity audience. What is admirable about *Choreartium* is the state of perfection into which the terpsichoreans have been rehearsed and the way musical themes are presented physically and developed." The distinguished music critic Ernst Newman declared, "The better we know Brahms's music the more pleasure we derive from the ballet *Choreartium*."[82]

The company also received splendid reviews from the *Menton News* on November 18, 1933: "In passing, we should like to offer M. René Blum our warmest congratulations on the marvelous success in Paris, and more especially in London of his Ballets Russes de Monte-Carlo. Only a few know how much M. René Blum has staked both in artistic and physical effort, and financially, but his belief in his company has been well justified."[83]

While the Blum/de Basil company beguiled Londoners with its exciting productions at the Alhambra, several dancers from the Ballets Russes were invited to perform before cameras for the BBC's year-old experiment in television. Janet Rowson Davis unearthed BBC records, discovering one of the earliest TV programs that focused on the "baby ballerina" members of the company and included broadcast excerpts from *Jeux d'Enfants, Le Beau Danube*, and *Petrushka*. Rowson Davis quoted the producer Eustace Robb's *A Day in My Life*, a memoir that offered details of this groundbreaking recording on November 2, 1933.[84]

It must have seemed not only inappropriate but downright insidious for de Basil to leave out Blum's name on all the advertising and programs as they toured London, Paris, and the United States—another reason why Blum's name has disappeared from the historical descriptions of events during the 1930s.

However, Blum's career as a producer progressed. From 1933 to 1934, he also worked in Paris as artistic director of the Théâtre Pigalle. On November 29, 1933, the newspaper *La Liberté* announced Max Reinhardt's *La Chauve-Souris* as the "inaugural performance produced by Wallace Haendler and René Blum," whose varied programs were also complemented by the famed director Nikita Balieff.[85]

The Blum/de Basil company began its New York season on December 22, 1933, at the St. James Theatre. After a lackluster New York stay, the troupe toured many cities, crossing America to San Francisco. Both Blum and de Basil teamed up with the indefatigable Sol Hurok, who made extravagant arrangements for openings and social events in order to appeal to the rich and famous. Everyone played a role in the whirlwind effort of raising money and developing audiences for the ballet. But New York and the St. James Theatre with its small stage did not provide the same exciting successes that the company experienced in London at the Alhambra.

Traveling by train across America generated a tremendous sense of adventure and merriment, despite the hard work of almost a hundred people associated with the Ballets Russes at that time. During the winter tour in St. Louis, Baronova remembered that in the middle of a snowball fight she fell awkwardly, fracturing her ankle. This injury would incapacitate her for months. It was also during this tour in Chicago that de Basil hired the soon to be famous Sono Osato, then a mere fourteen years old.

In the fall of 1933, Blum continued in his role as artistic director of the Théâtre de Monte-Carlo, creating an array of what were called "comédies lyriques." Using his pseudonym, René Bergeret, he helped rewrite the libretti for *L'Étoile* by Emmanuel Chabrier and *Dona Francisquita* to a new score by A. Vives. In 1934, Blum resumed his English comedy season featuring George Bernard Shaw, Sir Arthur Conan Doyle, and other lesser-known playwrights. Blum understood that younger, sophisticated English visitors to Monte Carlo would appreciate the biting satire of Shaw and also be drawn to the thrilling dramas of Conan Doyle.

Although de Basil was supposed to be in Monte Carlo for the 1934 season, the masterful Hurok, Sorley Walker wrote, "opened up the wide horizon of the United States for the touring company.[86] Breaking his contract with Blum in the spring of 1934, and relishing this new opportunity, de Basil lengthened his American tour, forcing Blum in Monte Carlo to seize other opportunities and find dancers and choreographers, one of whom was the brilliant but "terrifying" Bronislava Nijinska. Tamara Tchinarova Finch commented that working with Nijinska, especially as a very young person, was a most fearsome experience. When saying goodbye, she observed, "We should have thanked her that we had learned how to carry on in spite of our bleeding toes, wounded pride, diminished egos and the hate in our hearts."[87]

This was the beginning of the end for de Basil and Blum. Blum engaged Nijinska as the new ballet master in March 1934, and hired away from de Basil some of his best dancers: Danilova and Woizikovsky, Tchinarova, Jasinsky and Guerard, along with Mia Slavenska and Boris Kniaseff. Danilova later commented that this period also marked the beginning of the creation of Blum's own company, and since she was the star ballerina, "Whenever I sneezed everyone came running, 'Are you all right?'"[88]

Naturally, the repertoire included Nijinska ballets such as *Bolero*, which was originally choreographed for Ida Rubinstein's company in 1928, as well as *Variations* and the intriguing *Les Comédiens Jaloux*, two pieces created for her own company, Théâtre de la Danse, in 1932.

Les Comédiens Jaloux (The Jealous Actors), which opened on April 24, 1934, told the story of Flavio's valet Pedrollino, the dreamer who creates a play that is performed in a public plaza in the middle of a small town. Pantalone wants to marry off his daughter Clarisse to a wealthy man. Capitano Spavento and Capitano Cocodrillo hope to obtain the hand of Clarisse,

Figure 7.17
Portrait of Bronislava Nijinska by Gordon Anthony. Courtesy of V&A Images/Victoria and Albert Museum, London.

who is truly in love with Flavio, a strong, handsome, and unfortunately poor young man. Pedrollino, the poet, invents every sort of ruse to betray Pantalone, keeping him far from the rendezvous that Clarisse and Flavio have arranged. In a minor scuffle, Pedrollino knocks out Capitano Spavento, and leaves his body in Pantalone's garden. Pantalone discovers Spavento and, thinking him dead, fears that the crime will be attributed to him. The coy Pedrollino then threatens to reveal this secret if Pantalone refuses to accept Flavio as his daughter's fiancée. The terrified Pantalone agrees to this trick, and Clarisse falls happily into her lover's arms forever.

When the Blum/de Basil company sailed back to Europe from America, its first engagement was the bullring in Barcelona. It became a hilariously improvised affair as there were no proper places for either scenery or the orchestra, and bullring habitués were unclear about how to respond to ballet—something that they had surely never seen. Then the company moved on to Paris, opening at the Théâtre de Champs-Élysées on June 4, 1934, for a series of very well-attended performances. The Paris stay ended on June 16, 1934, and everyone looked forward to the London season and Covent Garden.

Many people recalled the gala opening night of the Blum/de Basil company at Covent Garden on June 19, 1934, when the troupe's stars received bouquets of flowers and tumultuous applause. They met their financial backers, Captain Bruce Ottley and Baron Frederic d'Erlanger, themselves musicians and composers who shared a love of ballet and opera.[89] Erlanger not only composed the score for *Les Cent Baisers*, a ballet in which Baronova performed the lead role, but he also funded the production. In London, the company revived Fokine's works as well as a new Massine ballet, *Union Pacific*, which it had rehearsed every evening while on tour in America. The season, in Baronova's words, was a "tremendous success, and all of us, individually and together, were applauded, admired and loved to bits."[90]

The ups and downs of the ballet *Union Pacific* are worth retelling, as they offer a lesson in "unintended consequences." Since no documentation exists of Blum's opinion about the endeavor, it is impossible to know how he viewed the raison d'être and concept of the piece. We know that Massine desired to create a ballet with an American theme, and the Union Pacific railroad, suggested by American poet Archibald MacLeish, seemed the perfect subject. Hurok knew Nicolas Nabokov, who composed the music for this work in a mere twenty-three days.[91] The score was inspired by songs and dances from the turn of the century, including African American jazz tunes from Chicago and New Orleans. It premiered in the United States on April 6, 1934, at the Forrest Theatre in Philadelphia, followed by a performance at the St. James Theatre in New York on April 27.

The plot for *Union Pacific* included stereotypical stories of Mexicans, Chinese, and Irish workmen, Mormon missionaries, ladies of easy virtue, and a bartender. Jack Anderson quoted Caryl Brahms who found it "raw," save for several moments like Baronova's Girl of the Golden West, the Barman's cake-walk solo, and the sleeping corps de ballet's variation.[92] Massine had studied "black dance" in New Orleans and Harlem in order to polish his much-noted Barman's dance. Interestingly enough, it caused a good deal of consternation among the modern dance crowd in New York, as witnessed by several editorials in the May and August 1934 issues of *Dance Observer*.

The editorial in the May 1934 *Dance Observer*, entitled "American Ballet?," offered a prescient if scathing commentary on the Ballets Russes' *Union Pacific*. The author informed readers that in the farewell program of the Ballets Russes de Monte-Carlo, de Basil wrote a polemic defending his decision to make an American ballet,"that the Russian ballet has broken contact with its native soil and sought to germinate in the soil of other lands."[93] We are told that since de Basil was fascinated by American folklore, he decided to produce this work. In a facetious quip, the author asks, "Why is the Ballets Russes leaving us then, if it wishes to create an American ballet?" The final sentence wonders cynically: "How can the Colonel, at this trying, crucial moment, when the current desire of Americans to have their own ballet is of such intensity, be so heartless as to forsake our shores and leave us to our own inept, untutored devices?"[94] A heated debate at the time professed that since America was the land of the future, it must develop cultural themes in contemporary dance delineating a new world suitable to the American ethos.

The same May 1934 issue of *Dance Observer* contains a disparaging review of *Union Pacific*. The critic Sophia Delza reproached the ballet: "For all the American quality achieved in *Union Pacific*, the Ballets Russes de

Figure 7.18
Union Pacific, with Léonide Massine as the Barman. Photo by Studio Iris, courtesy of Bibliothèque du Musée de l'Opéra.

Monte Carlo [no mention of René Blum] might easily have substituted the choreography of *Petrouchka*, the style of *La Concurrence*, and the costumes of *Les Matelots* without materially altering their interpretation of what they considered to be America in 1869. . . . The spirit of this ballet is as far removed from the America of 1869 as Buffalo Bill was from the Paris Opéra."[95] The review postulated that

> there were ample opportunities for rich characterizations—dances for Irish workmen, for Chinese, for ladies of "easy virtue," dances of rivalry, love, display and antagonism, dances of capitalists and barmen. The Ballet Russe maestro missed his chance every time or else failed to realize his chances. The Surveyor danced by Eglevsky, and the Barman played by Massine . . . everything about *Union Pacific* was extremely superficial, unimaginative and flat. What stilted similarity of conception, what loose formation of ensembles, what a display of old-fashioned musical comedy exaggeration, what weak formless organization! Where was its wit, its style etc.? Lost in the forests and wide plains of America. Are the leading spirits of the Ballets Russes de Monte Carlo unaware of the extraordinary developments in dance composition, do they not realize the widened perceptions of integrated form and design, of space construction and related group movements that have taken place in the last two decades? In conclusion, it may be said that it had a charm in its first scene, which though trite was pleasing.[96]

Continuing the diatribe against the Ballets Russes de Monte-Carlo, the editorial of the August–September 1934 issue of the *Dance Observer* blasted those critics who praised *Union Pacific*, and targeted John Martin (*New York Times*), Burns Mantle (*Daily News*), and Pitts Sanborn, who all found positive elements in the ballet. The *Dance Observer* editors were angered that they had "buttered up" the Ballets Russes.[97] Critics Jerome Bohm and Leonard Liebling also adored the choreography. Ridiculing these writers, the editor asked if they had seen the inside of the Roxy or the Paramount where "similar original and resourceful devices have occurred time and time again"[98]

Since critics and reviewers alike acknowledged that it was time for an American ballet company, how could they say that this ballet laid the foundation? The editorial stated that "neither the forms, style, spirit, nor type of technique employed in the works of the Monte Carlo Ballet or any other organization similar to it can possibly be utilized in the founding of a native American ballet."[99] The editors rather preferred Martha Graham and Doris Humphrey to lead the way to truly American works. The final argument condemned the fact that critics or reviewers in American newspapers suffer from a lack of knowledge about dance, and that the newspapers, the editors insisted, "have forced on the public music and dramatic critics who are often uninterested in the dance and who are by no means always competent to judge, and who misdirect the public which requires at this point intelligent leadership. For the sake of American dance—let us have dance critics whose education and experience have fitted them for the task of sitting in judgment on what is certainly one of the furthest advanced of native arts."[100]

Finding it impossible to work in tandem with de Basil, Blum had withdrawn from their collaboration as early as the end of 1933, although he remained artistic director of the company. On August 16, 1934, he and de Basil signed a one-year contract to terminate their partnership and the Blum/de Basil company as of May 15, 1935. Blum recovered 250,000 francs that he had poured into the new company, a sum that de Basil was able to furnish on April 30, 1935, the same date that Blum extricated himself from the partnership.[101]

In a letter to Alfred Delpierre, president of the Société des Bains de Mer organization, dated August 22, 1934, Blum stated that his liaison with de Basil would conclude in April 1935, and that he would create a new company "of at least an equal artistic value as the present company, but this company would be disengaged from any foreign influence, and would only have me as its director."[102] Blum began this contractual letter by acknowledging that he chose a totally unworthy Russian partner, and that "in order to limit his personal liabilities, [Blum] had to make over the ownership of the Blum/de Basil Company to de Basil."[103] This must have been an embarrassing and difficult move for Blum. But also, in order to recoup his investments, for the moment Blum had to continue a relationship with de Basil, and thus still assumed a kind of paternal artistic ownership of the company. In this letter he reassured M. Delpierre that he had found funding in England and in America to bring his new company to Monte Carlo in 1936. Blum referred to a previous letter from Delpierre informing Blum that he need no longer produce the season of plays and operettas, but rather could spend all of his time with the assurance of enough funding to plan the 1936 ballet season effectively. A formal contract followed this letter, stipulating that Blum would receive 450,000 francs including half of the performance receipts, travel funds to Paris, and other prerequisites. However, Blum would be responsible for paying all expenses for a troupe of fifty dancers as well as the choreographer, the scene designer, the costumer, the hairdresser, the musical scores and orchestra parts, and the editorial rights pertaining to publicity and the printed programs.

Even as the company began to formally dissolve in late 1934, the dancers kept to a challenging performance schedule. The company embarked for Mexico City to open on September 25, 1934. An altitude of 7,400 feet devastated the breath control of the dancers, but they loved the Palacio de Bellas Artes, a theatre built in the style of the Garnier in Paris and Monte Carlo. All performances were sold out and the company received standing ovations.

On October 25, after four weeks on stage, the troupe made its way to Montreal on a special train for another whirlwind North American tour that spanned 20,000 miles in seven months, ending in New York.

One of the great hits of the January 1935 opera season in Monte Carlo was Strauss's *La Chauve-Souris*, which had had such a startling success in Paris at the Pigalle Theatre a year earlier. As the season progressed, *The Menton News* praised the touring activities of the Ballets Russes but chided de Basil for blatantly excluding Blum's name:

> Only a few days ago we received a rapturous review from Vancouver. It should scarcely be necessary to say that René Blum is the Artistic Director and M. W. de Basil the General Manager. Many of us here resent the way in which René Blum's name is always omitted in London newspapers, for we know that their wonderful repertoire is primarily due to him. Honor where honor is due and in this case it should be René Blum and M. de Basil.[104]

Strained by his concerns about de Basil, and also preparing for what might be a very different ballet company, Blum rehired the National Lithuanian Ballet Company, with which he had an affinity and a long relationship. For the Monte Carlo season from January 16 to 31, 1935, the company led by Nemtchinova and Oboukhov danced *Carnaval, Raimonda, Giselle,* and *Swan Lake* to augment the usual slate of operas. One month later, it played in London at the Alhambra and especially for Nemtchinova's performance in *Giselle* received lovely praise: "She carried the piece past the perils of melodrama with complete success. She sustained the ghostly atmosphere without breaking the illusion for a moment; the bucolic maiden of the first act was a veritable disembodied spirit throughout the second."[105] Several weeks later on a more critical note, the *Times* rebuked her: "Once again, Nemtchinova received cheers, except for her 32 fouettés in the role of Odile, during which she fell off pointe"[106]

The new ballet company, now called the Ballets de Monte-Carlo, traveled by ship to France and then by train from Paris to Monte Carlo. Nijinska rehearsed the company in Paris, preparing it for a season premiere on April 4, 1935, in Monte Carlo. Boris Kochno accompanied the group when he thought his services as a dramaturge would be useful. It was at this moment that Massine began his *Symphonie Fantastique,* based on Hector Berlioz's score in five movements. With designs by Christian Bérard and costumes by Karinska and Mme. Larose, this spectacular production was to be premiered a year later, on July 24, 1936.

The 1935 Monte Carlo season, the last for de Basil, included Massine's *Union Pacific* with its unexceptional debut on April 4, as well as a lukewarm reaction to *Jardin Public,* which opened on April 13 (it had premiered originally on March 8, 1935, in Chicago). Though it had a scenario developed by Massine and music by Vladimir Dukelsky or Vernon Duke, the inspiration for *Jardin Public* came from a section of André Gide's novel *The Counterfeiters*. "A day in the life of a public garden" was meant to be a reference to the experiences that human beings endure, along with their unpredictability and odd permutations. Utilizing contrasts such as wealth and

Figure 7.19
Jardin Public, with Kyra Strakhova, Galina Razouma, and Mira Dimina. Courtesy of Jerome Robbins Dance Division, the New York Public Library for the Performing Arts, Astor, Lenox, and Tilden Foundations.

poverty, age and youth, innocence and decadence, and "those who wish to live, and those who wish to die," it seemed on the surface an interesting conceit. However, the points were heavily labored and the discordant music displeased the audiences. The French painter Jean Lurçat and American designer Hélène Pons created the decor and costumes, respectively.

After the long breakup, Blum needed a star choreographer and wrote to Balanchine on November 5, 1935, meditating on how happy he was to regain his cherished liberty whereby now he alone would direct his company and realize his artistic conceptions.[107] He told Balanchine that he considered this an opportunity to find his voice once again as a producer and director. In the past he was besieged by what he called "combinaisons," or cliques who worked against him, such that they dragged him down, as along with "the whole artistic enterprise." The letter suggested the trust and respect that had evolved in Blum's relationship to Balanchine over the many years of their professional association. Blum remembered that Balanchine wanted to collaborate when Blum no longer had "that partner." Blum continued: "I always hoped that together we might create beautiful productions, because our sympathy for one another has always been perfect, at least in the sense of creating true art."[108]

Balanchine cabled back on November 21, 1935, and said that Blum's resolution to create a new ballet company "makes me very happy. I am so grateful

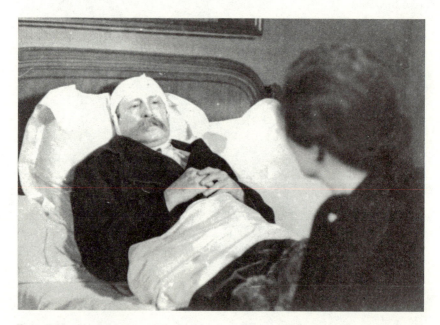

Figure 7.20
Léon Blum recovering from the attack by Action Française members. Courtesy of Centre d'Histoire de SciencesPo.

for your invitation, but at present I am very tied up in New York."[109] Balanchine had a contract to choreograph for the Metropolitan Opera. "I wish with all my heart that you will have a brilliant success, as you surely deserve!"[110]

At the same time that René Blum was strategizing the creation of his own company, a startling and disastrous event shocked the Blum family and especially Léon and René. On February 13, 1936, upon returning from the Chambre des députés and riding in Georges Monnet's car, Léon Blum, Monnet, and others came to the Boulevard Saint Germain. Léon Blum was by then the head of the French Socialist Party. At the corner of the rue de l'Université, a huge crowd of right-wing, militant pro-Fascists from the "Action française" had been following the funeral cortège of Jacques Bainville, a historian and partisan of the movement. When they saw the car with Léon Blum, they yelled, "Blum à mort" and "Juif assassin," and then shattered the car windows and beat him with an iron bar. He was saved by Monnet and others, and taken to a safe place where a physician treated his lacerated face. The reckless group had ruptured Léon Blum's temporal vein, but he had the good fortune to recover rather quickly.[111] Despite the storm of anti-Semitism assaulting western Europe, the trajectory of Léon Blum's political career was to soar when his party, the Popular Front, took over several months later and he was elected prime minister, the first Socialist and the first Jew to hold that office.

There is no mention of this devastating blow to Léon Blum in René's correspondence, but it must have shaken the whole family and particularly René. During the following months, all of Blum's energies were focused on developing the aesthetic plans of the Ballets de Monte-Carlo. In a Paris newspaper, he looked back and mused upon the creation of his new company: "In the beginning I thought I would assume an artistic position, but alas, I had to become an administrator. It was then that I created a second company, The Ballets de Monte-Carlo. I am deeply confident with the collaboration of one of the greatest modern choreographers for classical ballet, Michel Fokine."[112] Blum looked to Fokine, a true modern master who himself desired a forum for his new choreographies. Their partnership, though highly successful, only endured for one year before Fokine abandoned Blum for de Basil.

CHAPTER 8

Blum Brings Michel Fokine into the Fold

Although the Great Depression had begun in the United States with the stock market crash of 1929, the French economy and that of Monte Carlo, protected by high tariff barriers, remained somewhat insulated from the worldwide recession until after 1931.

Economic crisis and political turmoil reinforced each other. In 1932 the right-wing Bloc National lost control of parliament to the Radicals who then governed with the support of the Socialists, although the latter refused to be represented in the cabinet. In Germany, in part as a result of economic chaos and inflation, Hitler and the Nazis rose to power in 1933. Right-wing movements hostile to the Revolution and the republic had long existed in France, the most important of which was the Action Française, founded by Charles Maurras at the turn of the century. He believed that "four alien nations, Jews, Freemasons, Protestants and Métèques [immigrants] dominated and corrupted the nation."[1] He sought a return of the Catholic Church and the monarchy, appealing to conservatives and the military. The Action Française created the Camelots du Roi, a violent street gang that presaged the actions of future Fascist movements in Italy, Germany, and elsewhere.

With the rise of Hitler, and the popularity of other Fascist movements and their leaders such as Mussolini in Italy, authoritarian and Fascist movements like the anti-parliamentary Jeunesse Patriotes and the Croix de Feu emerged in France. On February 6, 1934, right-wing extremists managed to organize a huge demonstration at the Place de la Concorde. The crowd then crossed the Seine and tried to break into the Chamber of Deputies of the French Parliament. They were forcibly held back and were fired upon by the police. This caused Prime Minister Daladier to resign and brought to power a government of national unity. All the left-wing political groups united in a

Popular Front in 1935 that defeated the conservative Radical government then led by Prime Minister Pierre Laval, who had made the cardinal mistake of cutting government spending and raising taxes during a potential depression. As a result, René's brother Léon Blum came to power in 1936 as the first Socialist and Jewish prime minister of France. Unfortunately, the intransigence of the Communists, who refused to join the new government, led to sit-down strikes all over France and weakened the new government from the start.[2]

Blum's Ballets de Monte-Carlo began optimistically on April 3, 1936, with the ballet master Nicolas Zverev and dancers Vera Nemtchinova, Marie Ruanova, Nathalie Krassovska, Hélène Kirsova, Anatole Vilzak, Anatole Oboukhoff, and André Eglevsky. They surged ahead with Blum's almost divine plans to rescue a company that he so believed in. Soon a new ballet master, George Gué, took over. Other dancers were hired in June: Woizikovsky, Raievska, Tarakanova, and Igor Youskevitch. De Basil kept some of the repertoire and a number of the original performers, including Baronova, Riabouchinska, Lichine, and Danilova, who returned to Blum in 1938. As the company's performances increased in number and success, Blum engaged more dancers, especially English ones. Soon the company would have more than ninety dancers. The fact that some of his most celebrated soloists stayed with de Basil seemed not to distress the ever-optimistic Blum.

Blum was constantly appealing to his superiors for one thing or another, and in 1936 his tone reflected his oppressive sense of isolation. Writing from Paris on March 3, 1936, he asked Delpierre for more rehearsal time, and said that he was facing more difficulties during the spring season than ever before: "I have a new company, new choreography, and new productions. How can I get six different ballets ready for performance when there is so little rehearsal time in the theatre?"[3] Blum was convinced that a successful opening night was essential to attract the favorable attention of impresarios in London and New York. Once again, he reiterated the enormous sacrifices he had made for the new company, to the sum of 700,000 francs, not to mention the emotional toll it had taken.

Michel Fokine, by then fifty-six, took over as ballet master when René Blum finally extricated himself from his ties to de Basil. Fokine longed to reclaim his fame in European capitals, as his time in America had disappointed and exhausted him. With Fokine and the other Russian dancers, Blum tried to sustain the glorious tradition of Russian ballet despite world economics that stressed the very core of the company's ambitions. Blum refused to admit defeat, and plowed on to achieve his dream of a ballet company, with Fokine as the inspiration.

Fokine's first new work for Blum, *L'Épreuve d'Amour*, premiered April 4, 1936, with scenery and costumes by the exciting artist André Derain. The

Figure 8.1
Vera and Michel Fokine in *Carnaval*. Courtesy of Archives Monte-Carlo, SBM.

music, thought originally to be by Mozart, actually was by several composers for a divertissement performed in 1838.[4] The ballet came to be appreciated not as one of Fokine's most experimental or brilliant productions, but as a charming, beautifully arranged piece of "Viennese Chinoiserie." Jack Anderson quoted Cyril Beaumont, who noted poetically that "'it possessed the charm of porcelain vases,' while Fernau Hall thought that it was 'expertly crafted.' Most important, Fokine found a way to disguise the weaknesses of the young Blum company.... Unfortunately the American audience did not take to it."[5]

The ballet's elaborate story, created by Fokine and Dérain, includes four leading roles: the Mandarin, his daughter Chung-Yang, her lover, and an Ambassador from a Western country. The curtain opens to reveal a group of monkeys whom the pompous Mandarin soon dismisses. Maidens enter with the lover, whose duet with Chung-Yang is interrupted by her father. The Ambassador arrives with gifts, and executes some stunning virtuosic movements. While seeking the affections of the young girl, he is attacked by a dragon who is actually her lover. The Ambassador is frightened away, and then set upon and robbed by friends of the young girl. The Mandarin finally agrees to the marriage of his daughter to her beloved, whereupon the Ambassador's goods are returned to him. The devious Mandarin, seeing the Ambassador as a better prospect for his daughter, changes his mind. But in the end, the Ambassador refuses the marriage, feeling that he prefers to be loved for himself. The young lovers wed, leaving the Mandarin with his monkeys, a butterfly, and his dreams of a wealthy life. An old silent film *L'Épreuve* helps somewhat to understand the kinds of movement themes Fokine designed. For example, in the beginning he held close to reality with figurative and gestural motifs, while still using the ballet vocabulary. For the

Figure 8.2
L'Épreuve d'Amour, with Jean Yazvinsky and Hélène Kirsova. Décor and costumes by André Derain. Photo by G. Detaille, courtesy of Archives Monte-Carlo, SBM.

monkey group, Fokine chose stereotypical animalistic imagery. In the same comedic manner, he exaggerated the overweening qualities of the Mandarin, giving him the villainous qualities of a silent-film character.

The movements for the daughter also recall the caprices of film heroines, fawning and meek, with hollow "Oriental" poses, at the same time keeping to the ballet lexicon. Vera Nemtchinova, the original Chung-Yang, admitted in an interview to the "simpering" behavior that Fokine insisted on, in order to give the character a more farcical style.[6] the Dancing Times hailed "Nemtchinova for her brilliant dancing and miming as the daughter, and especially for her turns sur la pointe."[7] The review extolled the beauty of a lovely pas de deux with Eglevsky and Nemtchinova, and commented, "If the choreography of L'Épreuve d'amour is, as I heard some say, a trifle old-fashioned, then give me old-fashioned choreography. I enjoyed every minute of it."[8] The Paris journal L'Illustration adored Fokine's treatment of the music, extolling the ballet's "finesse, and light touch, following the score with an impeccable awareness of its details."[9]

Fokine's several new productions remain important contributions to the repertoire. Critic A. V. Coton spoke of this "resurrection" of Fokine by Blum as the major happening in the spring of 1936 and critics rejoiced on both sides of the Atlantic.[10] Dance writers called Fokine "the father of modern ballet" as he did not approve of using ready-made dance steps, short skirts, and pink dancing shoes. Fokine believed that the time period and character of the nation represented should be researched and reflected in the dance, and that the corps of dancers should be used for expression, not just ornamentation. He believed an attempt should be made to harmonize music, scenery, and choreography.

Fokine, as a dedicated and passionate composer of ballet movement, was praised by Cyril Beaumont who remarked that Fokine knew the music exceptionally well, and worked for days on its sequencing: "He knows what phrase of movement is to be interpreted, where there is to be a pose, and for how long. He composes like a painter, sketching a few movements here, arranging a few details of a pose there; it is one of the most entrancing experiences to see these apparently isolated elements gradually set in their proper order and combined to form a beautiful dance."[11]

Twelve-year-old Adda Pourmel (Gertner) was hired into the Blum company with an "exclusive contract." Asked about the difference between working with Massine and Fokine, she said she greatly preferred Fokine: "With Fokine, you always knew where you stood, never with Massine. When Fokine was selecting a cast for his ballets, he would have the entire company execute the most difficult combinations in his choreography and assign the solos accordingly."[12] Pourmel thought that Fokine's process was fair, but often not popular with dancers whose technique was weak. Unfortunately, she added, "With Mr. Massine, he based his choices on who he liked at the time, and thought nothing of replacing someone in a role that had been theirs for a long time, putting in someone of his own choice, whether capable or not."[13] Pourmel summed it up: "He liked girls with big boobs."[14]

Pourmel also preferred Fokine in other ways, especially because he was ready with choreography from the first rehearsal through performance, "so that his ballets are encrusted in my memory as if I had done them last week."[15] She deplored working with Massine, who changed details every day and never seemed satisfied.

However, Pourmel recalled, it was not physically easy to accomplish what Fokine asked. "He always demanded certain positions and did not care how painful these might be. While I was rehearsing *Schéhérazade* in the role of one of the boys, the high saut de basque, ending in an arch (the hat had to touch the floor), on one knee which also had to touch the floor, no cheating allowed, all this at great speed. I could not sleep with sheets over my body for several weeks, I was in such pain."[16]

Pourmel remembered Blum "as the boss in Monte Carlo, that he had total control of the company, and that everyone loved him."[17] Her mother was appointed costume mistress, and other mothers complained that Blum had given her mother the job, but Blum believed she deserved it. Pourmel recalled that "Blum didn't hurt anyone's feelings; he was a pure soul, never seemed to get angry with us, and he tried to attend every performance."[18] She said that at one point in New York in 1938, when Blum showed up at a rehearsal on the Metropolitan Opera stage, "The whole company stopped rehearsal and ran to hug him and begged him to stay and watch."[19]

Despite challenges, the reviews for the maiden Monte Carlo season hailed Director René Blum as a brilliant leader with great taste. Alfred Henderson in *Le Petit Niçois* praised the major players in this new enterprise: the great master Michel Fokine for his *Lac des Cygnes*; the extraordinary triumph of Vera Nemtchinova and Anatole Oboukhoff; the graceful dancer of the very highest class, André Eglevsky; and Balanchine, whose *Aubade* brought down the house.[20] Henderson admired Marie Ruanova, writing that "there are no words in the English language to describe her spiritual beauty; her unimaginable grace, her suppleness and her spirit of gaiety and youth which imbues every member of the company around her with the desire to do ever better work."[21] *L'Éclaireur du soir* concurred: "The brilliant series of the Ballets de Monte-Carlo continues along with triumphal successes. Ovations mounted, especially for *Les Sylphides*, but also for the ingenious *L'Épreuve d'amour*, and the ravishing *Aubade*."[22] The critic for the Paris magazine *L'Illustration* applauded the glorious opening of the Fokine season and particularly his *L'Épreuve d'amour*:

magnificently realized by the great Michel Fokine, with an enchanting libretto and designs by André Derain. . . . This fabulation was treated by Fokine with great finesse, lightness, cleverness and a true "esprit mozartien." . . . It is an enchantment for the eye and the ear. For a long time, since the premiers of Diaghilev's time, we haven't seen such a success of this quality. The young troupe of the ballets de Monte Carlo created by René Blum has shown in this interpretation, a remarkable youthfulness and discipline.[23]

On May 15, 1936, the London season at the Alhambra Theatre, with three new works and several of Fokine's more distinguished ballets, also achieved success with the critics. According to the *Dancing Times*, the "Corps de ballets has risen to heights of perfection which are a joy to watch."[24] Most of the critiques remarked upon Fokine's powerful presence in the remaking of these works. For example, the *Dancing Times* adulated Fokine's meticulous attention: "In *Petrouchka*, thanks to his scrupulous coaching, the crowd in the Fair scene became something truly remarkable, giving the impression that not one single movement, even of the humblest member of the company, had been left to chance, but that it had been specially arranged, in complete harmony with the music, to develop the story and create the necessary atmosphere."[25] A. V. Coton stated that "this was to be the first occasion since 1914 of Fokine's presence in London, directing his own works. . . . Whatever else was to fall short of the hysterical expectations of a large section of the audience, one could expect that at last *Les Sylphides* would be presented with some echo of the beauty of grouping and purity of line that must have marked the earliest performances in pre-war days."[26]

In the *Dancing Times*, a letter from Violet Rowbotham reminisced about Fokine:

> It was generally accepted among audiences and dancers that when Fokine himself conducted the rehearsals, *Les Sylphides* had a magic "out of this world." That I think, is what is lacking in productions today, the inspiration of the master artist working with the dancers. I would give much to see the Blum company again, not only for *Les Sylphides*, but for *Les Elfes*, the Mendelssohn ballet, and that masterpiece, *L'Épreuve d'amour*.[27]

The world premiere of Fokine's *Don Juan* occurred on June 17, 1936, at London's Alhambra Theatre. Based on the original Gluck/Gasparo Angiolini 1761 ballet, it was famous as a moving and important eighteenth-century classic that carried on the innovative structure and movement of the *ballet d'action*. Fokine's version took place in three tableaux; the first tableau is practically all mime when Don Juan serenades Elvira and visits her bedroom. Suddenly, he is interrupted by the arrival of Elvira's father, the Commander. When Don Juan fights a duel with the Commander, he

Figure 8.3
Don Juan. Décor and costumes by Mariano Andreu. Photo by G. Detaille, courtesy of Archives Monte-Carlo, SBM.

kills him, leaving Elvira to mourn his death. Oblivious to his evil act, Don Juan entertains friends and mistresses in the second tableau banquet scene. He tries audaciously to secure Elvira's favors, sometimes by force, and even succeeds in appeasing her anger. But unexpectedly, the Ghost of the Commander appears and admonishes Don Juan for his dissolute life. The guests are shocked and frightened as Don Juan accepts the Ghost's invitation to meet him at his tomb in the cemetery. In the third tableau, Don Juan stands close to the tomb and a statue of the Commander on horseback. Coming to life, the Commander implores Don Juan to admit his wasted life and many abandoned, forlorn mistresses. The unrepentant Don Juan is unable to yield, and consequently, the Furies chase him relentlessly to hell.

In an undated letter, Blum wrote Josette France enthusiastically that Fokine's ballet *Don Juan* was a major triumph and captivated Monte Carlo audiences, vouchsafing that the Monégasque season "is truly very brilliant; never have I had so much success, nor have I had such marvelous results in ticket sales, almost double last year's."[28]

The Ballets de Monte-Carlo programs from the London season featured photos of both Fokine and Blum, as well as their producer, Sir Oswald Stoll, who was the chairman and managing director of the Alhambra Theatre where they played. Programming for the season was impeccable, combining Fokine's new works with his older exotic ballets such as *Schéhérazade*, *Prince Igor*, and *Petrouchka* and the classics such as *Coppélia*, *Lac des Cygnes*, and *Les Sylphides*, along with *Spectre de la Rose* and *Carnaval*. In a sense, it was a perfect menu for a smaller company (forty-eight dancers) with few stars to bewitch the audiences, and especially for those who recalled the wondrous days of Diaghilev. The Jester in *Don Juan*, played by the youthful André Eglevsky, surprised and enthralled audiences and critics. *The Times* on June 26, 1936, congratulated Fokine for his *Don Juan*, noting that he exploits the idiosyncracies of M. Eglevsky's technique with admirable results," and adored Ruanova in her dance of the Furies that was "one of Fokine's finest inventions." It praised Fokine for his "unfailing creativity and his extraordinary sense of line, which give interest and beauty to every movement."[29] Eglevsky's dancing in *Les Sylphides* also received admirable notice in *The Spectator* on May 22, 1936; the critic noted that he showed himself to be an "excellent dancer in the technical sense, with a slow dream-like quality."[30] The new *Aubade* was the recreation of an earlier Balanchine piece that Blum loved to include in the program, but *The Times* in a May 28, 1936, column seemed disappointed in the way the choreography and the music by Poulenc came together.

Writing from London on June 2, 1936, Blum reopened his dialogue with Delpierre about dwindling finances. He cited his financial doldrums, having invested all his savings and more in this new company, but noted that the London tour began initially with only four weeks of scheduled performances, and that now it was bound to last much longer, a "grand success," and he hoped to recoup part of his losses. He recounted his continuing problems with de Basil, who was slated to bring his company to London at the same time as Blum's. Blum asked Delpierre to inform the newspapers that de Basil did not establish the company that was created after Diaghilev's death, as the "Colonel" continued to claim that he was the founder of the Ballets Russes de Monte-Carlo. Even in this moment of success, troubles never ceased to assault Blum's peace of mind.

The government of the Popular Front, run by René Blum's brother Léon, was elected on June 6, 1936. It endured but one stormy year, and fell in June 1937. Despite Léon Blum's short reign, he accomplished some of the most important social reforms for workers: the forty-hour work week, the month-long summer vacation, free health care, and social security. At the end of 1936, in what may have been an inevitable result of the worldwide depression that began later and lasted longer in France than elsewhere, Carmen Callil calculated that "a quarter of a million workers went out on strike, and Léon Blum was forced to devalue the franc."[31]

The careers of both Léon and René were never to recover from the dev-astating results of the Depression. Callil deduced that "all this caused terror amongst business leaders, and on the right."[32] Fear prompted widespread hatred for non-French citizens. By 1939, France was home to about 330,000 Jews, of whom some 30 percent were refugees.[33] Callil noted that the French Israelites, as they liked to be called, or those Jews who had been in France since the nineteenth century, had very mixed feelings about the poor Jews who were arriving from Central Europe and Russia.

Plagued by the economic crisis in France, the business of raising money and escaping de Basil's clutches placed a heavy burden on Blum. A contract dating July 13, 1936, disclosed that he was attempting to form an English Limited Company with an authorized share capital of 30,000 pounds for the purpose of taking over the activities and assets of the Ballets de Monte-Carlo, and all its costumes, scenery, and properties. Blum was to be credited with shares that were valued at half the share capital and would still be entrusted with the technical and artistic management of the Ballets de Monte-Carlo. A copy of this letter was sent to World Art, Inc. Complex negotiations begun between Denis Milner, David Milner, and M. Rubinstein continued until Blum successfully refinanced the Ballets de Monte-Carlo and tried to assure the future of his company in America.

Figure 8.4
René and Léon Blum. Courtesy of Centre d'histoire de SciencesPo.

Strong emotions were stirred up in August 1936 when the Blum company tour arrived in Glasgow and was banned from performing. This imbroglio demonstrated as well the complexity of the public relationship between René and his brother, the French Prime Minister Léon; neither wanted to appear to use the other for reasons of impropriety. Sadler's Wells Ballet, run by Ninette de Valois, was also on tour to Glasgow that August, and sought a permit to perform there the week after the Blum company's season. The Ministry of Labour believed the proximity of the two companies performing at almost the same time would compromise ticket sales for the Vic-Wells, since Blum's company had created such a stir in London.

The result was the cancellation of the Ballets de Monte-Carlo performances in August 1936 and a postponement until the following year in March 1937. An odd letter of apology and explanation followed from Ninette de Valois, director of the Sadler's Wells Ballet Company. To avoid conveying any sense of chicanery on her part, de Valois told the Scottish press that she was unaware of the Ministry's decision, and claimed "as a protest that any ill feelings should spring from an idea that artists of our country should stoop to pettiness towards our foreign contemporaries and friends."[34] Many angry remonstrances appeared in the newspapers, including a column that interviewed an indignant René Blum, who "is at a complete loss to understand the reasons for this step, especially as I have done so much for the British theatre."[35] Blum remarked that "he had taken great care to see that his brother, the French Premier, should in no way be troubled in the affair with which he is dealing as an ordinary citizen." At the end of the article, the paper presented a statement from the the French Prime Minister, Léon Blum, asserting, "The Prime Minister's part in this affair has been solely confined to the introduction of his brother, M. René Blum, to the British Embassy in Paris. The idea that the Prime Minister has even considered general acts of reprisal (such as banning British actors from the French stage) because of a measure regarding his brother personally, is not only quite absurd but offensive."[36]

In the fall, the company sailed to South Africa where they performed from September to December 11, 1936, returning to England for performances in February and March 1937. On his way to Johannesburg, Blum wrote Delpierre on September 10, 1936, requesting another 50,000 francs, as soon as possible, to be deposited with Madame Viel-Fiévet, his secretary. On September 15, Delpierre replied that he had sent the money, and described the very difficult fiscal times in Monte Carlo as, unfortunately, the powers in France were not helping the Société des Bains de Mer. He ranted that "France has incurred our enmity due to its unjust, harsh and self-interested laws that only serve to extend the crisis in the Principality of Monaco."[37]

In order to ameliorate the severity of France's behavior toward Monte Carlo, on December 2 Blum advised Delpierre to write his brother Léon at the quai Bourbon about the measures that France had enacted almost intentionally to hurt Monte Carlo. For example, Monégasques were not permitted to work in France, even though there was a 1919 treaty that reassured the Monégasque of France's "protection." In addition, France allowed more gambling than any other country, cutting the earnings from gambling in Monte Carlo, and France forbade the sale of lottery tickets from Monaco. All these acts worked substantially against the Monégasque economy.

When the company toured in South Africa, local groups gathered to act as tour guides and caring hosts, and the reviews were mostly gratifying. For example, *The Star* newspaper in Johannesburg on October 6, 1936, noted that during *Don Juan*, audiences were stunned "by the delightful and thrilling Spanish dancing by Maria Ruanova, the Argentine ballerina."[38] Also in *The Star* on October 27, in the ballet *Casse Noisette* (Nutcracker Suite), once again Ruanova pleased the critics: "Here, during this waltz and in the earlier snow storm, we see Maria Ruanova, splendid in her strength and skill, and for a moment we forget the exquisite decorations and the delightfully costumed bon bons as we appreciate her toe-balancings and her rhythmic leaping into the waiting arms of her powerful partners."[39]

One of the dancers in the company, Stanley Judson, wrote a letter to the *Dancing Times* describing the tour in South Africa. He noted that the opening night audience in Johannesburg was "unappreciative," but eventually, spectators warmed to the company. The most favored ballets of the long tour turned out to be *Schéhérazade* and *L'Épreuve d'amour*. Apparently in his role as Apollo, Eglevsky had injured the nerves in his foot, but improved quickly. Judson described a field trip: "Last Sunday we went to the Rose Deep Mines to see the Zulus dance. M. Blum was very impressed with their energy and rhythm and the way a long line of them could keep together."[40] Adda Pourmel confirmed that while the company was performing in South Africa, the dancers went on strike and told Blum they needed more money. Pourmel later stated that "he took money from his pocket and gave it to them."[41]

The Blum company returned to England where it performed for two weeks at the end of February 1937 with an enlarged roster of seventy.

Writing again to Delpierre on March 18, 1937, Blum requested an advance for some lighting gels that could only be bought in London. In order to minimize the stigma of his pleas for money, he reaffirmed the great advantages that his Ballets de Monte-Carlo bestowed on Monte Carlo as, "they have once again defended the honor of the 'house,' with the name Monte Carlo glistening on all the walls and columns as well as appearing in the newspapers."[42] On April 20, Delpierre wrote back, informing Blum that his contract for the Ballets de Monte-Carlo had been extended for three more years. He added that the "conseil" voted 50,000 francs for him to take the ballet company to the Paris Exposition from the 15th to the 25th of May.

From Manchester the troupe traveled to Glasgow, Scotland, where it performed on March 8, 1937, at the Alhambra. The reviewer for the *Dancing Times*, Francis Savage, painted an interesting comparison between the panoramic view of Glasgow, that is, "snow-covered hills, all gold and rose in the setting sun," and the "breathtaking vision of the first moments in *Les Sylphides*."[43] Savage wrote that Glasgow recognized their good fortune in being able to see the Russian ballets *Schéhérazade, Prince Igor, Petrouchka,* and *Spectre de la Rose*. He reiterated that inherent in every ballet is the coalescence of music, painting, and drama, along with the estimable dancing of the Blum ballet. Savage recounted the wonders of watching the perfectly synchronized corps de ballet, and variations that demanded the split-second timing of several people. The "blaze of rich color" in *Schéhérazade,* "the stolid dancing of Michael Panieff as the Negro, and the voluptuous acting of Jeanne Lauret, created a tempestuous canvas for this *Schéhérazade*."[44]

On the other hand, Savage did not find *Casse Noisette* appealing: "I was sorry not to see the old version, mainly because its good classical numbers are missing from the new. Admittedly, I do not consider the first two acts of either version worth doing, except for children, and if all the value in the last act is cut, the ballet seems a poor show indeed."[45]

Savage continued with a thorough analysis of the other Fokine staples, including *Carnaval,* which he did not think up to par, and *Spectre de la Rose,* which was very "poetic." *Un Soir,* a new ballet by Georges Gué with music by Florent Schmitt, was "so banal that one hoped the wrong couple would go back into the mirror to provide diversion"; however, "*Prince Igor* proved to be a decidedly entertaining and wild fantasy."[46]

Savage concluded with some very helpful remarks about the company. He found the corps disciplined and well-rehearsed, and indicated that the corps and the soloists performed mime artfully and skillfully. However, he was struck by the "weakness of the male dancers," and was annoyed that the advertised program sometimes changed at the last minute.[47] Other critics concurred about *Un Soir,* finding the choreography full of "attitudinizing and too little real dancing, and rarely a point of repose.[48] the *Dancing Times* of July 1937 pronounced that two astounding young artists had emerged from the Blum company: "André Eglevsky and Nana Gollner—Eglevsky, particularly in his character work, and Gollner, who has technical equipment second to none, an American Girl; a fine athletic body, charm and especially the aptitude for virtuosity. She is the first true American prima ballerina."[49]

In 1937 the company went to Monte Carlo, then Paris, London, and on a tour of the English provinces—including Brighton, Manchester, Liverpool, Glasgow, and Aberdeen—and finally to Amsterdam and in December to Zurich. The technician with the company, Jean Cerrone, recalled that "we were supposed to go to Italy in 1938, but at the last minute, we returned to Monte Carlo since Mussolini did not give the visa to Mr. Blum or to the company; we found out that it was because Mr. Blum was Jewish."[50]

The new season in Monte Carlo began auspiciously on April 1, 1937, when Pierre Michaut lauded the talents of Ruanova, who united "an impeccable virtuosity with a very personal temperament."[51] Michaut cited René Blum for having brought together a number of young choreographers, designers, and musicians to inaugurate a "new French School" that would be seen later at the Théâtre des Champs-Elysées in Paris. Although Maria Ruanova continued to be the hit of the company, the American Nana Gollner and the Russian Raisse Kousnetsova also received rave reviews.[52] L'Eclaireur du Soir spoke of their "ripe and elegant talent." The critics and audiences loved Petrouchka, the perfect alliance of music and mime, and the company's victorious continuation of the incomparable traditions of Diaghilev.[53] The company exuded a sense of internationalism. Many dancers from all over the world auditioned and some did make it into the company. Gradually, its russification abated, especially as the years wore on. Renée Stein asserted that "Monte Carlo and its ballet company accrued the reputation of being an international place where fruitful collaborations between different countries occurred."[54]

Blum's name appeared in all the columns, especially for the performance of Don Juan. The critic L. Gerbe in Le Petit Marsaillais, "La Vie Artistique," waxed poetic in his praise of Blum: "He knew how to bring brilliant, excellent new artists who have created ravishing theatrical sights, the beauteous South American Marie Ruanova, an incandescent dancer made of flexible steel, with pirouettes filled with grace next to a powerful verve. What a gypsy she is in Don Juan, and by contrast, what a tender young thing as the Chinese girl in L'Épreuve d'amour."[55] Gerbe extolled the abilities of the male dancers, MM Panaieff, Yazvinsky, Mouradoff, Beriosoff, and Ozohne, as well as the formidable talents of Eglevsky and Oboukhoff.

During the same period that Blum's company was touring Europe, Massine, eager to run his own company, began discussions in March 1936 with a wealthy American banker, Serge Denham, while touring with the de Basil company in the United States. Massine's deteriorating relationship with de Basil ended a year later, allowing for the seeds of a new company in collaboration with Blum and with Massine at the helm.[56] As Massine and Denham were making plans for their new alliance, Blum was working on another Paris Exposition to take place in 1937. Blum wrote Balanchine, once again, imploring him to "stage whatever he wants for the upcoming festival."[57]

The Blum Ballets de Monte-Carlo opened in Paris on May 16, 1937, at the Théâtre des Champs-Élysées on the occasion of the International Exposition. The critic Jacques Barraux, of the leftist newspaper *L'Intransigeante*, interviewed Blum on May 17, 1937, and began the meeting with an insinuation of trouble in the company, perhaps alluding to Fokine's imminent departure. Barraux suggested that Blum and Fokine had quarreled at the end of the Monégasque season, recalling that at the premiere of *Les Elfes* the audiences went wild, and Blum rushed foward to tell Fokine, "I am angry with you, but I cannot keep myself from throwing my arms around you to congratulate you."[58]

Blum spoke with Marcel Reichenecker, a Monte Carlo critic, explaining why "la grande saison" in Paris signified so much to him. He loved being in Paris and said, "In spite of the nomadic existence I have lived for four years, this is my true terrain where I took my first steps and where I feel totally at ease." Blum's long tenure as a critic in Paris prepared him to be respectful as well as apprehensive about other Paris critics. He admitted that "I do not forget that I myself judged very severely the works of others. I must add, without bitterness, that I carry alone the weight of this terrifying enterprise. Diaghilev knew many rich people, a now extinct race, because I search for them in vain in my country."[59]

This short interview revealed the challenges and strains that Blum had endured, in spite of his successes, due to the economic and political exigencies gripping the whole of western Europe. As discussed before, Léon Blum and his Socialist-Radical ministry persuaded parliament and the leading industrial leaders to increase wages, pass a forty-hour week, introduce paid vacations and collective bargaining, and partially nationalize the Bank of France, an agenda not very different from that of President Franklin Roosevelt in the United States. Unfortunately, these desperately needed social programs were not supported by increased industrial production, while high unemployement and the flight of capital out of France persisted. Blum and his cabinet were dismissed in 1937 as the Socialists and the Radicals came into conflict over Blum's policies. From April 1938 until 1940, the Radicals were returned to power, suspending the Socialist programs. Although production did rise in the face of German rearmament and aggression, the French were never able to catch up with the German juggernaut. For René Blum, trying desperately to keep his ballet afloat, the Depression and the slow French recovery were mortal financial blows.[60]

With all of Europe in turmoil, it also explained why he needed to discover a more solid means of support that necessarily had to be connected to the American business world. In an interview with Georges D. De Givray from the *Chronique Théâtrale*, Blum was adulated for his expansive background in the arts, one that fully prepared him for his rise to prominence as a producer: "René Blum is a prodigious producer. Trained by the greatest artists of the century, the Guitry, among others, he surpassed them with experience as a journalist and theatre critic. This formation permitted him to develop his exquisite sensibility, and his charming humor."[61]

It is remarkable that Blum and his company continued to create and to perform to appreciative audiences and critics. Émile Vuillermoz, a sophisticated and often difficult-to-please critic for Paris's *L'Illustration*, had nothing but superlatives for the Blum/Fokine season in Paris. In the June 5, 1937, issue, he spoke highly of Fokine's contributions to the company, and applauded his new works as well as his old ones. He said that *Les Elfes* satisfied audiences for its pure choreography with "poetic virtuosity, and grace," while *Don Juan* displayed Fokine's exceptional and extraordinary mastery of "gesture, attitudes and choreographic rhythms." In discussing *L'Épreuve d'amour*, he disclosed that all of the above qualites shined more brightly, especially Fokine's light irony, in this "irresistible" fantasy.[62]

Because Fokine used classical composers such as Gluck and Bach, a reviewer on May 26, 1937, questioned why Blum had not engaged contemporary composers for his company. Blum responded that indeed this was a critical point, as he had trouble finding appropriate modern musical works. He reassured the critic that he would soon be working with choreographers "sensitive" to contemporary music, but he also understood that classical works taught the young dancers in his company, sixty-three artists from ten nationalities, "the cohesion and discipline" that they needed.[63]

Jean Dorcy, in *La Tribune de Danse* of May 20, 1937, delighted in the way Fokine carefully reconstructed the choreography in his *Les Elfes* and *Don Juan*, and claimed he deserved the title "Le Hugo de Ballet." Dorcy indicated that Fokine preferred a strong dramatic theme, and that he poured all his talents into a brilliant realization of *Don Juan* as a tragicomedy. He noted insightfully that "*Don Juan* is the work that best lends itself to an analysis of Fokinnienne composition, and Fokine threaded together a series of expositionary kind of dances, using pantomime, as only he can." Dorcy also compared Fokine to the legendary poet and storyteller La Fontaine, explaining that "one speaks of the free verse of La Fontaine, just as one acknowledges the free dance of Fokine."[64] He wrote that both are classicists—in their rhythmic enunciations, in the stories that they tell, and in the sonority of their narrations. Dorcy perceived a continual flow from dance to dance in Fokine's work and posited that Fokine's greatness lived on in these newer works.

The Fokine/Blum company returned once again to London where they opened May 31, 1937, at the Coliseum. Fokine's *Les Éléments*, set to J. S. Bach's Second Suite, held its first performance in London in June 1937. Based on a series of dances in a suite, the ballet's protagonists seem to emerge from an eighteenth-century painting, with mythical heroes such as Flor and Zephir, along with personifications of natural events such as rain, flowers, wind, and volcanoes. A rehearsal film in the New York Public Library offers a glimpse into some of the ballet's movement ideas. The silent production, filmed in black and white, begins with several dancers asleep downstage. Groups of dancers enter and leave the stage seamlessly: one intriguing section is devoted to wavelike motions of the arms. Two rows of women, eight all told, sit with their legs crossed and begin to rock back and forth as their arms move in a circular motion. Eight men and four women skillfully slip in and out of the two rows of women. Fokine envisioned a Boucher painting come to life, enhanced by a carefully manipulated Baroque score.

Despite the acerbic comments of certain critics, London audiences found Fokine's *Les Éléments* very compelling, especially the way Fokine wove the complex movement combinations to Bach's B minor suite. According to *The Times* on June 25, 1937, the ballet presented a cycle of nature, drawn from Greek and eighteenth-century classicism. Raindrops were played by dancers looking like maidens from an ancient frieze, and flowers were represented by women dancing in court costumes with immense skirts and low-heeled shoes. The first part of the ballet cleverly suggested the patter of rain as a single dancer appeared at each fugal entry,

Figure 8.5
Les Éléments. Photo by G. Detaille, courtesy of Jerome Robbins Dance Division, the New York Public Library for the Performing Arts, Astor, Lenox, and Tilden Foundations.

keeping the countersubject going with tapping of the hands on the boards to evoke the sound of a driving rain. The critic asserted that "Mr. Fokine has been successful in fusing through dancing, the decorative, musical and dramatic elements into a unity and has created a substantial one act ballet that interests the mind, charms the eye, and, with some reservations in the matter of the climax, is effective on stage."[65]

Les Elfes continued to baffle audiences as well as to please them. In a June 1, 1937, review in The Times, the critic praised the choreographer who "marvelously visualized for us the insubstantial dreams of Fokine. If he has failed with Mendelssohn, it is in part because he has been ill-served by the designer of the costumes, and in part because, instead of being content with short pieces of music—he has made a very whole-hearted attempt to be symphonic."[66]

Some reviewers preferred Ygrouchka, such as the critic from The Times on June 9, 1937, who pronounced that the ballet had "a child-like plot, easy themes, simple steps and vivid colours borrowed from Russian folk art and raised to a higher power by a process of stylization." Impressed by Nana Gollner, the critic believed her charming portrayal of the Goose Girl had surpassed her performance in Swan Lake. But he also found the Four Swans charming as well as "neat and nimble," and especially lauded Krassovska's dancing in Spectre de la Rose.[67] Les Éléments received good reviews on June 27, 1937, in The London Observer, which praised the piece and the "delightful dancing and clever choreography that mimicked the contrapuntal nature of the music."[68]

Jean Cerrone (the future manager of the Ballets Russes in America) wrote a letter to Janet Rowson Davis in response to her queries about René Blum. Cerrone met Blum in 1936 when he applied for a job with the Ballets de Monte-Carlo. He had no prior experience backstage, but as he recalled, "Mr. Blum was a very kind and generous man and after six months working there, he told me that he was very pleased with my work and that I would get a raise to 10 shillings per week" (which was a very good salary in 1937). Also when Blum introduced him to others, he never referred to him as an employee, but rather as his collaborator. Cerrone remembered that when the company was in London at the Coliseum, "Every Sunday Mr. Blum asked me to take care of his son Minouchou who was 11 years old at the time, and I would take him around London to lunch and movies and return him in the evening at Mr. Blum's expense."[69] Cerrone commented that Josette rarely took responsibility for the boy; rather, it was the grandmother who raised him.

When the company performed in Edinburgh and Aberdeen, Francis Savage was less flattering in his critique. He compared, unfavorably, the new ballets in the repertoire with Fokine's earlier creations, L'Épreuve and Don Juan. He said that Ygrouchka, with music by Rimsky-Korsakov, although

Figure 8.6
Les Elfes, with Alicia Markova. Photo by Gordon Anthony, courtesy of V&A Images/Victoria and Albert Museum, London.

perhaps the best, was inconsequential. *Les Elfes* was good, but the decor was disappointing. Savage observed that in his opinion the choreography in *Les Éléments* was disconnected and the dances outdated and trivialized, despite the "most satisfactory" music and the "beautiful costumes." Savage was harshest in his assessment of Glinka's *Jota Aragonesa,* which "should be given a painless death as soon as possible, for it is totally lacking in interest."[70] On the other hand, Savage had nothing but compliments for the dancers' technical ability and their consummate, vital sense of theatre.

The dancer Frederick ("Freddy") Franklin recalled the amusing story of the *Ygrouchka*, "that it was a folk tale; and that Choura [who played the girl later] had a big costume, and she came on to the stage with a flock of geese; she beats them like this" (Franklin gestured with quick hand movements). "She wants some water, and a young man falls down the well. She was marvelous. Just lovely. That was Fokine. Someone had said that they had to do something like Massine's *Coq d'Or*, which was a terrible flop, although they had great costumes."[71]

Although little is known about Fokine's departure from Blum's company, vestiges of a disagreement with Fokine were hinted at in a letter Blum wrote to Josette France on August 14, 1937, after the Monte Carlo season. Fokine's "deceit" centered on the fact that when Massine decided to leave de Basil in 1937, de Basil hired Fokine as his ballet master. Blum disclosed that "Fokine was rather crestfallen when Blum confronted Fokine with his deceitfulness in their relationship. Although Fokine refused to discuss it."[72] Blum was bitter as a result of what he called, "the ingratitude, the egotism and the duplicity of those whom he supported."[73] However, as Blum contemplated the larger picture, he added that Fokine's artistry was decidedly superb, and that "Fokine knew how to work with and train our dancers to bring them to an excellent level."[74]

Frederick Franklin believed that Blum and Fokine had an amicable relationship, and they often exchanged funny stories. When Fokine created his *Aragonesa*, which became *Capriccio Espagnol*, it was a slight piece, only twelve minutes long. Franklin recalled that "after watching the ballet, Mr. Blum said to Mr. Fokine, 'I thought that it was going to be a full ballet; you know it's not nearly long enough.' To which Mr. Fokine quipped, 'Never mind, we play it twice in a row. They will dance it twice.'"[75]

CHAPTER 9

The New World Calls!

Blum Sells the Company to Americans

S everal months before Fokine's contract was due to expire, Blum began a correspondence with World Art, Inc. concerning the sale of his company. The letters spanned the period from March 1937 to January 1940. There were grave doubts about moving the Ballets Russes to the United States, but having Serge Denham, a Russian-American banker, and Julius "Junkie" Fleischmann as underwriters for the company, along with the great impresario Sol Hurok, who arranged tours to America, helped this fledgling idea come to fruition.[1]

Rumor had it that Massine was looking for a company with stable finances where he could at last fully achieve his choreographic ambitions. During the American tour in the spring of 1937, Massine encountered Julius Fleischmann, a Cincinnati industrialist who was heir to a yeast and liquor fortune. Massine arranged for Fleischmann and Denham to meet with Blum; they all agreed that the Ballets de Monte-Carlo with Massine as artistic director would have great success based on American soil, while still offering annual seasons in Monte Carlo and other European cities. On November 19, 1937, Blum sold the Ballets de Monte-Carlo to World Art, Inc., later called Universal Art, with the official purchase to take effect on February 1, 1938.[2] Blum's decision created the conditions for Massine's career to flourish in the United States. In part because of Blum, Massine and other choreographers and dancers would revolutionize ballet in America.

A. V. Coton tells the story of this culmination of Massine's professional life:

At last, after all the years with Diaghileff, the broken years in revue, cabaret and super cinema, to the great revival of 1932, through the five full years during which we saw the greatest stimulus to ballet expressed in all its history in his ten new works, Massine had achieved a pinnacle—a dancer still as neat and finished as ever, a choreographer with more living successes to his name than any one has ever done before, now to be launched with a company he could select from the cream of Europe, and with the prospect of a full winter season in America, Monte Carlo in the spring, and London in the summer.[3]

The transfer of power and funds began in the spring of 1937, well before the actual purchase. Even though Blum parted from de Basil, the ghost of de Basil still haunted him. In a grim letter dated March 1, 1937, Blum wrote Denham from Manchester, England, of his discovery that de Basil had inserted the title "Monte Carlo" in his own letterhead and advertisements, probably under the advisement of Sol Hurok whom Blum did not trust. Blum declared this infringement wrong, if not illegal, since de Basil had renounced the title "Monte Carlo" some time ago in favor of the Colonel de Basil Ballets Russes Company.[4]

In what amounted to a game of musical chairs, lead choreographers shifted their allegiances. The May 1937 issue of *Dancing Times* announced Fokine's move to de Basil's company, while Massine returned to Blum, assuming creative direction of the new company with Blum's blessing.[5] A bevy of British dancers who had been hired into the company by Blum and Fokine were let go by Massine, except for Alicia Markova and Frederick Franklin. Adda Pourmel noted that "Massine weeded out many of the British dancers at the end of the season in Monte Carlo in 1938. Blum tried to accommodate their English rituals such as allowing for tea to be served when they asked for it."[6] The situation seemed paradoxical: Blum's World Art, Inc. would possess many Fokine ballets, but without Fokine, while de Basil would have a number of Massine ballets without Massine.

Confused about these new developments, dancers were at a loss as to where to go. By the time the Blum and de Basil companies consolidated, they made their decisions: on Massine's and Blum's side were Alexandra Danilova, Tamara Toumanova, Alicia Markova, Mia Slavenska, Eugénie Delarova, Lubov Rostova, Nathalie Krassovska, Jeannette Lauret, Milada Mladova, Nini Theilade, Igor Youskevitch, Serge Lifar, Frederick Franklin, George Zoritch, Michel Panaieff, Roland Guerard, Marc Platoff, Simon Semenoff, and Jean Yazvinsky. The dancers who decided to stay with de Basil included David Lichine, Irina Baronova, Tatiana Riabouchinska, Tamara Grigorieva, Olga Morosova, Nina Verchinina, Lubov Tchernicheva, Sono Osato, Yurek Shabelevsky, Paul Petroff, Yurek Lazowski, and Roman Jasinski. Efrem Kurtz left de Basil to become the Blum company's leading conductor.

Blum discussed his plans for choreographers. His contract with Fokine lasted through June 1937, but Blum was hoping Fokine might be retained for several more years, since it was Blum who had helped to restore Fokine's prestige the past year. Blum also suggested that Fokine make a ballet to the music of Mendelssohn's *Italian* symphony; he admired Fokine's *Les Elfes* and hoped Fokine would create three new works. In his writings, Blum stated that he continued to have excellent relations with Monte Carlo and that he would prolong his contract there. Then he detailed specific information about his productions. He wanted Mme. Nijinska to do her *Bolero*, a chef d'oeuvre in his opinion, and *Aubade*. Originally, he wanted Balanchine to create a ballet to the music by Delannoy with scenery and costumes by Raoul Dufy, but Balanchine was unable to return to Paris from America.

In a March 1, 1937, letter to Denham, during the interim before the merger was completed, Blum indicated his intention to give the dancers short contracts because he did not know how long he could retain them, yet the reigning principal soloists had to be assuaged.[7] He praised Nana Gollner's successful *Swan Lake* and Tarakanova's *Coppélia*. He expressed the need to be diplomatic with Ruanova because she might leave to perform at the Theatre of Colon in Buenos Aires. He hoped Toumanova would join the company as she had left de Basil, but she failed to contact Blum, as she said she would; the same was true for Shabelevsky.

Ever busy with future productions, in his letter to Denham, Blum discussed the 1937 Exposition. Blum contemplated hiring Lifar to take the place of Balanchine, as Lifar was very excited at the prospect of working with Blum. But would Lifar leave the Opéra where he was the "spoiled child"? Blum expressed hope for great success in Paris where he noted that he had "so many friends among the artistic circles."[8]

Blum's Ballets de Monte-Carlo was to open the 1937 season at the Théâtre des Champs-Elysées in Paris on May 18, featuring the orchestra of the Théâtre de Monte-Carlo, keeping his strong Monégasque ties. As was typical of Blum's pride and lifestyle, he requested that Denham reserve only the best travel accommodations. At the heart of the conversation in the March 1 letter, Blum alluded to money. The impending contract with the new company was figured at 400,000 francs for the month of performances in Monte Carlo, with author's rights and publicity to be paid by the casino. Blum expressed concerns about when the new company would start functioning, and how he would be able to keep charge of the repertory as well as his "new ballets."[9] Oddly, he signed the letter Durand Senior, a pseudonym he occasionally used. Why the secrecy? One senses that at this point Blum had become paranoid about his finances as well as his "enemies."

On April 27, 1937, Blum wrote Massine in Beaulieu, to confirm the financial arrangements for the new company. Blum reminded Massine that he would retain control of the new company, now owned by Denham and Fleischmann. Blum was to be paid the sum of $30,000, half of it payable on June 1, 1937, and the balance on February 1, 1938, but Blum held the performance rights to these ballets until February 1, 1938. In addition, $800 for two or three ballets was to be paid to Fokine in July 1937.

Despite the fact that its new home would be in New York City, the new company was expected to continue its seasons in Monte Carlo. Blum guaranteed a contract with the Société des Bains de Mer for four years of ballet seasons, that is, until 1942, with certain provisions. He confirmed that his name must precede Massine's on all stationery and publicity, and he must approve of all repertoire to be performed in Monte Carlo. Any contracts with SBM de Monte-Carlo must bear the title "Ballets de Monte-Carlo" when referring to the company. If the society changed the title to "Ballets Russes de Monte-Carlo," Blum repeated that he would not be legally responsible, as at this time he no longer had the right to call his company the Ballets Russes de Monte-Carlo. At every stage of the contractual agreements, he was afraid of being short-changed or cheated, or having his status reduced. And as history has proven, Blum later relinquished some of these demands.[10]

As Blum's correspondence with Delpierre and Denham attested, his finances were increasingly at risk. On July 20, 1937, Blum again wrote to Delpierre with dire predictions. The company was leaving London after a "brilliant season," having not made enough on ticket sales to defray expenses. Blum knew that the future of the company would be assured with American support, but he bemoaned his current financial woes as well as the last two years of losses, which added up to 700,000 francs. He complained that the devaluation of the franc had dealt him a mortal blow, and importuned Delpierre to advance him funds to support the company.

Many financial and contractual issues were strategized in a series of letters that flew back and forth on August 2, 1937. Early that day, Blum asked Denham to settle a debt of 1650 pounds with 5 percent interest due his "English creditors." He requested that the sum of $2,000 be paid to him in the form of twenty shares of preferred stock in World Art, Inc. But Blum also confirmed that he was committed to Denham's purchase of his company.

Later on August 2, Blum offered as a guarantee for their deal various properties he owned in L'Étang-la-Ville, a little village outside of Paris, acquired from M. and Mme. Meniad in 1925. These pieces of property could be sold as needed to protect his contract with Denham, and Blum indicated that if someone bought the properties, he would reimburse Denham in order to erase his debt with his creditor. The same day, Blum wrote that if Denham wished to purchase the company before February 1, 1938, it could be arranged. Increasingly, we sense the anguish and anxiety caused by Blum's precarious financial situation, a condition that mirrored the economic and political crises in France.[11]

Feeling discouraged at having to sell his company, Blum wrote Delpierre in an apologetic tone on August 3, 1937. He told Delpierre about his enthusiastic American friends (Denham and Fleischmann), and sang the praises of the Ballets de Monte-Carlo as it continued to "flaunt the glory of your company to the four corners of the world."[12] He added that occasionally there were incommodious difficulties, but certainly all would be ironed out in time. Blum requested that the new company's season in Monte Carlo be prolonged, especially given the success of the Beethoven piece. He reassured Delpierre that he would never forget that he worked for the Société des Bains de Mer, and not for the Americans.

In the next letter, on August 9, 1937, Blum elaborated on certain issues of his future contract. He requested 120,000 francs for eight performances, but stipulated in another paragraph that this sum was based on the pound or livre being worth 75 francs, its value several months prior, and not its present worth of 175 francs. In other words, the contract should not be tied to the current value of the French franc, which was considerably lower, in which case René would receive a fair recompense. One can only imagine the anxiety provoked by the tumbling value of the franc. He also asked Delpierre if the season could begin on April 2 and run through May 12.

Three days later, Blum requested that yet another contract be written, indicating that because of inflation, the original 120,000 francs should be increased to 160,000 francs, and that the contract should be renewable until 1941. In the past Blum had taken all the receipts from ticket sales, but now he would offer half to the Société des Bains de Mer. Making sure that the Ballets de Monte-Carlo would continue to receive ample exposure in London, for the months of September and October, Blum arranged first that the company play at the Drury Lane for five weeks and then move on to Covent Garden for another three.

With a company promised to him, Massine proceeded to plan the new seasons. Naturally, his own works would be the mainstay of the World Art company. When he left Blum to work with de Basil, the overly ambitious Massine quickly learned the pitfalls of that relationship. His contract with de Basil was due to expire September 15, 1937. Of course, Massine wanted exclusive rights to all his ballets, including those he had choreographed for de Basil.[13] De Basil, however, repudiated that arrangement and brought a suit against Massine in London's Chancery Court.

The case is controversial even today as it questioned whether "the choreographer as author of the ballet" should be considered its owner.[14] Massine stated, "I am the servant of nobody. I devise my ballets when I can, and when the spirit moves me."[15] The judge who presided over the trial, Justice Luxmoore, disagreed. He divided Massine's repertoire into three groups: those ballets created before he knew de Basil or before June 1, 1932; those ballets made under contract with de Basil from November 17, 1932, to August 10, 1934; and the ballets created after August 10, 1934, which were made for a director of the Ballets Russes and whose contract states that full and exclusive rights were given to the director.

Predictably, in such a scenario where art seemed to be a commodity, Massine was deemed to own those ballets in the first group, with the ballets in the last two groups going to de Basil. The reasoning centered on the belief that a ballet is composed of many arts, and that the director "owns" most of those arts, but that the choreography could not exist without the other arts. Despite the outcome, Massine fulfilled his contract with de Basil when the company toured the United States, beginning at the Metropolitan Opera in October 1937 and traveling across America to San Francisco at the end of January 1938.

A description of the European transcendence of René Blum and the Ballets de Monte-Carlo appeared in an interview with the *Edinburgh Evening News* on September 16, 1937. Knowing that he would soon be deferring to his American colleagues, Blum permitted reporters to review a little of his past. Alongside a photo of himself with his dancers, Blum spoke modestly about his career. Until the death of Diaghilev in 1929, he had no idea he would take over the promotion of ballet. Blum recalled that:

> I was Director of the Monte-Carlo comedy and theatre season and became a great friend of Serge Diaghileff. When Diaghileff died, it was thought that it would be the end of the ballet. They came to me and said, "you have to try the ballet." I always liked the ballet, but it would be stupid for me to say that I was Diaghileff, because I am his successor. What I did do was to try to keep the best things of the repertoire.[16]

He reported that of the troupe's current fifty dancers there were sixteen nationalities, including a dozen British members. During the same interview, he hailed the beautiful American ballerina Nana Gollner, who was rapidly becoming a Hollywood film star. He cautioned that ballet was not "a commercial enterprise, rather it is an artistic creation."[17] He observed that the company loved the British Isles, where a true sympathy existed between the dancers and the audiences. Blum liked statistics and he noted that "the current repertoire cost 15,000 pounds," adding that "the one thing that is hard to find is a talented choreographer, of whom there were very few in the world."[18]

In another article in Edinburgh's *The Bulletin* on September 17, 1937, the critic commented whimsically that "Blum was the brother of the jaunty Léon, for so short a time Socialist Premier of France. The Blums have not gotten over their astonishment over the head over heels fact that Fate has performed with their lives."[19] Blum disclosed that "at one time Léon was writing and studying literature, while he, himself, had political aspirations." This was something that had never been mentioned before. René added, "Then suddenly, it was the other way around—Léon had plunged into politics and I had taken up stage production." The interview concluded with Blum plumbing the purpose of the professional dancer's life, observing that "they believe their life mission is to entertain people who have been working hard and require relaxation." [20]

On the same day (September 17), the *Edinburgh Evening Dispatch* related other curious facts about the Blum family. René confided that his brother Léon was, as he described, "a fond admirer of the ballet, and that he attended his performances of the Ballets de Monte-Carlo when it appeared at the World Exhibition in Paris in May."[21] René told readers that he held a passionate love for the theatre and added that "it is creation rather than exploitation that I strive for on the stages, and pure art separated as much as possible from materialism."[22]

Blum spent every day of his life as a producer of ballet worrying about money, and yet he eschewed adulating its commercial value. He asserted that he had been director of ballet since 1929 in Monte Carlo, but that his real interest in the art form dated from 1909 when the Russian ballet was introduced to Europe by Serge Diaghilev. Blum rhapsodized that ballet was a perfect fusion of all the arts—including music and poetry. He declared, "My true interest is to find new dancing, new painters and new musicians."[23]

In the same article in the *Edinburgh Evening Dispatch*, Blum also discussed his love of film and the cinematic art. He indicated that he was one of the first in France to promote film, and that he was president of the first club of cinema artists. He was keen to experiment with ballet and film, and stated that "there are such wonderful opportunities for the screen to demonstrate the artistry of ballet, by concentrating the camera on features which are often lost in the vastness of the stage and by its limitation to three walls."[24] At the time, he was making arrangments for the Monte Carlo ballet to appear in a film for which he was writing some screen scenarios. To our knowledge, these plans were never fulfilled.

On October 10, 1937, from the Garrick Theatre in Southport, England, Blum sent Denham a long, emotional letter addressing his fear that he was perceived by the company as a failure with no credibility. He asked Denham to please safeguard his "dignity" and asked him "to help avoid the disastrous effects of a conspiracy of which I am the object."[25] He added that he had written his lawyer Rubinstein and hoped that, finally, his adversaries would be quieted. Are these the ghosts of de Basil once again? Or had Blum, as a consequence of his continued obsession with his depleted finances, finally become paranoid? Blum battled his demons, writing:

Figure 9.1
Massine showing ballets on film to the company. Photo by G. Detaille, courtesy of Archives Monte-Carlo, SBM.

> They cannot struggle against your organization [World Art, Inc.], or destroy my business. They think they can. They wanted an association with us and I can get all the money that is necessary from them. I am defending myself with all my strength, but I just lost 1,500 pounds or 225,000 francs. The franc has gone way down. I do not lack tenacity, or courage and although I must monthly get out of being "ruiné," I have decided to struggle to the end against them. If this goes on, without anyone coming to my aid, I do risk succumbing. Please think about this because you are involved with this, and if they are trying to ruin me, they are trying to ruin you as well.[26]

Furthermore, Blum implied that his music publishers, Breitkopf and Hartel, were troubled too. They did not believe that their rights were protected since World Art, Inc. certainly was not the Ballets de Monte-Carlo. Blum accused Massine of being underhanded for telling people that Blum would not play an important role in the new World Art, Inc. administration. Blum cited rumors that de Basil might join Massine in the creation of a new company, and complained that Massine's activities were "not nice."

On November 25, 1937, tensions soared. Despite Denham's efforts to soften Blum's opinion of Massine, Blum sent a letter from Amsterdam reiterating that Massine seemed very sincere but that behind this façade, he was untrustworthy. Massine had hoped for years to run his own company, and he probably saw Blum's role as considerably diminished. Blum warned that "Massine must not endanger the Société and work against my interests;

he cannot create a new company, because it is my company which continues under my administration with new 'collaborateurs.'"[27]

More than anything, Blum was intimidated by Massine's haughty pride or "grand détachement."[28]

Blum reminded Denham that his contract stipulated no ballets could be produced without his stamp of approval—not the scenarios, or the scenery, or anything else. He believed people thought that the company was being liquidated, and therefore had cancelled some of their bookings, thereby increasing his debt. By then he had lost almost 400,000 francs and, though exhausted from the struggle, wrote that he would hold on until the February 1, 1938, launching of the new business or société. It was not just a question of quieting his bitterness, René explained: all involved must accept his or her responsibility to help him during the next two months. The impending loss of his beloved company was a grievous blow to René's mental health. These dramatic confessions reinforced the sense that time and events were closing in on him.

In another letter soon thereafter, Blum pondered how he would fulfill his financial obligations, or payment dates, as he did not have the money to cover them. Fortunately, he had befriended the immensely wealthy South African diamond entrepreneur, Lord Oppenheimer, although he feared his enthusiasm for the ballet might not endure.

While Blum gave interviews to reporters about his heartaches over money, when his administrative apprehensions drifted into the background, he admitted some fascinating facts that he did not normally provide. For example, in the *Manchester Daily Dispatch* of November 5, 1937, Blum told R. J. Finnemore that most of his dancers were too young to have performed during the Diaghilev period. He said he spent hours auditioning dancers in the five or six important ballet studios in Paris; he tried to characterize the quality of their dancing by their nationality and found that the Russians had superiority over the French. He said that "to the French technique, the Russians added the Slavic temperament, something vast, not so stylised, something more vibrant. There is a difference in their sensibility of expression."[29] He then revealed what he thought about several of the greatest living choreographers: "Take Balanchine. He is wittier, more artistic, lighter. Massine is deeper. As an architect of the ballet, he is stronger. Nijinska has a kind of genius. She has vision. When her work comes off, it is perfection, but when it doesn't—."[30]

The journalist reminded Blum that the last time Blum's company played in Manchester, it lost a lot of money, and asked why he had returned. Blum responded, "I am very obstinate, and I believe that each time I come back I will do better. I received many hundreds of letters from Manchester this year asking when I would return." After hinting that a ballet company incurs great expenses, Blum postulated, "I am a poor man. I have spent all I have on my ballet. But I shall continue because I have made an arrangement with a private society in America of people interested in art, and the new arrangement comes into operation in February." [31]

Glorious news for Blum arrived on November 8 at the Alhambra Theatre in Glasgow. Although many troupes from Europe and America had been invited to perform before judges, the company received a telegram stating: "The Committee of the Paris International Exhibition (1937) at a meeting today awarded the Grand Prix to the Ballets de Monte-Carlo for the performance given at the Théâtre de Champs-Elysées."[32] It was well known that Diaghilev's Russian ballet promoted worldwide passion for ballet, and that dance studios sprouted in many of the cities where they had toured. The same was true for the several companies with which Blum was associated. The *Brighton Supplement* on November 13, 1937, echoed this observation: "The present company has revived an interest in ballet everywhere on its route, cities that had no dancing schools now have several and it is the ambition of every pupil to join the Ballets de Monte Carlo."[33] The critic explained the success of the Ballets de Monte-Carlo as due to the ardor and intelligence of René Blum: "He has made ballet a fine art by choosing the right artists and especially the most talented dancers: some are needed for their brilliant technique, some for their spirit, some for their memory and very many for what they promise in the future."[34]

Good news for Blum continued on November 19, when the World Art, Inc. sale was finalized. On November 20, 1937, the *New York Times* announced:

> The Blum Ballet was sold to a company here! World Art, Inc. formed by Julius Fleis-chmann, the Cincinnati sportsman and world traveler, takes over the Monte Carlo troupe. Purchase price put at $30,000 plus $10,800 to René Blum, the brother of the Vice Premier of France. The news declared that they filed a registration statement with the Securities and Exchange Commission in Washington. Blum would provide the official site for the company in Monte Carlo and direct the season there, according to Sergei J. Denham, the vice president of World Art.[35]

The article made clear that "the company has no connection to the Colonel de Basil's Ballet Russe de Monte Carlo" (which had recently arrived for the fifth time in the United States), and indicated that the purchase would take place on February 1, 1938, and World Art would present five weeks of ballet in Monte Carlo each spring from 1938 to 1942. Interestingly, the long and detailed contract for the sale of the Ballets de Monte-Carlo to World Art, Inc. was published in its entirety in the *Journal de Monaco* on March 10, 1938.

The prospect of the new collaboration gave heart to both dancers and audiences alike. In her autobiography, *Markova Remembers*, Alicia Markova wrote about the history of the recent Ballets Russes, acknowledging her excitement at being invited by Massine to Monte Carlo in November 1937. She spoke about Blum, "a most delightful man," whose original partnership with de Basil was not a happy one, and, she recalled, neither was Massine satisfied to work with de Basil. Massine had wanted Markova to come to Monte Carlo years before in 1932; however, she said that at the time her "home was with British ballet"[36] as well as her great friends Danilova, Youskevitch, and Frederick Franklin in Monte Carlo. "This was an extraordinary time for the Ballets Russes," she explained, as dancers "were shuttling between de Basil and Blum/Massine, and even Fokine going back briefly to de Basil because Massine was in artistic control of the new Ballet Russe de Monte-Carlo (a name automatically inherited and greatly valued by our impresario, Sol Hurok)."[37] She extolled the new repertory of works by Massine, some created for de Basil, others from the Diaghilev years, as well as ballets by Fokine and others.

The Blum Ballets de Monte-Carlo returned to Paris on December 30, 1937, after a four-month journey to England, Holland, and Switzerland, and arrived in Monte Carlo at the end of January 1938. In a letter to Delpierre

Figure 9.2
Blum conferring with Massine and Markova. Photo by G. Detaille, courtesy of Archives Monte-Carlo, SBM.

from Zurich on December 20, 1937, Blum admitted being depressed about not making enough money on the many performances the company had given, however positive the audiences and critics. He also admitted his annoyance at not being provided the necessary permits to travel to Italy where the company was scheduled to perform for the whole month of January.

On December 30, 1937, Blum wrote the Argentine ballerina Maria Ruanova in Buenos Aires that he would "mount several new ballets with Massine. Our artistic success has been extraordinary wherever we have toured, and now we are hastily putting togther new works. We are preparing for a large tour of North America, and maybe one day we'll go to Buenos Aires."[38] Ruanova was no longer dancing with Blum, but a month later he responded to her kind note about the death of Léon Blum's wife. He continued with news of the growing company, now ninety-seven dancers, and added that "he would not cause her any pain by speaking about Massine."[39] Ruanova decided to return to the Teatro de Colon for the sake of a more secure and stable future. One might ask why Blum did not reduce the size of his company to decrease his financial strain.

As the time for the merger grew near, the contractual correspondence increased. A rather insidious note was written by Denham to Jacques Rubinstein suggesting that he not pay Fokine special fees for the rights to the three ballets that he had choreographed for René Blum. Rubinstein responded quickly to Denham, saying he intended to work only for a "correct" organization, and indicated that Fokine had to be paid for his work with Blum and such antics should not be imagined again.

It is interesting to read the part of Blum's 1937 personal contract with World Art, Inc. that protected him from possible neglect or denial of access to publicity. It stipulated that "for performances outside Monte Carlo, René Blum will be designated in the publicity and in the programmes by the title, 'Founder of the Company, Director of the Ballets de Monte-Carlo.'"[40] However, in Monte Carlo itself, the name René Blum would figure alone in the publicity, with the title of director, and M. Massine would be called "maître de ballet." The contract also stated that "starting from the second year, another name can be added to that of René Blum, but René Blum's name will figure in the first place, and will be the only one to carry the title of Director."[41] Here we witness again Blum's wary and careful approach to legalities, having suffered the betrayal of Colonel de Basil.

Another interesting specification acknowledged Blum's contributions to his other companies. The paragraph noted that World Art, Inc. "will examine, with as little delay as possible, all the artistic proposals submitted by René Blum and will study them in the spirit of collaboration concerning the productions in Monte Carlo,"[42] thus recognizing the value of René Blum's creative sensibility and administration. Thirteen Fokine ballets, along with their costumes, decors, accessories, and photos, were at the heart of this legal agreement, with both new and old Fokine creations. Administrators from World Art, Inc. included a curious clause in this contract. Fearing the misuse of film technology, they restricted Blum or anyone from utilizing films exceeding two minutes of ballets for the purpose of reconstructing them for another company.

After the merger was completed, on February 16, 1938, Blum signaled Denham about problems with several ventures, including the fact that Fleischmann wanted Gertrude Stein to write a scenario for a ballet to be choreographed by Massine. Since Blum had spent many years as a literary critic, he was somewhat abashed by this suggestion. Blum asserted that he knew Stein's work better than Massine and called Stein's poetry "this interminable *fatras* of English words about which Massine understands nothing."[43] As for other scenarios suggested by Massine, Blum found them "rather imbecilic and naïve, as was typical of Russians."[44] Blum chided Massine for not considering who his public was, especially his English or American public. One begins to understand Blum's intense sense of isolation. He encountered a strong Russian culture during his career. Denham, Massine, Hurok, and de Basil were all Russians and did not take very kindly to Blum's leadership. They were wary of his refined French aesthetics and taste, while he found them crude and uneducated.

In another diatribe on April 23, 1938, about de Basil, Blum complained that M. Rubinstein was obstinately silent about the administrative plan for the new company. Blum said, "As an *honnête homme* I was not informed about the details of the ballets to be presented or about the infamous de Basil." Blum threatened that if de Basil's name appeared, he would not offer any help from the Théâtre de Monte-Carlo. He explained that "though I was completely correct with M. de Basil in my four years of association with him, he was not, he did not observe the same ethics and I want nothing to do with him, and certainly not in my house."[45] Often ignored in these complex financial arrangements were the dancers who bore the burden of the success and failure of performances. Blum noted that "the dancers were apprehensive because they feared losing their jobs and their roles in the changeover to a new organization." Blum mentioned that he was delighted with the new, young Frederick Franklin, that he was a wonderful person and dancer.[46]

Perhaps one of the most revealing letters was written by Blum to "Junkie" Fleischmann, the president of World Art, Inc.[47] On August 2, 1938, Blum indicated that he wanted to speak confidentially to Fleischmann before he left for America. Many people, including Blum, considered Fleischmann a very special and sympathetic person. Blum told him that the company performing at that moment in Covent Garden was founded and financed by

Blum for at least two years. He said he gave up his old contract with the Théâtre de Monte-Carlo because he was told to do so by Sol Hurok. Having spent 2 million francs on the adventure with great artistic success, René lamented that during those two years, he had been assailed by his adversaries and old associates, even Massine who had convinced Blum to work with him.

In this narration, Blum recounted the history of his introduction to World Art, Inc. At the time Massine was forming a new company in America with Denham and World Art, Inc., and since Blum wanted to tour America, he decided to go along with their plans, but that he then lost 800,000 francs. He spoke about his emotional and psychological difficulties as Massine, Kochno, and Denham conversed constantly in Russian, and kept him out of the loop; he was patently shunned. Then de Basil showed up and was brought into the "mess."

The August 2 letter continued: Blum was furious because a photo of him and his brother Léon was used in a souvenir program against his wishes. No one apologized for having done this. In addition, he said that his name was summarily removed from the program as not being part of the "artistic personnel." Here Blum spoke frankly to Fleischmann: "What am I exactly? Nothing it seems! And when I leave the theatre that I direct, I am thinking that I am someone annoying and everyone is waiting for me to leave."[48] He repeated that he had invested large sums of money in order for the company to play at the Drury Lane, and worried that his Monégasque following would deplore this improvidence.

According to Blum, the problem with the new company arrangement was that Denham did not have enough authority and that Massine had too much. Blum cautioned that it was a dangerous precedent to permit a choreographer so much administrative authority. He commented that the dancers in the company also harbored many complaints against Massine and his colleagues, such as not being treated properly, enduring too much work and too many long rehearsals, and being shown too little respect. In conclusion, Blum defended himself:

> After all, it is thanks to me that the Ballets Russes survived after Diaghilev died, and I have the weakness to love these young people whom I have seen grow up as if they were my own children. It is my duty to support them and defend them. As little as I know you Mr. Fleischmann, I have the impression that you are a fine person and will stay close to the dancers. And I have a love for this art and for the artists for whom I have sacrificed almost everything, without any hope for a return.[49]

Studying the correspondence between Denham, Massine, and Blum, one realizes that several issues were at the heart of René's desperation. There is the sad knowledge that Blum had lost too much money and too much heart to continue to run his company with his own funds, especially as France was in the midst of a grave depression. Blum suffered a great emotional toll as the consequence of a few of his relationships. There was the constant hurt from, and hostility toward, de Basil, whose name crops up consistently as an adversary and an enemy who fought against Blum's interests. Blum had a history of complex love/hate relationships with Fokine and Massine, including intense encounters and the fear that they would undermine him. Though Blum loved dancers, he also knew they would flee to wherever the money was more plentiful, and that if they could get a better contract with another company, they would leave him. Sometimes they would agree to stay on with him, but then try to work another job on the sly.

While the struggle to survive in the ballet universe was heartless, another compelling factor was the larger picture of a crumbling Europe, where Fascism and war were beginning to destablilize world relations and politics. This was the canvas, background to the lives and the series of letters that passed between these serious men who sought to keep a fine ballet company alive and well.

This author also believes that Blum, who turned sixty in 1938, had been suffering physically; his health was deteriorating without his understanding how that affected him. Blum was a sensitive person and stress bore down on his physical as well as his emotional being. Finally, Blum became increasingly isolated and alone, even though he spoke often of friends and family.

Being important public figures caused both René and his brother Léon a good amount of distress in their lives, but they shared a healthy and continuous correspondence, often with René asking for advice and counsel from his older brother. Unfortunately, many of their letters have been lost. On March 27, 1938, René wrote a curious letter to his brother Léon. He asked to visit Léon at the Quai Bourbon in the middle of Léon's crushing worries, as he had just been the victim of a terrible hate crime, in order to reiterate his problems with the octogenarian Gunsbourg, the director of opera and music at Monte Carlo. Oddly enough, Gunsbourg had pled with René to speak to Léon about his desire to leave Monte Carlo and move to Palestine. There, he wanted to represent France in some manner and to spend his final days. With serious self-interest, René recognized that if Gunsbourg left, he might replace him as head of the Opéra. René assured his brother that despite his antidemocratic enemies who cast aspersions and gravely injured Léon, he had a "cohort of very close friends, whom you cultivate anew every day."[50] He also told him how happy he had been to spend his birthday with him and their other brothers on March 13.

Soon after this letter, in March 1938, an article appeared in *Le Petit Niçois de Nice*. Here critic Marcel Reichenecker reported the new plans for Blum's (*le magicien*) ballet company, and reminisced about his last interview with him when he sensed the estimable René Blum was struggling with a certain disquiet, one that constrained him from speaking freely. But he reassured the reader that now Blum had an expression of serenity, and that he had achieved a sense of harmony, having lived through some of the most difficult times in keeping his company together. Reichenecker indicated that Blum was able to realize "his desire for perfection by accepting the proposals for a new American company instigated by M. Denham of World Art, Inc."[51] The journalist emphasized the tremendous possiblilities that awaited the company in going to America and traveling freely for six months to eighty-four cities, where audiences would certainly applaud the beauty of its work. He mentioned that Blum was convinced that artists, no matter what they cost, would desire to collaborate with this new group.

Reichenecker commented on the difficulty of staging ballets, and how they quickly lose their allure, become "déformé," and disappear into history. But he applauded Blum for rectifying the problem by creating a film library of all the company's ballets, thus creating a means of preservation and renewal hitherto unheard of in the ballet world. Reichenecker concluded his homage to Blum: "But M. René Blum estimated, very reasonably, that it was enough for his glorious reputation to have been an innovator in an art that always risked being forgotten."[52]

In the spring of 1938 when the company of one hundred dancers arrived in Monte Carlo, they knew that something momentous might occur. Massine went there with a number of dancers, including Markova, Danilova, Youskevitch, and Franklin. They soon discovered that some forty dancers would have to be fired. In addition, Massine was convinced that he needed a Russian-based company and therefore asked the dancers to Russianize their names; for example, Natalie Leslie became Natasha Krassovska.[53] Frederick Franklin said, "It was a very sad moment, as so many were let go. When we got to Monte Carlo, we arrived at midnight on the blue train from Paris. We had to find places to stay. There were 110 people in the tiny Monte Carlo studio including five people from the States—Rosella Hightower, Dorothy Etheridge, Bob Madren, Charlie Dixon and Milas Milanova." Franklin voiced the dangers of being jobless during this difficult time in the Depression.[54]

Rehearsals progressed under the talented leadership of ballet mistress Mlle. Tatiana Chamié, preparing performances for a season in Monte Carlo from April 4 to May 14, 1938 of Nijinsky's *Afternoon of the Faune, Prince Igor, Le Tricorne, Gaîté Parisienne, Giselle, Blue Danube, Swan Lake*, and *Bogatry*. Massine's *Gaîté* by Offenbach was bound to be a sensation.

At this time, Massine's extensive negotiations with World Art, Inc. surfaced, while the impresario Sol Hurok took over as he was accustomed to doing. In a moment of appalling stinginess, Hurok told Blum that he refused to retain any of the technical crew from the Ballets de Monte-Carlo. Nevertheless, Mr. Blum insisted that Jean Cerrone and wardrobe mistress Madame Pourmel remain.[55]

During the extensive, twenty-four-performance spring season in Monte Carlo, everyone adored *Gaîté Parisienne*, "Massine's New Triumph" according to the *Dancing Times*. With lighthearted music by Offenbach, and "charming and attractive costumes and décor by Étienne de Beaumont . . . it is Massine at his gayest and wittiest."[56] Though the role of the glove-seller was given to Nina Tarakanova, a less startling and engaging dancer than Danilova, the ballet still charmed. The journal stated that Youskevitch "established himself as a dancer with merit, and Franklin as the Baron opposite the Glove seller had grace and ease of movement, and a great feeling of strength."[57] Of course, when Massine danced, the world applauded. In the role of the Peruvian, he created what was described as a "perfect character study, a stranger in the café with two carpet bags; he does not know which lady most warrants his attention in the enchanting *Gaîté Parisienne*."[58]

One of the more startling of the new works, Massine's *Seventh Symphony*, had its premiere on May 5, 1938. The brilliant designer Christian Bérard created the scenery and costumes with the help of Karinska. Massine infused this remarkable and rather stern 1812 score by Ludwig van Beethoven with a deep sense of religiosity, perhaps because it was considered such a classical masterpiece. Interestingly, the great composer Richard Wagner, years before Massine's creation, called the "Seventh" the apotheosis of dance.[59]

In the libretto of the *Seventh Symphony*, the eternally troubled human condition preoccupied Massine; he recognized the dangers of German Fascism, and the futility of hopes for peace during the late 1930s. For the first movement, the program alluded to the biblical theme of the creation of the universe, with chaos transformed into a structured harmony by the Spirit of Creation, played "zestily" by Frederick Franklin. Baird Hastings in *Ballet Review* described the dancers and stirring events in the narrative. The Sky was danced by the gossamer Alicia Markova, and the Stream was performed by the "mysterious and fragile" Nini Theilade. Eventually, "Plants, Birds, the Serpent, the Fishes, the Sun, the Woman, the Man come to life."[60] "Earth was the subject of the second movement, predicting a dreadful fate: after the first crime is committed, all humanity is plunged into despair and guilt (evoking the descent from the cross)."[61] The third movement, Sky, was suffused with an ethereal glow; it was danced by Markova and Youskevitch, and later by Markova and Dolin. The Bacchanale and Destruction were the

Figure 9.3
Gaîté Parisienne, with Jeanette Laurent and Igor Youskevitch. Décors and costumes by Étienne de Beaumont. Photo by G. Detaille, courtesy of Archives Monte-Carlo, SBM.

themes of what was a "spectacular finale." Massine conjured up a human orgy that inevitably led the gods to initiate a fiery immolation of all who have forgotten the commandments. Hastings concluded that at times Massine's themes seemed "contrived," but the sets by Bérard enticed all the senses. In hindsight, Massine's fourth attempt at the symphonic form seems a fitting prophecy of the events of the time. A critic from the *Daily Herald* concerning his "customary treatment of concert music"observed: "Once again Léonide Massine put forward his theory that symphonies should be Massine as well as heard."[62]

Not all the financial news was glum. Blum wrote Josette France that this triumphant season finished with extravagant ticket sales exceeding 25,000 francs in Monte Carlo, and that the *Seventh Symphony* was responsible for the record sales and windfall.[63]

After Monte Carlo, the troupe went to London to play the Drury Lane, on July 21, 1938. There Massine created *Nobilissima Visione* to a libretto and score by Paul Hindemith. In the United States, the work was titled *Saint Francis*, and despite its lack of toe shoes, which suggested a modern dance piece, Massine's choreography fascinated audiences. Taking his inspiration from early Italian paintings, Massine presented the figure of St. Francis, who first wished to become a military hero, but finding the practice of war violent and ugly, dedicated himself to a religious life, as Jack Anderson

Figure 9.4
Seventh Symphony, studio rehearsal. Photo by G. Detaille, courtesy of Archives Monte-Carlo, SBM.

wrote, "a religious renunciation of all worldliness—an ideal most ordinary mortals probably could not attain."[64] The man tames an attacking wolf, and envisions the abstract characters of Poverty, Chastity, and Obedience, finally uniting with Lady Poverty played by the alluring Javanese dancer Nini Theilade.

Reactions to the ballet were mixed. Some found Massine's presentation of St. Francis sacrilegious and the music monotonous. Others, including John Martin of *The New York Times*, declared it one of the most beautiful pieces he had ever seen. Hurok, of course, called it a masterpiece. But it never became a popular triumph with audiences.

The season in July at the Drury Lane included Serge Lifar's capable staging of *Giselle*, with the effervescent Alicia Markova in the title role and Serge Lifar as her partner Albrecht, though Lifar seemed not to please the public. In his book *The One and Only: The Ballet Russe de Monte Carlo*, Jack Anderson mentioned that "Frederick Franklin called Lifar 'a drooly sort of dancer,' fond of flamboyant gestures that the English deplored."[65]

Lifar was known to behave impudently. During curtain calls he insisted on taking all the bows with Markova, never giving her a chance for a solo bow. This was truly unheard of. Many years had passed since companies had performed *Giselle*, and despite its "unblushing romanticism," it captivated the London audiences and confirmed what most balletomanes knew: that the piece was a historical jewel.[66] Perhaps because Markova was

Figure 9.5
Nobilissima Visione, with Roland Guirard and Milada Mladova. Courtesy of Jerome Robbins Dance Division, the New York Public Library for the Performing Arts, Astor, Lenox, and Tilden Foundations.

English, or perhaps because the British had an undying love for the romantic ethos, she elicited enthusiasm and adoration beyond all expectation. According to *The Times*, "Her miming has gained enormously in conviction so that for instance the pathos as well as the fact of mental derangement was suggested in the mad scene without any forcing of expression. Then too her dancing is lightness itself."[67]

Dance lovers lived out their wildest dreams when both de Basil's company and the Massine/Blum company found themselves in London at the same time in July 1938: one at Covent Garden, the other at the Drury Lane. The Educational Ballets, Ltd. was the moniker under which de Basil's company performed. On some evenings, people dashed between the two theatres, trying to take it all in. Since the company directors were known to be rivals, spectators who preferred one or the other began to take sides. For the most part, the dancers stayed friendly. According to Anderson, a few upsets occurred. Markova was told that she was to perform first, but there was a problem. The costume people misunderstood and thought it was Toumanova who would dance first, and Markova's costume was not ready. Fortunately, she had her own Giselle costume from the Markova-Dolin Ballet. There were other contretemps, but somehow the two companies managed to meet the obligations of their contracts.[68]

In April 1938, a series of striking political events began to shake the ephemeral peace that both England and France thought they enjoyed, and Léon Blum was forced to resign. His political enemy, Daladier, formed a right-wing government. When Hitler announced his plans for the Sudetenland (a region in the north and northwest of the People's Republic of Czechoslovakia), France called up 1 million men. In September 1938, Chamberlain and Daladier met with Mussolini and Hitler in Munich, and negotiated the infamous treaty they believed would forestall any further annexations of territory in Central Europe. Britain and France acknowledged the annexation of the Sudetenland to Germany in exchange for Hitler's promise to make no more territorial claims. Peace seemed provisionally secured, and Britain and France hoped they would have time to rearm in the event of war.

In October 1938, the company sailed to the United Sates with the new Ballets Russes de Monte-Carlo under the artistic direction of Massine and Blum, who was billed as founder of the Ballets de Monte-Carlo. At the same time, Blum received a visa from the U.S. embassy on December 10, 1938, for his mission as technical counselor for the French Pavilion at the New York World's Fair. The visa provided that he was proceeding to the United States on a mission for the French Ministry of Commerce, arriving on December 21, 1938, on the SS *Champlain*.[69]

In a brief feature in *The New York Times* on December 22, 1938, a photo of René Blum, captioned "Ex-Premier's Brother to stage shows at Fair," indicated that René arrived to supervise the theatre, music, and ballet programs planned for the French Pavilion at the World's Fair. The following statement defies credibility: "He said that he frequently disagrees with his brother on political policies and that the former Premier often spent a great deal of time trying to change his views." Recognizing the gravity of

Figure 9.6
On their way to the United States, Natalie Krassovska, Mia Slavenska, Nini Theilade, Tamara Toumanova, Alicia Markova, and Alexandra Danilova. Cosmo-Sileo Co., courtesy of Jerome Robbins Dance Division, the New York Public Library for the Performing Arts, Astor, Lenox, and Tilden Foundations.

current events, Blum announced that "there would be no frivolity in the presentations and that he planned to stay until January 1939 at the Savoy Plaza Hotel."[70]

The season in New York startled everyone, as Serge Denham boasted in a letter to Blum on December 7, 1938: "I think it was the first time in the history of ballet that the enormous Metropolitan Opera House was completely sold out for the whole three weeks that we played there."[71] The May 1939 *American Dancer* contained a long review, by Albertina Vitak, of the season at the Met, which celebrated the Ballets Russes engagement, especially highlighting the stars. Vitak noted that Markova "danced exquisitely in *Le Lac des Cygnes*, while Massine threw himself with daunting power into *St. Francis* (with Hindemith present at the debut), and Mia Slavenska and Roland Guerard outdid themselves in 'Bluebird Variations.'"[72]

Vitak was especially taken by the panache of Danilova and Massine: "Danilova startled her audiences with coquettery and verve in *Gaîté Parisienne*. Who but Massine could dance the noble St. Francis, and the delightfully absurd little Peruvian all within an hour?" Guerard was also a favorite of the critics, who sighed at his hovering jumps and adulated his "diagonal line of brisé volés, with the body describing a graceful arc for each backward beat." Vitak praised Slavenska, "strong technically with unusual balances in arabesque, she once achieved seven pirouettes under Guerard's arm, which I have not seen anyone do in this dance before." She also lauded Krassovska who "stands out over all and is one of the most valuable assets of the company."[73]

Not all her comments were positive. Vitak remarked that Slavenska was "rather too Sylphide-like, while Tatiana Grantzeva was not good enough for the featured part in *Lac des Cygnes*." She noted that there were "over lavish decors in *Bogatyri* and the finale was too long in winding up" and lamented that "Fokine's *Les Elfes* choreographic designs are pretty, but nothing more." Vitak's last remarks about ballet rituals were hilarious; she exclaimed that she was "going to start a crusade against male dancers always leaving the stage with a leap, whether in solos or after bows, and I do wish the custom of tearing a flower out of bouquets to present to male partners might also be dropped."[74]

A document that Janet Rowson Davis acquired from the Franklin Delano Roosevelt Library in Hyde Park, New York, indicated that on January 7, 1939, George F. Summerlin, Chief of Protocol, U.S. Department of State, wrote to the presidential secretary Marvin McIntyre informing him that a note had been received from the French ambassador regarding René Blum's desire to be received by President Roosevelt. According to the presidential diary, Blum met with Roosevelt from 12 noon to 12:15 p.m. on Friday, January 13, 1939. No information is available concerning the purpose of the visit, although it may have been to discuss the success of the World's Fair, or to inquire about his work for the Comédie Française, or perhaps in the interest of helping his brother Léon in one way or another. This is but guesswork. What we do know is that René kept a signed photograph of FDR on his mantlepiece and loved to tell people about his meeting with the distinguished president.

After a six-month tour in the United States, the ballet company began its Monte Carlo season optimistically on April 4, 1939. Massine created two new ballets: Rimsky-Korsakov's *Capriccio Espagnol* with the scintillating La Argentinita that premiered May 4, 1939, and on May 11 the more dour *Le Rouge et le Noir*, a symphonic ballet to Shostakovitch's Symphony No. 1. Henri Matisse created the sets and costumes, but when the ballet played in Paris that June, a new title emerged: *L'Étrange Farandole*. Various newspaper articles indicated that the change acknowledged the fact that the great painter Matisse used to sing a farandole while he painted.

Both René and Léon Blum adored the writings of Stendhal; they had deep roots in French literary traditions and knew his work well. Indeed,

Figure 9.7
Capriccio Espagnol, Massine and La Argentinita. Décors and costumes by Mariano Andreu. Courtesy of Archives de Monte-Carlo, SBM.

Léon had written a book about Stendhal's views of love and had presented lectures on the author at various times. Though Massine's *Le Rouge et le Noir* had little to do with Stendhal, it is certain that the French audience expected to see the novel's story. Its premiere took place in Monte Carlo on May 11, 1939. In the scenario, Massine concentrated on an "abstract vision of Man" as a poetic spirit who, in the first movement, is overtaken by crude forces. Bright colors light up different groups of dancers in spare white, yellow, red, blue, and black; the whole stage seems to be a moving mural. Massine was enthralled by the struggle between good and evil, and his second movement dwells on the Materialistic Men of the City (led by Frederick Franklin), who dominate and enslave the Men of the Field. The third movement (Solitude) is a lament as the Woman in White (Markova) becomes separated from her partner by dancers in black (led by André Eglevsky). Destiny is determined by the battle between "Man's" spiritual and terrestrial values. Man and woman are reunited but for a moment, as Fate intervenes, consuming the whole world—another sad prediction of events to come.

Figure 9.8
Rouge et Noir, Markova and Matisse. Photo by G. Detaille, courtesy of Archives de Monte-Carlo, SBM.

This was to be the last season that Blum directed in Monte Carlo. Due to world events including the war, the casino closed from August 31 to November 16 in 1939, and again from June 10 to November 18, 1940. When it reopened, it functioned with a greatly diminished budget and only several minor repertory companies and concerts. René Blum had been dismissed.

With the Spanish Civil War raging, the German invasion of Czecholslovakia, Anschluss, the march into Poland and France, Dunkirk, and the bombing of Britain, hopes for sustaining the arts were dashed. The rise of Hitler and the Nazis had prompted the French to seek alliances with Poland, Russia, and Italy, but after Mussolini invaded Ethiopia in 1935 and Hitler reoccupied the Rhineland in March 1936, France did not mount a coherent policy. In 1936 Léon Blum and his government, confronted by the resistance of the Radicals, could not even support the Spanish Republic against the Fascist invasion of Franco, whose forces were aided heavily by Mussolini and Hitler. Through most of the decade the Americans remained isolationist, the British argued for appeasement, and the French were too divided to stand up to Hitler alone, retreating behind what they believed to be their impregnable Maginot line of fortresses. Hitler was a gambler and at

Figure 9.9
Matisse at a well-attended dinner with Nijinska, Blum, and Danilova. Courtesy of Jerome Robbins Dance Division, the New York Library for the Performing Arts, Astor, Lenox, and Tilden Foundations.

any point a strong and united Anglo-French response might have had a good chance of stopping Germany, but exhausted and divided since World War I, the French and British set their hopes on appeasement.[75]

Despite the threatening clouds of war, before the company played the Palais de Chaillot in Paris in June 1939, it revived *Cimerosiana*, a ballet Massine had made for Diaghilev that the company performed in Florence. With the outbreak of the war, its London season was cancelled. In the Massine collection at the New York Public Library of the Performing Arts, a contract between the Ballets de Monte-Carlo and Universal Art for the Covent Garden appearances on June 31, 1939, is available. There was to be a weekly payment of 1,000 pounds to Covent Garden, but of course the season never happened. Most of the scenery and costumes that had been in London were forwarded to New York, and the administrators scrambled to get the company there as well. With few ships able to cross the Atlantic, the dancers struggled to find passage. Finally, most of them took the last ship, the *Rotterdam*, arriving in New York just in time for opening night.

A number of men stayed behind, while some were conscripted into the army. The company's property man, Jean Cerrone, was dismayed at being drafted, but was very grateful that Blum gave him an extra month's salary before his departure. Blum even wrote him during the four months that he served in the army, to keep up his morale.

On November 17, 1939, Blum wrote a letter to financial advisor Maître Rubinstein in Paris, noting that the president of the Société des Bains de Mer de Monte-Carlo had refused him permission to produce a season in Monte Carlo in the spring of 1940. Blum requested that Rubinstein communicate this decision because of "la guerre" to the administrators of the Society of the Ballets of Monte-Carlo. This trenchant refusal by SBM was the coup de grâce for his association with Monte Carlo. (Perhaps as an act of contrition, in March and April 1953, the Société des Bains de Mer sponsored an exhibition honoring the work of both Serge Diaghilev and René Blum; a stamp with their photo memorialized the two masters.) English and French ballet lovers, represented by Cyril Beaumont, honored René Blum's memory in 1950 by establishing an annual award in his name for the most promising French dancer of the year; it was discontinued for lack of funds in 1968.

On January 18, 1940, the last letter from Blum to Denham disclosed that Blum had loaned Mme. Karinska $161 and that he was grateful to Denham for reimbursing him. He mentioned that he intended to be in New York at the end of January. He thanked Denham and sent his regards to madame and their charming daughters.[76]

Blum received another visa for a trip to America on March 3, 1940; he was slated to perform a mission of propaganda for the French government, organizing a tour for the troupe of the Comédie Française. However, the war also interfered with these plans for the estimable theatre troupe.

While in New York at the St. Regis Hotel, René wrote his brother Léon on March 12 that conditions for the publication of Léon's autobiography were ripe. It included a chapter on "L'Affaire Dreyfus" that Léon had published much earlier in France. René instructed his brother to send a letter authorizing the Dwight Literary Agency to engage in negotiations for this book of memoirs in English. He confided that he was enjoying himself, doing good work, and might well stay a long time. He asked Léon to please send news of Léon's son Robert, who had enlisted in the army. Six months later, Léon was arrested by the Vichy government, while his son Robert was taken prisoner during the war and sent to Germany.

After spending considerable time in the United States, Blum decided to express his concerns about his reputation, and wrote a "Letter of Protest" to the magazine *Dance* in April 1940. He referred to their publication of two articles in February 1940—"one on the Original Russian Ballet" and the other on "the Ballet That Massine Built." He objected to the fact that both essays neglected to mention his name, asserting, "I must confess, in all humility that I am not quite as modest as certain people seem to believe," and that he had a strong penchant for accuracy.[77]

He observed that if anyone had succeeded Diaghilev, it was he, as he "was appointed Director of the Ballets de l'Opéra de Monte-Carlo by the Société des Bains de Mer de Monaco," and, he stressed, "I have held this position ever since."[78] He assured readers that the Ballets Russes de Monte-Carlo was already well established by the time Colonel de Basil arrived on the scene. De Basil and the Prince Zeretelli, it seemed, were never able to come up with any serious money to back the venture. Blum retold the story of his adventures with de Basil, adding that they would eventually appear in his autobiography, *Memoirs on the Ballet*, soon to be published in London.

According to the same letter, Massine claimed that he built the company, which was untrue, as it was Blum who organized the Ballets de Monte-Carlo while Massine was still ballet master for de Basil. Fokine was hired to create what Blum indicated were "indisputable masterpieces"—the three ballets: *L'Épreuve d'Amour, Don Juan*, and *Les Éléments*. Blum noted that he carried the whole weight of the enterprise, a burden too heavy for his feeble shoulders, and that he exhausted all of his small capital and much more, until the day, he said,

I yielded to the entreaties of my friend Libidins and Massine, who came to see me in Monte Carlo, assuring me with sobs in his voice that his greatest desire, the most cherished dream of his life, would be to collaborate with me again, and begging me to deal with a company, the World Art, Inc., which had just been organized in New York, and of which he was artistic director.[79]

Figure 9.10
Advertisement for Blum's autobiography published in program for the Ballets Russes de Monte Carlo, June 1939. Courtesy of Janet Rowson Davis collection.

Perhaps the most interesting part of this declamation was Blum's description of Léonide Massine's character and talents. To one familiar with the private letters of Blum to Denham and Fleischmann from earlier months, these comments come as little surprise. Blum recalled his long-standing relationship with Massine, since Massine's stunning performances with Diaghilev's Ballets Russes full of "ardor and fervor" in *The Legend of Joseph*. In a consummate assessment of Massine's artistry, Blum struck a truthful chord about Massine:

> Although his character may not be to my liking—he is neither very sincere or coura-
> geous—and I am further tempted to reproach him for his carelessness and offhand
> manner when dealing with the works of his colleagues and of his masters, I neverthe-
> less admire his great inventive and studied talent, his deep sense of choreographic
> rhythm, his inspiration, pathetic and spiritual by turns, his erudition, his architectural
> genius—for perspective and imposing ensembles (which he owes no doubt to the
> influence of Fokine) and to which most other choreographers bow. I also appreciate
> his endurance, that inner fire which consumes him when he is at work, that desire
> for perfection which he is then able to impart to his dancers . . . if the work is one of
> his own.[80]

Blum stated that he ceded the ownership of his ballet to Denham and World Art, Inc., soon to become Universal Art. The company performing that spring at the Metropolitan Opera was therefore built by Blum and not

Massine, although Massine broadened it and contributed great works to it. Blum reiterated the same old wounding comments: "The reading of posters and programs is somewhat misleading. . . . You may well be forgiven for having forgotten me, inasmuch as the necessary data was missing." Blum pleaded for justice, requesting that *Dance* magazine rectify the facts given by others. He concluded, "It is no doubt a pity, for the recital of the bare facts, without any recourse to flights of fancy, would suffice in composing such a striking chapter in the Human Comedy."[81]

The final letter to René Blum in the archives of the Monte Carlo casino came from Delpierre. He wrote, on December 16, 1940: "Mon Chèr Directeur that according to their conversation, they are in agreement that the circumstances of war prevent the SBM from producing a season of the Ballets de Monte-Carlo in the spring of 1941."[82]

Further correspondence with the administration of SBM concerned Blum's ownership of costumes not wanted by the new American company. They were to be kept in the storehouses of the casino theatre. The remaining letters in the archives pertain to a special prize that was created in René Blum's name: "Le Prix René Blum." Established by Delpierre after the war, it was to be awarded to talented ballet dancers. A jury of writers and dance critics, headed by Pierre Michaut, would decide which lucky ballet dancer received 10,000 francs each year. Unfortunately, soon after Delpierre retired in the early 1950s, monies were no longer allotted to the prize.

The new de Basil Ballets Russes company, without Massine or Blum, was led by Gerald Sevastianov and Fokine, who tried foolishly to make arrangements to perform in Berlin in September 1939. The threat of war continued, and one is startled by their naiveté in planning such an engagement. In the company's earlier 1938 trip to Berlin, writer Kathrine Sorley Walker recalled that only one ballerina, Sobinova, a Canadian, seemed disturbed by the Nazis and their grotesque hatred for the Jews. Kristallnacht, during which three thousand synagogues were burned, occurred soon after this visit, in November 1938. Sorley Walker said, "Russian artists had no particular political stake in any country."[83] Perhaps there was a touch of anti-Semitism in their attitudes. Several years after the break between de Basil and Blum, Blum's fears about de Basil's cunning actions behind the scenes proved quite valid. De Basil tried once more to ally himself with Hurok and Blum, and he continued to call his company the Ballets Russes de Monte-Carlo. However, in principle, he was not allowed to set foot in Monte Carlo again.

Sorley Walker also recounted a fascinating story, one that resembled Lifar's poor recollection of this event, which concerned Gerald Sevastianov. In his unpublished diary, she said Sevastianov wrote, "He [Sevastianov] cabled German authorities to the effect that he regretted, but he did not have enough Aryans in the company to fulfill the contract."[84] Goebbels responded that it was up to him [Goebbels] to decide who was Aryan, and from Goebbel's point of view, all members of the Covent Garden Russian Ballet were pure Aryans.[85]

One shudders to think that people lived in such a narrow world at that time and believed their performances or pursuits would go on uninterrupted. Fokine was already rehearsing *Tannhauser*, set to Wagner's "Venusberg," and thought it could be performed in Berlin for the company's season. But one must not criticize this choice too quickly. The Russians were avid lovers of Wagner and German music, as were the Americans. Massine, too, was creating in New York a bacchanale to the same music for a debut at the Metropolitan Opera on November 9, 1939.

When Blum toured America with the ballet company in March 1940, many people importuned him to stay with the company as the news from France and Europe was becoming more disastrous with each passing day. But in a proud and self-destructive gesture, he rejected the offer to stay in New York. He returned to Paris, where, after the Nazis invaded, he retreated into a kind of purgatorial hiding before his arrest. Why Blum returned is uncertain, although he insisted to his friends that his son remained in Paris. Perhaps, having won the Croix de Guerre in World War I, he felt himself a true French patriot. It may also be that once confronted with the Occupation and the Vichy regime, he did not flee to Spain or North Africa because his brother Léon was by then imprisoned and put on trial by the Vichy authorities.

One of the people whom Janet Rowson Davis contacted in the course of her research on Blum was the narcississtic but ingratiating Serge Lifar. There are many versions of Lifar's meteoric rise to fame in Diaghilev's company, and later at the Paris Opéra. Ivor Guest offered one interpretation that claimed him as a veritable savior of the company during the Occupation. Many disagree, but time will tell. Frederick Franklin boldly reported on Lifar's collaboration with the Nazis, declaring that several dancers, Valodia Skouratoff, for example, revealed "Lifar was a great friend of Goebbels, and that these Russian dancers preferred to starve doing nightclub work rather than work at the Opéra with Lifar."[86] Indeed, in 1963, when this author studied dance with Skouratoff in Geneva, he told the same story. But it was quite sad, as Skouratoff had to pass the hat after his dancing number, and often did not collect enough money to feed his mother and himself.

After reading Lifar's autobiography, *Ma Vie*, Janet Rowson Davis wrote him in 1978 in order to verify a story on page 282 about the demise of René Blum, and anecdotes concerning his son Claude-René.[87] Lifar did not mention the Blum family name; rather, he referred to it as an episode in a Greek-like tragedy that occurred during the Occupation when Lifar was in charge of the Paris Opéra. On May 24, 1978, Lifar's letter to Davis recalled, "The son Claude was extremely embarrassed that his father was a Jew, that his uncle Léon was a socialist and a Jew of the Popular Front, and that the family was involved in a lucrative business Blum Frères; as a teenager Claude-René favored the most radical right political party, Charles Maurras and L'Action Française."[88]

Details from Lifar's letter remembered "the most regretted René," whose amicable friendship with him lasted from 1923 until 1941. Lifar called Blum "a man with an exceptional nobility of soul and heart, of a crystalline purity."[89] He then recounted the sad events of the relations between René and his son. Lifar called himself a "witness" to this harrowing story, in which he was approached by one of Blum's relatives to announce to the world that Claude-René had informed on his father. Blum's current relatives denied the truth of these comments. There were three brothers who survived the Occupation: Marcel, Léon, and Lucien. None of these men would have conceivably contacted Lifar about René's son.

Lifar continued that "for the sake of history and truth, I will tell you what happened. Until spring 1941, René was living in Paris."[90] In fact, René lived in Paris until December 1941, when he was arrested. Lifar then listed various pieces of information about Blum's life—for example, the whereabouts of Blum's apartment, the fact that he was separated from his wife, that he attended the Opéra, and that he always sat in the first row of the orchestra. Lifar declared proudly that Blum came to the premiere of Lifar's ballet *Le Chevalier et la Damoiselle* on July 2, 1941, and was most enthusiastic about the work. Then Lifar said, "Blum began to cry when he confided to me that his son denounced him to the Gestapo, that Claude-René announced, 'Je suis monarchiste, Maurassien et mon père est Israelite.'" Lifar recalled that after the Liberation the son Minouchou "volunteered in Le Clerc's army and that he was shot dead and therefore the 'procès' or trial never took place."[91] One asks oneself, what "procès"?

Lifar added that René Blum was contacted by Goebbels' office, which offered him the chance to leave for the United States via Spain. (This is another tall tale, according to Blum's nieces.) Lifar noted that Blum immediately refused, saying, "I have no right to desert my country because I carry one of the most significant names of anyone of my race." Lifar then questioned, "Why this kindness on the part of the Germans, vis-a-vis the Jews?" Lifar answered by asserting that just before the war in 1939, Blum brought his company, the Ballets de Monte-Carlo, to Berlin, and after triumphant performances, he was greeted and congratulated by Goebbels. This is another fantasy, because the Ballets de Monte-Carlo did not go to Berlin in 1939. Lifar was confusing Blum with de Basil. After separating from Blum/Massine, de Basil took his company to Germany several times, according to

Sorley Walker.[92] In the fall of 1937, de Basil toured several German cities and continued to have high hopes for a London season that, of course, did not happen. De Basil's company appeared in Berlin in 1938, and tried to return in 1939, even sending the music ahead, but with the German invasion of Poland, war broke out on September 3, 1939. Lifar ended the letter to Rowson Davis noting that Blum's "wife" and the mother of Claude-René or Minouchou must still be alive.[93]

Lifar was quite correct about Claude-René's angry behavior, as the family admitted that his room contained posters, flags, and objects touting the right-wing platform. When his father was taken in December 1941, Claude was only sixteen years old. Because his opinions, to anyone who would listen, were viciously transparent and very vocal, some assumed that Claude informed on his father, and told the authorities where to pick him up. This is utterly absurd, since the police knew all they needed to know about René, and when they rounded up the Jewish intellectuals in Paris, no one was surprised that René was among them.

After World War II, Lifar's reputation suffered greatly, especially with the artists who worked with those who had fled to America to escape the Nazis and the conflagration of war. Nathan Milstein, the brilliant violinist and close friend of Balanchine, painted a particularly insulting portrait of Lifar, whom he knew for many years. He confessed,

> To tell the truth I did not like him. Lifar came from Kiev, and I called him the "fake Ukrainian," because everything about him was fake and affected. Later he attended my concerts, and it was always a major production—Lifar carrying himself into the dressing room with wide-spread arms and exaggerated delight that began with his shrieking, "Nathan!" Lifar always had to be the center of attention, always in the spotlight. And that, alas, led him to collaborate with the Nazis during World War II. One doesn't like to judge others. The whole business with Hitler's arrival in occupied Paris with Lifar showing him around the grand opéra was, after all, Lifar's personal affair. But then he shouldn't have felt insulted when some people refused to shake his hand.[94]

When Jean Cerrone, the property man for René Blum's company, was in New York in 1941, he remembered that René's niece (probably his brother Marcel's daughter Simone) visited him and "asked to see me wanting to know why Mr. Blum's name was no longer on the credits. She was very upset and told Cerrone that Blum did not really sell the company, but that he gave it away to save the company and to relieve himself of the financial burden." Cerrone explained to Rowson Davis that he knew Blum was having financial difficulties in 1937, but, he wrote, "We always got our salaries, and Mr. Gautrin, who was the Administrator, told me that it was with the help of the Americans and also of his brother Léon Blum."[95]

Was this a happy ending for Blum's Ballets de Monte-Carlo? As we have seen, Denham's new American company, allied with Massine, was now the Ballets Russes de Monte-Carlo. Their marvelous dancers, including Danilova, Markova, Toumanova, Tarakanova, Slavenska, Rostova, and Krassovska (Leslie), along with Lifar, Frederick Franklin, Panieff, Guerard, Platoff, and Youskevich, rallied on. The new ballets, *Gaîté Parisienne* and *Seventh Symphony*, were both stunning and quite successful in their own rights. Blum did retain his title as founder and director and still held some stocks in the enterprise. Massine was artistic director, choreographer, and the maître de ballet, as well as the leading dancer. Efrem Kurtz became musical director and David Libidins (Blum's revered long-time friend) took over as company manager.

Financial infusions came from the celebrity/sportsman "Junkie" Fleischmann and World Art, Inc., while the not so proud Denham chased after de Basil's dancers in order to lure them to World Art. The ever-vigilant Sol Hurok, always looking for the better deal, decided to support the Denham company.

De Basil's legal issues, and the desire for a U.S. performing contract, haunted him. He became embroiled in a merger with Denham, whose contract he claimed to not understand. Many publications such as the *Dancing Times* in London advertised that "the most glorious ballet company was about to be created, Reunion of Ballet Companies; De Basil, Massine and Blum to Work Together; Array of Talent for London Season."[96] In June 1938, the contract was officially revoked. The backers still wanted to effect a merger but without de Basil. The new company, without him, would be called Educational Ballets Ltd. Sevastianov, de Basil's student, became the adminsitrator of this new and perfect organism, which then left de Basil in the lurch. However, the indomitable de Basil prevailed: he recovered the company and took it on a successful tour to Australia, arriving in Los Angeles in 1940, with his company now called the Original Ballet Russe. It performed in October 1940 at the Fifty-First Street Theatre in New York to sold-out houses. With two Russian ballet companies, de Basil's Original Ballet Russe and the Ballets Russes de Monte-Carlo, competing for American audiences, the abundance of talent belied the "deviousness" and difficulties that continued to plague both dancers and directors. John Martin quipped that "it is a brave man, indeed, who will stick his nose into such matters as these, unless he is himself a Muscovite."[97]

In an interview on October 10, 2001, in New York City, Frederick Franklin was most warm in his comments about Blum. He called him "one of the most gracious gentlemen that I'd ever met." He noted that he was very excited to join Blum's company when he auditioned for Massine in 1937 and was given a contract for five years as "premier danseur." He said that "Blum was so good to the dancers, a truly paternal figure. He instigated the idea of having tea after class which we all adored. Blum offered advice to everyone." Franklin recalled how significant this moment was for the world and said: "It was the end of an era when Blum sold his company to World Art, Inc. René Blum had run the company in every way; it was a huge company. He chose the ballets; he hired excellent dancers including Eglevsky, Krassovska/Leslie (who was but a child), and Nemtchinova. It was in direct competition with de Basil, and Danilova left the Colonel and came over to us as well."[98] Franklin believed that Blum had a great affinity and affection for his dancers, and that he lived to be with the company. For example, he mentioned that Blum was always alone, never with anyone else, but spent a lot of time at rehearsals and performances.

Franklin recalled that later on Blum seemed to be absent from the company's activities. He said, "We knew that Blum had gone to be with his family in Paris, and especially with his brother Léon. 1939 was the last time the Ballets Russes were in Europe; we played the Palais de Chaillot in Paris. When we arrived in New York, we went straight to the Met and danced Frederick Ashton's *The Devil's Holiday*. Because half the company was new, we had to rehearse and rehearse."[99]

In those days, Franklin pointed out, the dancers were taken to many parties: to make themselves known, to help ticket sales, and to do whatever Hurok told them to. The company went to Cannes and then it had another season at Covent Garden. René Blum virtually disappeared, according to Franklin. Then Franklin recalled an "awful moment. We were all outside Covent Garden, all the loudspeakers were on, blaring about the war." The troupe got on one of the last boats to the United States. He said, "It was tragic, we never saw Blum again."[100]

CHAPTER 10
Blum's Final Days

Little has been documented about René Blum's final days in Paris, although his niece Françoise Nordmann has vivid and loving memories of her uncle. She spoke to the author about his concern for family members who remained in Paris in the early days of the Occupation. René's brother Lucien kept a journal that followed their daily life from 1940 to 1942. In those memoirs, René's name is mentioned several times with great sadness, as if Lucien sensed his brother's fate after his arrest in 1941.

Blum had been in the United States with his ballet company when the Germans invaded France. The company remained in the States, but he returned to France to be with his family (especially his brother Léon and his son Claude René and to "be with the French"). According to Georges Wellers, Blum asserted that "I and my family are too well known to flee from the Germans, or to ask for protection by the Vichy authorities."[1] In 1941, just before he was taken, his friends begged him at least three times to go to the Zone Libre—the free zone in the South. Perhaps Blum assumed that although he was a Jew, the French would not forget his heroism as a French soldier who had been decorated for valor in World War I.

His great-niece Francine Hyafil recalled that in 1940 René tried to visit his brother Léon in Riom, where he had been incarcerated since September 1940, awaiting his trial for treason by the Vichy government. René was refused a visitor's permit and was extremely distraught to think he would never again see Léon. René Blum told his friend René Bruyez: "My brother is ill. I tried to attain an *ausweis*, or permission to visit him." The authorities informed Blum that this would be possible only if he promised never to return. Blum countered that such an action would ultimately be disgraceful. He told Bruyez, "I could not do this as it would seem that I was a coward and that I would flee if I had the chance. I said no. I will stay here."[2]

According to a biographer of Léon Blum, Ilan Greilsammer, René's brother had intended to go to the United States for several months just before war broke out in Europe. René wrote his brother Léon from New York on March 12, 1939, suggesting that a literary agency was interested in publishing Léon's memoirs, but nothing came of this project. That same year, President Franklin Roosevelt invited Léon to visit him at the White House; his bags were packed and he was ready to go, but his friend and fellow Socialist George Mandel advised that, given the prevailing international situation, he was needed in France.[3] Sadly, Mandel was later deported by the Germans to Buchenwald and murdered.

In a brief handwritten journal dated May 19–23, 1940, after his return from America, René wrote poignantly about his life. He was struck by the intractability of his loneliness as idleness and depression overtook him. His account tells how each morning at 8:30 a.m. (very early for him), he shopped for bread, paid his bills, and mailed letters. He confided that he coped by reading and still found joy in returning to Euripides and Greek antiquity. By this time, Monaco and the Monte Carlo casino were occupied by the troops of Vichy France, but as if in an argument with himself, he wrote, "There is still a true France, and the 'Boches' (Germans) will have much to pay."[4] Suddenly, he heard sirens—a possible bomb alert, but he feared arrest if he went to the Red Cross bomb shelter. Paranoia overcame him, but he reassured himself by recalling that only once had he been asked for his identity papers.

The tone of his journal darkened as he described his approach to a very dangerous place, the Gare St. Lazare, where there were many German soldiers. "I'll avoid it by taking a detour," he said. He expressed his longing to visit his small getaway home outside Paris in L'Étang en Ville, where he dreamed about walking freely through the forests. The next day, he complained that his legs hurt as he sat in a church during Mass. Churches were still quiet and relatively safe resting places for the hunted. He praised a good sermon, but bemoaned his deteriorating health. He traveled about Paris by circuitous routes and on one occasion he took the train to St. Cloud, after which, Blum revealed, "There was another alert, and I had to walk home. But all went well."[5] These pages implied that his behavior was not as brazen as some have described and that he tried hard to avoid confrontations with the French police or the German patrols.

Paris was his home, and he continued to go to opening nights at the theatres, to visit his family, and to give solace to the very ill, such as his great friend Édouard Vuillard, who died in June 1940. Despite his tribulations, Blum was not idle; he was working industriously on a film about Molière, as one of his letters to Josette France attested.[6]

A police report in the Archives de la Préfecture dated August 6, 1941, just months before his arrest, simply referred to René Blum as "an Israelite, a bachelor, and the brother of Léon." It gave his address and noted that he lived with the mother of his mistress and their son Claude, a student. It indicated that he conformed to the "German Racial Laws concerning Jews," which meant that he wore a star and did not work in administration to supervise non-Jews. In their observations of him, the police cited a trip that he made in June 1940 to the Midi (the south of France), but stated that he returned and "he is often seen walking between his apartment in the 17th to his office at 60, Rue de la Chaussée d'Antin." The report went on to say that "he was the director of the ballet and the theatre at Monte Carlo and that he made many trips there, but since the arrival of the Germans, and because of the measures made against the Jews, he ceased his 'functions' and no longer goes to Monte Carlo."[7] The end of the report maintained that he was no longer on good terms with his brother Léon, since René did not agree with Léon's politics. It was unlikely that René disagreed with Léon's politics; this may only have been a ruse to divert the attention of the Vichy police.

There were many examples of Nazi brutality. In October 1941, the French Nazis mirrored Kristallnacht, which had occurred on November 9 and 10, 1938, in Germany, by setting fire to seven synagogues in Paris. Although few knew that the Holocaust had already begun viciously in Eastern Europe, the first "Aktion" occurred in the Ukraine on October 28, 1941, when 720 men were rounded up, tortured for 36 hours, forced to dig their own graves, and shot. The writer and poet Daniel Mendelsohn wrote about the town where his family lived: "The Germans were going around with Ukrainian policemen, because at first they had a list. On the list, were the names of prominent Bolechower Jews: doctors, lawyers, and businessmen. The idea was to demoralize the town by eliminating its leading citizens."[8] The same scenario was repeated two months later in Paris when the Germans and their Vichy allies arrested more than seven hundred leading Jewish citizens, including René, and imprisoned them, first in Compiègne and then in Drancy, from where the majority were shipped to death camps.

Georges Wellers, author of a book on the Holocaust in France, *De Drancy à Auschwitz*, wrote that in his three and a half years of captivity, there were many remarkable people in his life, but René Blum in particular stood out. In describing Blum, he wrote: "What equilibrium, harmony and courage, and a great sensibility and profound intelligence as well as a fundamental sincerity and a charming simplicity characterized this very cultivated man."[9] Wellers told the story of Blum's arrest on December 12, 1941. He was picked up at his apartment by a German military policeman accompanied by a French gardien de la paix. The guardian acted as an interpreter and ordered Blum to dress in fifteen minutes and to bring some food, a blanket, his identity papers, and his food-rationing card with him. He was taken to the Municipal Building along with thirty to forty other Jews and then to the École Militaire. There he walked through two lines of Germans who laughed raucously and yelled vicious remarks at the Jewish prisoners. After being kept in a vestibule, he was directed to remain in one of the horse rings at the school. During the morning, more groups were brought in. They were Jews from different quarters of Paris, and they were all French citizens. At the end of the day, the prisoners totaled 743.[10]

Wellers tried to explain their capture on December 12 as a political strike waged by Hitler. Months before, Hitler promised retribution against the Jews if any country declared war against Germany, which indeed happened when the Japanese bombed Pearl Harbor and the United States declared war against Japan and Germany. He described where the prisoners were taken:

> Soon, we met the German chief of Jewish Affairs, Lieutenant SS Dannecker who was railing against some French physicians dressed in French uniforms. There were two powerful German commandants, Danneker and Kuntze who both were fearsome figures. . . . The train left with all of us at 11 pm and in the silence we rolled through the countryside for two hours when we arrived at Compiègne. [11]

Figure 10.1
Plaque honoring 743 French Jews, including René Blum, who were deported to Auschwitz and killed there. Photo by David Bennahum.

At Compiègne, Wellers was introduced to René Blum and described their effort to stay alert, while being held captive, by holding classes of up to one hundred people who would be taught by the "intellectuals" among them. No paper, no pencils, no books were available; the lectures were given without any notes. Blum quickly became one of the most renowned presenters, as Wellers explained:

> His language was admirably lucid, elegant and always spiritual; his thinking was profound, elevated, generous and his manner full of simplicity and nobility. He loved to speak about the *Fables* of La Fontaine; he was knowledgeable without having one note of text. He filled his talks with stories about ballet and his role in forming his company, and his contact with ballet designers, composers and dancers since he was a youth at the *Revue Blanche*. [12]

When Blum lectured on the Russian ballet, he also criticized prison policies and the captives' wretched treatment. The next morning, he was chastised as it was perilous to speak negatively of the authorities. Blum responded: "Yes, twelve people have already been to tell me I was wrong.... Perhaps I was, I easily get worked up. I am not always master of myself when I am speaking."[13]

Wellers remembered that Blum lauded the role Russia was playing in the war against the Germans and proclaimed his conviction that the Germans would be defeated. Several prisoners tried to warn him that "mouchards" or informers were among them, and cautioned him to be more prudent. He responded: "Do you really think they would arrest me?"

During the winter at Compiègne, a minimum of a hundred deaths occurred in the camp from cold, lack of care, and starvation. Among them were some "scoundrels and miscreants" who abused the other prisoners by stealing food from the kitchen and withholding it from reaching people who were starving, and who also seized possession of the few clandestine goods that prisoners coveted, such as liquor and cigarettes. Most of the prisoners lacked the energy or the character to fight them. René Blum, starving, emaciated, and sick but with a determined sense of moral authority, assumed the job of identifying and accusing the thieves. They refused to admit their guilt, but Blum's strong center and gravitas caused others to refrain from committing the same acts. René earned the reputation of a man with the highest ethical standards.[14]

During the course of research, Rowson Davis discovered an anonymous letter dated November 22, 1961, which honored the memory of Gregory Sedoï, a fellow captive at Compiègne.[15] It documented his imprisonment from 1941 to 1942 in a hidden encampment surrounded by high barbed-wire fences. In the narrative, the anonymous writer indicated that he met

Sedoï when he escaped his quarters and miraculously avoided the patrols, dogs, and all the lookouts in order to bring food to fellow inmates who were starving.

Sedoï knew that René Blum intended to write a memoir that would be a witness to those appalling days. He declared that "by some sort of miracle, several of us have been spared, so that we can disclose the story of these very cruel and odious times at Compiègne; they were just a debut to the terrifying steps to Auschwitz and toward the definitive horrors."[16]

The prisoners' daily ration was one piece of bread; it barely kept them alive through the night. In the morning, they received a bowl of what might have been called soup, but was only water with a few pieces of carrot and a few grams of vermicelli thrown in. Occasionally, a small cube of margarine was added.

The "giving of the bread" became a very serious rite. The bread was cut equally and then passed out. One day, an elderly man burst out in anger when he saw a few tiny crumbs that had been overlooked. He was told that he could have them, so he gathered them avidly and ate what in reality were only small splinters of wood. Later in the evening, he cried out from stomach pain. One of the inmates purchased a can of herring from a German guard for an extravagant price and he shared it with the elderly professor who by that point was raving. The complaints were silenced and the dignified engineering professor, who was known far and wide, finally recovered his bearings.

The same writer painted a sad picture of his roommate, René Blum, who became quite ill in the concentration camp. Every evening Blum would try to lift himself from the straw floor mat and put his painful, swollen feet into shoes hardened from the cold. Blum would sigh and then make his way outdoors, leaving a burst of cold air behind. He continued this narrative, "Half asleep, I spied his silhouette in the light diffusing from the corridor, then the door closed and the sound of his footsteps disappeared as he made his way toward the latrines."[17]

The description disclosed the difficulties Blum had to endure as he made his way through the filth and smells, and then the same miserable return. "At the end of a long moment, we would hear Blum approaching, then the same screeching door, followed by the cold wind on my face. I opened my eyes to see the same fugitive image pass by my feet in the penumber."[18]

They heard more sighs as Blum tried to comfort himself from the severe pain in his feet, which resulted from an acute protein deficiency or perhaps heart failure. The narrator commented that "his breathing eventually seemed to reach its rhythm of sleep and he found some peace. But not for very long, because several times in the course of the night Blum had to go through the same exhausting challenges, with their continuous and unchanging certainty."[19]

"Never," the writer proclaimed, "did we hear one complaint from René Blum. He was a continuous ray of light that sustained our hope and our confidence. He thought always of others before himself. Many other anguished images often return to me. I know that in spite of the many deaths that occurred there, especially of the sickest and weakest, it is I who was spared these horrors and at a time when I had no idea really of the grave dangers surrounding me."[20]

In *The Camp of Slow Death* by Jean-Jacques Bernard, we learn more details about Blum's incarceration. Bernard, the son of Tristan Bernard, arrived at the enormous expanse of camps at Compiègne (in Royallieu near Paris) at the same time as Blum. The morale of the Frenchmen, Bernard recounted, "brutally snatched from their daily life and affections, however, remained on the whole very high. Very few admitted, 'If only I had known.'"[21]

When Bernard met Blum, he brought him to his cellblock that held thirty-five men. He noted that a small group of acolytes surrounded Blum—clerks, young workmen, and others who admired him and his brother Léon. Blum was adored for his courage, kindness, and affection and the younger men tried to care for him.

Blum was sixty-four years old and ill. Yet he worried about his friends and thought constantly of Bernard's health. Everyone acknowledged his stoicism, but it was evident how much he suffered from the wretchedness around him. Even when he was in severe discomfort, he smiled affably. A disheartening story was told of a young man in the block who had been torn from his dead mother's bedside for no reason. Blum consoled him, "We must keep a record of all these things."[22]

Blum's block included a high proportion of foreigners, while Bernard's bunk was full of angry Frenchmen. They allied themselves with the French nation and considered themselves French above their Jewish-ness. Bernard said to Blum, "Let it be understood that if I have to die in this place, I shall have died for France; I don't want to be claimed by Judaism as a martyr."[23]

Others, Central European foreigners who identified themselves as Jews and Zionists, sought hope in France, but wanted a Jewish homeland or state. It was they who Bernard and probably Blum believed fed right into the hands of the Nazi propaganda that all Jews were foreigners. With surprising scorn for their Zionist ideals, Bernard called them "frightful wretches lost to the Jewish cause."[24]

Although Bernard displayed disdain for these prisoners' longing for a Jewish state, nonetheless, he was dismayed that the Central Europeans had been treated shabbily by France. He admitted, "However, it was impossible to tear France out of our hearts."[25] At the time of the Dreyfus trial, and even long after, assimilated French-born Jews had difficulty accepting the fact that anti-Semitism persisted in much of Christian France, not to speak of Germany, Poland, and elsewhere in Europe.

When Bernard and René Blum gave literature lectures to their fellow prisoners, they relied on their memories from earlier school days and were able to paint a picture of French poetry from the sixteenth century to the Symbolists. They owned only one book by La Fontaine. They taught for two evenings, but sudden lapses in memory, telltale signs of starvation, often left them incapacitated. Before their internment, poetry had been at their fingertips.

Bernard began to feel very weak; walking and climbing steps were practically impossible. Because he was not eating meat or other protein, his health was dwindling. A biscuit or a piece of chocolate, although not the best nutrition, was considered a magnificent "meal." When Bernard visited with René, he tried to offer Blum a bar of chocolate. Blum protested at first, but after a little walk and some conversation, he asked if Bernard would mind if he ate the whole bar at once.

Everyone knew Blum was a sick man. After he'd been at Compiègne for only one month, Blum's friends begged him to go to the infirmary. When Bernard also encouraged him to go, René repeated his statement that he was the brother of Léon and therefore held a special position. In truth, he was close to death and was finally excused from roll call. Permission to stay in bed was required from the camp doctors, and without it, the Germans became furious. This, in turn, caused dire consequences for other prisoners.

Blum requested such permission and stayed in bed for two or three weeks. When he was so sick that he could not leave his room, he summoned the doctors and instead of speaking for himself, told them how ill Bernard was. Soon after, a doctor went to visit Bernard at his bedside and sent him to the infirmary for Russian internees where better care was available.[26]

The Russian infirmary was heaven. Bernard wrote that this transfer was essential to his survival. Those sent there were fed soup twice a day and their prison stay was considered bearable. Bernard could barely walk or gather his belongings at this point, but he paid Blum a final visit. Blum reassured Bernard that he too would join him at the infirmary if his health continued to decline. Illustrative of Blum's typical good nature, he warranted: "Anyway, I am sure that we will be dining together in Paris before a month is up."[27] Bernard was released and sent back to his family.

Unfortunately, Blum was sent to Drancy on March 19, 1942, along with 150 others over the age of fifty-five. Originally, he thought he was going to be released from prison and told George Wellers that he would visit Wellers's wife the next day, but he was not liberated.

On March 26, a group of 550 prisoners were deported to Auschwitz. The next day, 1,050 men were sent—half from Compiègne and half from Drancy. Those were the first Jews deported from France.[28] Soon it was Wellers's turn to be deported. René went to see the head of the camp and tried to stop his deportation, but to no avail. Blum spoke to Wellers with tears streaming down his face:

> It is ignoble. It is shameful to have to remain a powerless witness to such horrors. If one day I get out of here, I will fly to America, to Russia and everywhere in order to tell this story, how they treated people who have caused no harm to anyone, and who often have committed many acts of kindness. Listen well and tell everyone that we must hold on and we must not despair. All the same, humanity cannot possibly be as villainous as these Germans.[29]

These words deeply affect all of us who know the truth about those years.

Wellers was lucky. He was sent back to Compiègne and to the same barracks, three weeks after he left there. Eventually, he returned to Drancy where he again met with Blum. Wellers was saved with eighty others because they were married to Aryans, which under the racial laws offered some exceptions. Wellers ventured a visit to Blum whose legs by then were enormously swollen, and he asked how all of this could be happening. With his usual sensitivity, Blum intuited that his friends had been deported. Wellers, who had witnessed the move, began to narrate the saddest moments. When he finished his story, Blum was silent. Finally, he said, "There are crimes which have no name. I have only one consolation; this ignominy is German. Never would the French be capable of such crimes. The more hate one feels toward the Germans, the more one is proud to be French."[30]

Wellers warned Blum about his outbursts: "This is impossible; everyone knows you; they hate your brother Léon, whom they feel had done so much wrong to France; the inspectors and the gendarmes know you, Rothke and Heinrichsohn come through here often. Do everything you can to make yourself forgotten by them."[31]

That spring, four thousand Jewish children arrived at the prison and Wellers was forced to take care of them. At the end of the summer, he asked René for guidance and to visit the children with him. They entered a barracks with 110 children between two and twelve years of age. Women monitors washed them with cold water, without soap, and wiped them dry with dirty towels. Their bodies were covered with inflamed red marks from lice and their living quarters were suffocating, full of filthy odors. Wellers began a heartbreaking story:

> We noticed a young boy of seven or eight years with a head full of beautiful curls, a torn shirt so that his chest was exposed, and one shoe missing from his right foot. "What is your name, little one?" asked Blum. "Jacques Stern, M'sieu." Blum continued, "How old are you?" The child responded, "Seven years, M'sieu." Blum tried to engage him in conversation, "Oh my, you are a very big boy! Do you live in Paris? What do your parents do,

my child?" The boy looked at them very directly and answered, "Papa goes to the office, and mommy plays piano. She plays very well, you know. M'sieu, when can we leave this place?" Blum tried to comfort him, "Why, do you want to go so quickly?" Of course, the boy said, "I want to see my maman." Blum looked at Wellers with dismay. He said to the child, "Don't worry my child, you will soon join your maman after tomorrow." "Is that a long time, m'sieu? Look what I have to give to maman."[32]

The child showed them a cookie shaped like a soldier that had been distributed to all the children as if it were a special gift. He had chewed on the corners of the cookie, but saved the rest in his vest pocket. The child burst suddenly into tears and Blum held him close to his chest.

Nearby were two sisters who lay on a bed on the floor. The oldest was twelve and the other was four or five. The younger one was sleeping in her excrement. She woke up and looked fearfully at Blum and Wellers until she saw the Jewish star on their clothes. She held a page from a German newspaper, *Le Cri du Peuple*, dated August 28, 1942. Blum noticed that the paper was German and asked her about it. She cried out: "I no longer want to be French. The French are evil, I detest them."[33] She was stoic and her eyes were without tears. Blum reminded her that it was the Germans who did terrible things. She answered angrily, "Not true, it's the French who came for us, who heard my little sister and took her; they then came to get me at school." Blum spoke gently and said that they were the French who sold themselves to the Germans, and that they had become Germans themselves. Blum tried to calm her, "True French are as revolted by these actions as we are. But sadly, at the moment, they cannot do anything."[34] The child asked Blum and Wellers to leave because she wanted to sleep.

They went outside where the air was fresh and walked across the courtyard in silence. Wellers said to Blum, "I suppose that this visit is enough to show you what goes on here. If you wish to return, please tell me." Wellers continued, "Blum remained quiet. His mouth was trembling and he seemed deathly pale. We shook hands and he dragged himself to his stairway. He never asked to return to the children."[35]

Drancy could not sustain the number of its French prisoners and the authorities decided to send many of them to Pithiviers, which became a gathering place for two thousand French prisoners. Deportations became inevitable, and finally, René Blum was among them. He had stopped eating, his raincoat was torn, and his face was covered with dirt. His hair and mustache had been shaven. "He said, very quietly, that going to Pithiviers meant imminent death. When he left, the guards murmured, 'There is Blum. He is the brother of Léon.'"[36] Wellers and Blum embraced as he walked toward the prison exit in a slow, very determined walk. Wellers recalled that "later, at Auschwitz, some friends told me that René Blum was taken alone by the Germans immediately from the train. They knew not what became of him."[37]

Different stories have been offered about Blum's last day of life. Some say that he was immediately taken off the train to Pithiviers and killed. Others insist he was shot to death. A letter to Janet Rowson Davis on April 18, 1978, from the Sécrétaire d'État aux Anciens Combattants that consulted the German government about Blum's demise, states simply that Monsieur Blum was transferred first to Beaune-la-Rolande on September 20, 1942, and then to Drancy several days later where he was shipped to his death.

Ilan Greilsammer, in his book on Léon Blum, gives another account: from Pithiviers, Blum left on the convoy train (transport 901/31) along with a thousand other Jews, on September 23, 1942. A telegram to Adolphe Eichmann signaled his presence as the brother of the former president of the Conseil français.[38] Greilsammer continued his narrative: "An SS officer yelled, 'Where is the Jew René Blum?' when the train entered the Birkenau station. He was taken from there to an unknown destination."[39] His brother Léon, in his efforts to find out what happened to René, wrote to an authority who researched these questions after the war ended in 1945. He contacted Dr. S. Steinberg, former chief of medicine at Drancy, who was also a survivor of Auschwitz. Steinberg reported the following story. He knew a prisoner named Samuel Jankowski who was deported from France in April 1942 and who worked in the crematorium 100 meters from the entrance to Auschwitz. Greilsammer recounted that "Jankowski heard that on the evening of September 23rd, the SS took Blum into the courtyard of the crematorium and undressed him and threw him into an oven where he was burned alive with other corpses."[40] Steinberg swore that Jankowski told the truth. But Blum's family never acknowledged that this letter existed.

As this author discovered the gradual disintegration of this generous and courageous man, it has colored all that she learned and knows about Blum's life as a writer, critic, and producer. It is more than we can bear that such a marvelous person could be killed, as were so many millions, and begs us to question the human capacity for cowardice and cruelty. His accomplishments have perhaps been forgotten precisely because the world responded too late to injustice. In that sense, René Blum should stand as a reminder of what a creative life can be.

EPILOGUE

LÉON BLUM

Léon Blum was arrested on September 15, 1940, and sent to detention in the sixteenth-century Chateau Chazeron. After a period of time, he was moved to Bouressol, where he remained throughout his trial at Riom, which began February 20, 1942. Gestapo agents took control of the prison at Bouressol on March 15, 1943. Blum was then flown to Buchenwald, where he remained for the duration of the war with his wife. After the war, Léon became head of the French government, from December 1946 to January 1947, and continued to wield strong political influence until his death in 1950. His son Robert spent the war in a German prisoner of war camp, but emerged to begin a new life in the automobile and aviation industry.

FRANCINE HYAFIL

Francine narrowly escaped losing her life. She had befriended several young men in Paris who were involved dangerously in the Resistance. She was arrested, with her mother, and sent to prison for several months. Freed by a righteous German woman who worked for her father and who swore that Francine was innocent of any clandestine acts, Francine and her mother were fortunate enough to be released, but lived through some very frightening times when she and her family were in hiding. Francine sadly admitted to this author that she had lost out on her chance of becoming a pharmacist, as the Occupation prevented her from attending school. Unfortunately, the Vichy government had imposed a statute on October 4, 1940, that required one to prove "genealogically" that one was French in order to enter many professions. During those trying years, Francine did meet the love of her life, Marc Hyafil, whom she later married. She still marvels at how lucky she was not to lose her parents or her brother.

Her grandfather, Lucien Blum, was forced to resign his job at the Paris-France department store on July 14, 1941. Francine mentioned that "it was l'Oncle René's Christian friend, Jacques Richet, who helped my grandfather."[1] Richet was a charming and courageous man, and with great delicacy and friendship he offered support to her very chagrined grandpa. We do not know if he provided money, but her family, as well as that of her great-uncle Marcel Blum, were able to go into hiding in the Zone Libre and survived the war.

FRANÇOISE NORDMANN

Françoise's war history was less fortunate than Francine's, which evoked great sadness as we spoke. Her father Georges Blum stayed in Paris during the early years of the Occupation and there led a very tense and agitated life. He died in a tragic elevator accident, while her mother Germaine, in another ghastly turn of events, was later picked up almost by accident by Germans who had come to take a different woman, but when they determined that Germaine was also a Jewish woman, they sent her to her death at Auschwitz.

Figure 11.1
Claude René Blum, who died heroically on the battlefield, April 17, 1945. Courtesy of Arts du Spectacle, Bibliothèque Nationale.

CLAUDE-RENÉ BLUM

Claude-René, the son of Josette France and René Blum, wrote his last will and testament in 1943 when he decided to enlist in the army. He joined the Assault Troops of General LeClerc's army and died gloriously for France on April 17, 1945; he was just twenty years old. Apparently, he destroyed a German machine gun post, and like his father and uncle, he received the Croix de Guerre for bravery under fire. He died in the village of Gundelfingen, on the way to Munich. The war ended a few weeks after he was killed.

JOSETTE FRANCE

In 1940, Josette played a minor role in the movie *Face au Destin* directed by Henri Fescourt, and in 1943, she acted the principal role of Zerbina in the film *Capitaine Fracasse*, directed by Abel Gance, and was also one of the movie's producers. She continued to work in films and to take on positions of authority for large film organizations, such as production manager and producer. She acquired the publishing house Éditions Choumine from René Blum, and later founded her own Éditions Josette France, which published musical scores and libretti connected to cinematic production. She also translated and wrote subtitles for films, especially those in Italian. She died at the age of eighty-eight in Picardie.

Productions in Monte Carlo, 1924–1939

This list of productions includes straight plays, comedies, films, operas, operettas, and ballets at the Théâtre de Monte Carlo. The word "Création" is meant only to indicate the first performance in Monte Carlo, not its premiere debut. According to George Dorris, the British plays were quite up to date, having had recent West End shows. The lists for theatre productions, operas, and ballets may be incomplete.

PLAYS, MUSICAL COMEDIES, OPERETTAS, OPERAS, AND FILMS

1924–1925

La Corinthienne by Raoul Charbonnel (Création), Music by Francis Casadesus, Starring Madeleine Roch, Henry Mayer, Jean Hervé, and Louis Ravet, December 19, 1924.

La Beaute du Diable by Jacques Deval (Création), Starring Madeleine Renaud and M. Roger Gaillard, December 24, 1924.

Les Bulles de Savon by V.-A. Jager-Schmidt, Starring Jeanne Provost and Harry Baur, December 30, 1924.

Henri IV by Luigi Pirandello, January 3, 1925.

La Griffe by Henry Bernstein, January 6, 1925.

Le Gendre de M. Poirier by E. Augier and Sandeau, January 11, 1925.

Les Bleus de L'Amour by Romain Coolus, Music by Victor Alix, November 14, 1925.

Le Couvre-Feu by Boussac de Saint-Marc, November 25, 1925.

L'Homme du Destin by George Bernard Shaw, French Version, November 25, 1925.

Destinée, Film by Henry Roussell, Music by André Gailhard, November 28, 1925.

Un Mari Idéal by Oscar Wilde (Création), December 5, 1925.

Bertrand de Born by Raoul Charbonnel (Création), Music by Francis Casadesus, December 12, 1925.

La Viveuse et Le Moribond by François de Curel (Création), December 29, 1925.

1926–1927

Le Roi des Schnorrers by Israel Zangwill, Music by Octave Crémieux, January 5, 1926.

L'Âme en Peine by Jean-Jacques Bernard (Création), Starring Ludmilla Pitoeff, January 12, 1926.

Qui Êtes-Vous? by Paul Gavault and Georges Berr (Création), Music by Charles Cuvillier, November 13, 1926.

Le Marchand de Lunettes by Georges Delaquys (Création), Music by Marcel Delannoy, November 20, 1926.

La Grande Cathérine by George Bernard Shaw (Création), Music by Rimsky-Korsakoff and Mussorgsky, November 27, 1926.

7, Rue de la Paroisse by Rober Ferdinand (Création), November 27, 1926.

Carmen, a Film by Jacques Feyder after Mérimée, Music by Ernesto Halffter Escriche, December 2, 1926.

Jazz by Marcel Pagnol (Création), Starring Harry Baur, December 9, 1926.

Au Grand Large (Outward Bound) by H. Sutton Vane (Création), Starring Louis Jouvet's Company, December 16, 1926.

Démétrios by Jules Romains, December 16, 1926.

Lorenzaccio by Alfred de Musset (Création), December 23, 1926.

Le Chevalier à la Rose by Hugo Von Hoffmansthal (Création), Opera by Richard Strauss, January 13, 1927.

Chanson D'Amour by Hugues Delorme and Léon Abric, Comédie Musicale, Music by Franz Schubert, November 15, 1927.

Miche by Etienne Rey (Création), November 29, 1927.

Pas Une Secousse by Romain Coolus and Henry-Jacques (Création), Music by Victor Alix, December 6, 1927.

Choisir by André Charmel (Création), December 17, 1927.

La Valse de l'Adieu, Film by Henry Rousell, Based on the Life of Frederic Chopin, December 20, 1927.

Dans les Orangers by Henry Ferrare (Création), Music by Albeniz and Turina, December 25, 1927.

Le Messie d'Amour by Raoul Charbonnel (Création), Music by Francis Casadesus, January 5, 1928.

Le Condottiere by Pierre-Paul and Henry Turpin (Création), November 27, 1928.

Le Souper Interrompu by P. J. Toulet (Création), with the Théâtre du Rideau, December 4, 1928.

Le Retour de L'Enfant Prodique by André Gide (Création), with the Théâtre du Rideau, Music by Claude Debussy, December 4, 1928.

L'Auberge de la Poste by Carlo Goldoni (Création), with Marcel Herrand's Théâtre du Rideau, December 4, 1928.

L'Aube, Le Jour and *La Nuit* by Dario Niccodemi, December 9, 1928.

Chez les Chiens by Alfred Savoir, December 9, 1928.

Bretagne by André Dumas (Création), Music by Francis Casadesus, December 15, 1928.

Carmosine after Alfred de Musset, by Charles Monselet and Eugène Adenis, Comédie Musicale, Music by Ferdinand Poise, December 22, 1928.

Rose-Marie by Otto Harbach and Oscar Hammerstein, Comédie Musicale, Music by Rudolf Friml and Herbert Stothart, with 40 Mogador Girls and Boys, January 19, 1929.

Hélène en Égypte by Richard Strauss, January 23, 1929.

Une Nuit á Vénise by Johann Strauss, January 23, 1929.

L'Équipage by Georges Delance (after the book by Joseph Kessel) (Création), Music by Ph. Parès and G. Van Parys, December 3, 1929.

The First Mrs. Fraser by St. John Ervine (Création), with Edward Stirling's Company, December 19, 1929.

La Tempête (*The Tempest*) by William Shakespeare (Création), Translated by Guy de Portalès, Music by Arthur Honegger, December 26, 1929.

Zaïde by Jean Chantavoine, Based on the Opera by Mozart (Création), January 4, 1930.

Le Mariage by Gogol (Création), and Translated by Raoul d'Harcourt, Based on the Opera by Mussorgsky, January 4, 1930.

Le Capitaine Fracasse (after the novel by Théophile Gautier), by Paul Ferrier and René Bergeret (René Blum) (Création), Music by Mario Costa, December 9, 1930.

Le Chant du Désert, Based on the Operetta by Sigmund Romberg, French Version by Roger Ferréol and Saint Granier, n.d.

Boccace, Operetta by F. De Suppé, French Version by H. Chivot and A. Duru, December 2, 1930.

Les P'tites Michu, Operetta by Henry Meilhac and Albert Millaud, Music by Hervé, November 15, 1930.

La Poupée, Operetta by Maurice Ordonneau, Music by Edmond Audran, November 16, 1930.

Mam'zelle Nitouche, Operetta by Henry Meilhac and Albert Millaud, Music by Hervé, November 18, 1930.

La Belle Hélène, Operetta by Offenbach, Lyrics by Henry Meilhac and Ludovic Halévy, November 27, 1930.

Le Jour et la Nuit, Operetta by Albert Vanloo and E. Leterrier, Music by Charles LeCocq, n.d.

Rip, Operetta by Henri Meilhac and Philippe Gille, Music by Robert Planquette, n.d.

Véronique, Operetta by Albert Vanloo and Georges Duval, Music by André Messager, n.d.

On Ne Saurait Penser à Tout, No Author Indicated, December 16, 1930.

L'Amour Medecin by Molière, December 16, 1930.

On the Spot by Edgar Wallace, December 18, 1930, Mystery, Opened in London, April 1930.

The Silent Witness by Jack de Leon and Jack Celestin, December 20, 1930, Opened in London, April 30, 1930.

Arms and the Man by George Bernard Shaw, December 21, 1930.

The Vulture, an English Production by John Pollak, December 28, 1930.

Saint Joan by George Bernard Shaw, January 1, 1931.

La Belle Hélène, Operetta by Jacques Offenbach, January 3, 1931.

Le Chant du Desert, Operetta by Sigmund Romberg, January 8, 1931.

L'Arlésienne by Alphonse Daudet, January 13, 1931.

Le Loup, Based on a Play by Molnar, by Denys Amiel (Création), n.d.

Amants by Maurice Donnay, n.d.

1931–1932

Les Amours du Poéte by R. Blum and G. Delaquys, Music by R. Schumann, Choreography by G. Balanchine, January 5, 1932.

English Repertory Productions at the Théâtre des Beaux-Arts

To See Ourselves by E. M. Delafield (Création), February 1, 1932, Opened in London, December 11, 1930.

Counsel's Opinion by Gilbert Wakefield, February 3, 1932, Opened in London, August 26, 1931.

Payment Deferred by Jeffrey Dell, February 5, 1932, Opened in London, May 4, 1931.

Candida by George Bernard Shaw, February 7, 1932.

People Like Us by Frank Vosper, February 8, 1932, Opened in London, March 11, 1929.

Arms and the Man by George Bernard Shaw, February 10, 1932.

The Second Man by S. N. Behrman, February 17, 1932, Opened in New York, November 1927, in London, April 28, 1928.

Big Business, No Author Indicated (Création), February 22, 1932.

The Mollusc by Hubert Henry Davies, February 28, 1932, Opened in London, October 23, 1928.

Gala de L'Humour par l'extraordinaire humoriste, Betove, April 4, 1932.

1933

English Comedies

Musical Chairs by Ronald Mackenzie, January 5, 1933, Opened in London, November 15, 1931.

While Parents Sleep by Anthony Kimmins, January 7, 1933.

The Green Pack by Edgar Wallace, January 8, 1933.

The Soul of Nicholas Snyders by Jerome K. Jerome, January 10, 1933.

1934

Theatre and Operetta

Anthony and Anna, January 16, 1934.

L'Auberge du Cheval Blanc and *Les Biches,* January 17, 1934.

L'Auberge du Cheval blanc, January 18, 20, and 21, 1934.

Les Brigands, Operetta by Offenbach, December 27, 29, and 30, 1934.

1935

English Comedy Season

The Maitlands by Ronald Mackenzie, January 5, 1935.

The Village Wooing by Bernard Shaw, *The Dark Lady of the Sonnets* by Bernard Shaw, and *Waterloo* by Sir Arthur Conan Doyle, January 8, 1935.

Franz Liszt by Robins Millar, January 10, 1935.
The Private Road by John Carlton, January 12, 1935.
Le Nouveau Testament by Sacha Guitry, January 17, 1935.

Operas

La Chauve-Souris by Johann Strauss, January 1, 3, and 6, 1935.
Faust with Dancer Mlle. Lorcia, March 23, 1935.
Samson and Delila, March 24, 1935.
Madame Butterfly, March 26, 1935.
Siegfried in German, March 30 and 31, 1935.

BALLET PRODUCTIONS AND DANCERS

1928

December 22: Lecomte de Lisle's *Parfums Antiques* with choreography by Mme. Nevelskaya from the Théâtre Moscou.

1929

Ida Rubinstein's Repertory

January 10: Rubinstein performed the following works—Nijinska's *Les Noces de Psyché and de l'Amour*—along with Massine's *David* by the composer Sauget, Nijinska's *Bolero* by Ravel, *La Bien Aimée* by Schubert and Michaut. Rubinstein also performed *Nocturne* by Borodine, Nijinska's "Princesse Cygne" from *Le Tsar Sultan* by Rimsky Korsakov, *La Valse* by Ravel choreographed by Nijinska with décors by Benois, and Nijinska's *Les Enchantements de la Fée Alcine, Le Baiser de la Fée* by Igor Stravinsky, after *Contes d'Anderson.*

1930

Dancers and Operas

Many of the dancers working with the touring ballet companies in Monte Carlo also performed in the operas, including *Manon, La Traviata,* and *Carmen.* Here is a list of the dancers who performed from January 23 to April 8: Maître de Ballet, Paul Petrov; Mlles.: Darvasch, Natalia Branitska, Tatiana Chamié, Ludmilla Schollar, Choulgina, Alexandra Danilova, Goulet, Klemetska, Maikerska, Alicia Markova, Eleanora Marra, Miklachovska,

Lara Obidenna, Sonia Pavlova, Mia Slavinska, Toumankova, Lubov Tchernicheva, and Vera Zorina; Mns.: Rupert Doone, Michel Federov, Jan Hoyer, Kocharovsky, Marian Ladré, Lapitsky, Lisanevich, and Anatole Vilzak.

The operas performed included: *Madame Butterfly, Mefistofole, Walkiere, Rigoletto, Barbiere de Seviglia, Die Agyptische, Hélène, La Bohème, Quo Vadis, Turandot, La Damnation de Faust, Carmen, Boris Goudenov, Eine Nacht in Venedig, Tosca, Satan—Faust,* and *Don Quichotte.*

Mme. Vera Nemtchinova

April 24: *Le Lac des Cygnes, Aubade, Suite de Danses,* and *Islamey.* April 27: *La Reine des Ombres, Quatuor* (Création), *Suite de Danses,* and *Grande Couture.* April 29: *Le Lac des Cygnes, Quatuor, Aubade, Suite de Danses,* and *Grande Couture.* May 1: *La Reine des Ombres, Quatuor, Suite de Danses, Grande Couture,* and *Islamey.*

1931

Boris Kniaseff

On January 18, Kniaseff returned with his company to interpret *Rendez-vous manqué* to music by Debussy, *Jeux d'automne* to music by J. Satz, *La Légende de Beriozka* to music by Konstantinoff, and *Tzigane airs populaires romains et russe,* choreographed by Boris Kniaseff. On January 19, the troupe performed *Rêverie lunaire, Rendez-vous manqué, Obsession, Au temps des tartars* to music by Spendiarov; on January 20, it performed *Mascarade* to music by Schumann, *Jeux d'automne, la Légende de Beriozka,* and *Au temps des Tartares.* Kniaseff himself performed on April 10, with *Mascarade* by Schumann, *Devant le Sphinx* by Arensky, *Legendes de Berioska,* and *Rêverie Lunaire,* and *Au Temps des Tartares.* On April 11, the company did *Tosca* and *Prince Igor Dances* with Danilova, Tchernicheva, and Vilzak. Kniaseff returned on April 14 with *Rêverie Lunaire, Le Temple Abandonné* (Création), *Devant le Sphinx,* and *Tziganes;* on April 15: *Mascarade, Légende de Bérioska, Au Temps des Tartares,* and *Obsession;* on April 16: *Le Temple abandonné* to music by Max d'Ollone, *Légende de Beriozka, Obsession,* and *Tziganes.*

Ballets Performed by the Théâtre de l'Opéra de Paris

Soir de Fête choreographed by Léo Staats, to music by Delibes; *Impressions de music-hall* choreographed by Bronislava Nijinska, to music by Gabriel

Pierné, with costumes by Maxime Dethomas; *Les Deux Pigéons* choreo-graphed by Albert Aveline, to music by Messager; *La Nuit Ensorcelée* choreographed by Léo Staats, to music by Chopin, with a décor by Léon Bakst; *La Tragédie de Salomé* choreographed by Nicolas Guerra, to music by Florent Schmitt, with costumes by René Piot; *Coppélia* choreographed by Arthur Saint-Léon, to music by Delibes, with the soloists Carlotta Zam-belli, Camille Bos, Suzanne Lorcia, MM.Aveline, Peretti, and the corps de ballet. Several days later, the National Ballet Company of Lithuania starring Vera Nemtchinova performed *Aubade* and *Islamey*.

Ballets Performed by the Ballet de l'Opéra Russe à Paris

On April 25: *Le rêve de Ratmir-Pulcinella—Danses Polovtsiennes du Prince Igor;* on April 26: *Pulcinella, L'Amour Sorcier,* and *Danses Polovtsiennes du Prince Igor;* on April 28: *Le rêve de Ratmir-Chout (Le Buffon)* and *L'Amour sorcier;* on April 30: *Pulcinella, Danses Polovtsiennes du Prince Igor,* and *L'Amour sorcier;* on May 2: *Chout (Le Buffon), L'Amour sorcier,* and *Divertisse-ment;* on May 3: *Le rêve de Ratmir, Chout (Le Buffon),* and *Divertissement.*

1932

Ballets Performed by the Ballets Russes de Monte Carlo in Monte Carlo

April 12: *Les Sylphides, La Concurrence* (Création), and *Cotillon;* April 14: *La Concurrence, Jeux d'Enfants* (Création), and *Les Sylphides;* April 16: *Chout, Jeux d'Enfants,* and *Cotillon;* April 17: *Chout, Les Sylphides,* and *La Concurrence;* April 19: *Jeux d'Enfants, Petrouchka,* and *Cotillon;* April 21: *Chout, Le Lac des Cygnes,* and *Petrouchka;* April 23: *Le Lac des Cygnes, L'Amour Sorcier,* and *La Concurrence;* April 24: *Petrouchka, La Concurrence,* and *Les Sylphides;* April 26: *Les Sylphides, La Concurrence,* and *Jeux d'Enfants;* April 28: *Chout, Le Lac des Cygnes,* and *L'Amour Sorcier;* April 30: *Pet-rouchka, Pulcinella,* and *Cotillon;* May 1: *Pulcinella, Jeux d'Enfants,* and *Co-tillon;* May 3: *Pulcinella, Le Bourgeois Gentilhomme* (Création), and *Le Lac des Cygnes;* May 5: *Cotillon, La Concurrence,* and *Suite de Danses.*

1933

Ballets Performed by the Ballets Russes de Monte Carlo in Monte Carlo

April 12 and April 16: *Les Sylphides, Les Présages* (Création), and *Petrouchka;* April 15: *Les Sylphides, Le Beau Danube* (Création), and *Concurrence;* April

17: *Cotillon, Le Beau Danube,* and *Concurrence;* April 18: *Cotillon, Beach* (Création), and *Le Beau Danube;* April 20: *Le Lac des Cygnes, Beach,* and *Le Beau Danube;* April 22: *Cotillon, Les Matelots,* and *Les Présages;* April 25: *Le Lac des Cygnes, Scuola di Ballo* (Création), and *Petrouchka;* April 27: *Les Matelots, Jeux d'Enfants,* and *Le Beau Danube;* April 29: *Concurrence, Scuola di Ballo,* and *Petrouchka;* April 30: *Jeux d'Enfants, Beach,* and *Scuola di Ballo;* May 2: *Les Matelots, Scuola di Ballo,* and *Les Présages;* May 4: *Cotillon, Beach,* and *Jeux d'Enfants:* May 6: *Les Matelots, Scuola di Ballo,* and *Jeux d'Enfants;* May 7: *Le Lac des Cygnes, Les Matelots,* and *Le Beau Danube;* May 9: *Le Lac des Cygnes,* Les Présages, and *Le Beau Danube.*

1934

Ballets Performed by the Ballets Russes de Monte-Carlo in Monte Carlo

April 7: *Scuola di Ballo, Variations,* and *Boléro;* April 8: *Le Lac des Cygnes, Variations,* and *Boléro;* April 10 and April 15: *Scuola di Ballo, Étude,* and *Danses Polovtsiennes du Prince Igor;* April 12: *Les Sylphides, Scuola di Ballo,* and *Boléro;* April 14: *Étude, Les Biches,* and *Boléro;* April 17: *Le Lac des Cygnes, Les Biches,* and *Variations;* April 19: *Étude, Petrouchka,* and *Boléro;* April 21: *Les Sylphides, Carnaval,* and *Scuola di Ballo;* April 22: *Les Biches, Petrouchka,* and *Carnaval;* April 24: *Le Lac des Cygnes, Les Comédiens Jaloux,* and *Variations;* April 26: *Les Sylphides, Les Comédiens Jaloux,* and *Carnaval;* April 28: *Petrouchka, L'Oiseau de Feu,* and *Danses Polovtsiennes du Prince Igor;* April 29: *Les Sylphides, Les Comédiens Jaloux,* and *L'Oiseau de Feu;* May 1: *Le Lac des Cygnes, Étude,* and *Carnaval;* May 3: *Varations, L'Oiseau de Feu,* and *Boléro.*

1935

Ballets Performed by the Ballet de l'Opéra National Lithuanien

January 16 and 20: *Carnaval* (Fokine), *Les Fiançailles* (Zvereff), *Suite de Danses* (Zvereff), and *Islamey* (Zvereff); January 19 and 24: *Coppélia* (Zvereff); January 18, 27, and 31: *Raymonda* (after Petipa by Zvereff); January 22 and 29: *Le Lac des Cygnes* (after Petipa by Zvereff); January 26: *Gisèle* (after Petipa by Romanoff).

Ballets Performed by the Ballets Russes de Monte-Carlo

April 4 and 7: *Le Mariage d'Aurore, Union Pacific,* and *Le Beau Danube;* April 6: *Les Sylphides, Les Présages, La Boutique Fantasque,* and *Les Sylphides;* April

9: *Contes Russes* and *La Boutique Fantasque*; April 11: *Scuola di Ballo, Le Tricorne,* and *Les Présages*; April 13: *Contes Russes, Jardin Public,* and *Le Beau Danube*; April 14: *Contes Russes, Le Tricorne,* and *Le Beau Danube*; April 16: *Scuola di Ballo, Le Tricorne,* and *Le Prince Igor*; April 18: *La Concurrence, Les Présages,* and *Le Beau Danube*; April 20: *Le Mariage d'Aurore, Contes Russes,* and *Le Prince Igor*; April 21: *Les Sylphides, Jardin Public,* and *La Boutique Fantasque*; April 23: *Cotillon, Le Tricorne,* and *Le Mariage d'Aurore*; April 25: *Carnaval, La Boutique Fantasque,* and *Beach*; April 27: *La Concurrence, Beach,* and *Shéhérazade*; April 28: *Scuola di Ballo, Cotillon,* and *Shéhérazade*; April 30: *Cotillon, Beach,* and *Shéhérazade*.

1936

Ballets Performed by the Ballets de Monte-Carlo

Les Sylphides, L'Épreuve d'Amour, Petrouchka, L'Amour Sorcier, Coppélia, Le Lac des Cygnes, Le Prince Igor, Aubade (Balanchine), *Le Spectre de la Rose, Carnaval,* and *Casse—Noisette.*

April 11: *Carnaval, Le Spectre de la Rose, Antoine et Cléopâtre, L'Amour Sorcier,* and *Aubade*; April 12: *L'Amour Sorcier* and *Coppélia*; April 14: *Les Sylphides, Aubade,* and *L'Épreuve d'Amour*; April 16: *Le Spectre de la Rose, Le Prince Igor Danse Polovtsiennes, Carnaval,* and *Le Lac des Cygnes*; April 18: *Petrouchka* and *Coppélia*; April 19: *Carnaval, Le Lac des Cygnes, Le Spectre de la Rose,* and *Aubade*.

1937

Ballets Performed by the Ballets de Monte-Carlo in Monte Carlo

April 1: *Les Sylphides, Don Juan,* and *L'Épreuve d'Amour*; April 3: *Le Lac des Cygnes, Don Juan, Le Spectre de la Rose,* and *Le Prince Igor*; April 4: *Les Sylphides, Don Juan,* and *L'Épreuve d'Amour*; April 6: *Le Lac des Cygnes, L'Épreuve d'Amour,* and *Don Juan*; April 8: *Un Soir* (Création), *Shéhérazade, Le Spectre de la Rose,* and *Le Prince Igor*; April 10: *Les Sylphides, Petrouchka,* and *L'Épreuve d'Amour*; April 11: *Le Lac des Cygnes, Shéhérazade, Le Spectre de la Rose,* and *Le Prince Igor*; April 13: *Don Juan* and *Coppélia*; April 15: *Un Soir, Casse-Noisette,* and *Le Prince Igor*; April 17: *Soirée de Gala, Les Sylphides,* and *Don Juan*; April 18: *Petrouchka* and *Coppélia*; April 20: *Carnaval, L'Épreuve d'Amour,* and *Casse-Noisette*; April 22: *Les Sylphides* and *Coppélia*; April 24: *Shéhérazade, Les Elfes,* and *Prince Igor*; April 25: *Casse-Noisette, Les Elfes,* and *Le Prince Igor*; April 27: *Les Elfes, Petrouchka,* and *Le*

Prince Igor; April 29: *Carnaval, Don Juan,* and *Suite de Danses;* May 1: *Les Sylphides, Shéhérazade,* and *L'Épreuve d'Amour;* May 2: *Carnaval, Don Juan,* and *L'Épreuve d'Amour;* May 4: *Les Sylphides, Don Juan,* and *Le Prince Igor;* May 6: *Shéhérazade, Les Elfes,* and *L'Épreuve d'Amour;* May 8: Soirée de Gala: *Les Sylphides* and *Coppélia;* May 9: Matinee: *Shéhérazade, Les Elfes, Le Spectre de la Rose,* and *Le Prince Igor;* May 13: Soirée de cloture: Représentation de Gala en l'honneur du couronnement de S. M. Le Roi d'Angleterre, Georges VI: *Hymne Monégasque,* "God Save the King," *Les Sylphides* and *Coppélia.*

1938

Ballets Performed by Ballets de Monte Carlo in Monte Carlo

Les Sylphides, Gaîté Parisienne (Création) on April 7, *L'Épreuve d'Amour, Lac des Cygnes, Le Spectre de la Rose, Le Prince Igor, Carnaval, Les Éléments,* Debut in London on June 24, 1937, *Petrouchka, Don Juan, Shéhérazade, Igrouchka (Poupées Russes),* Debut on April 19, *Les Elfes, Septième Symphonie,* Debut on May 5, and *Coppélia.*

April 26: *Les Éléments, Don Juan,* and *Gaîté Parisienne;* April 28: *Carnaval, L'Épreuve d'Amour, Igrouchka,* and *Le Prince Igor;* April 30: *Les Elfes, Petrouchka, Le Prince Enchanté,* and *Gaîté Parisienne;* May 1: *Le Lac des Cygnes, Shéhérazade, Le Spectre de la Rose,* and *Le Prince Igor;* May 3: *Les Elfes, Petrouchka, Le Prince Enchanté,* and *Gaîté Parisienne;* May 5: *L'Épreuve d'Amour, Septième Symphonie,* and *Gaîté Parisienne;* May 7: *Le Lac des Cygnes, Septième Symphonie,* and *Le Prince Igor;* May 8: *Les Sylphides, Septième Symphonie,* and *Gaîté Parisienne;* May 10: *Les Sylphides* and *Coppélia;* May 12: *Le Lac des Cygnes, Septième Symphonie,* and *Gaîté Parisienne;* May 14: *Coppélia and Septième Symphonie;* May 15: *Les Elfes, Gaîté Parisienne,* and *Septiéme Symphonie.*

The New Ballets Russes Season at the NYC Metropolitan Opera

The following is Sol Hurok's souvenir program for the four-week season in October and featuring a repertoire with twenty-four ballets:

President: Julius Fleischmann
Vice-President: Serge Denham
Founding Director: René Blum
Principal Dancers: Serge Lifar, Tamara Toumanova, Alicia Markova,

and Alexandra Danilova. Soloists: Nini Theilade, Roland Guerard, George Zoritch, Irina Faberje, Nina Tarakonova, Simon Seme-nonoff, Jean Yazvinsky, Eleanora Marra, Nathalie Krassovska, and Nina Strogonova.

Painters: Henri Matisse, André Derain, Christian Bérard, Georges Braque, Eugene Berman, and Ben Shahn.

Music: Paul Hindemith, Francis Poulenc, Georges Auric, William Walton, Nicolas Nabokov, Zoltan Kodaly, and Igor Stravinsky.

Choreographers: Léonide Massine, George Balanchine, and Michel Fokine.

An image of René Blum with his brother is included among the many photos.

The Repertoire: *Beethoven's Seventh* with décor by Christian Bérard; *Don Juan* with music by Gluck; *St. Francis* with music by Hindemith; *Éléments* with décors and costumes by Dimitri Bouchène; *Aubade* with décor by Cassandre; *Czar Saltan* with décor by Gontcharova; *Borodin Second* with décor by Gontcharova; *Coppélia* with music by Delibes; *Gay Mabille* with music by Offenbach; *Giselle* with décor by Alexandre Benois and music by Adolphe Adam; *Faun* with music by Debussy and décors by Christian Bérard; *Igrouchka* with music by Rimsky-Korsakov and décors by Gontcha-rova; *Paganini* with choreography by Balanchine and music by Tommasini; *Farandole* with décor and libretto by Henri Matisse; *Lorelei* with music by Weber; *L'Épreuve d'Amour* with décor by Derain; *Carnaval* with new décor by Léon Bakst; *Spectre* with music by Weber; *Dali* with décors by Salvador Dali and costumes by Schiaparelli; *Les Elfes* with décors by Christian Bérard; *Petrouchka* with décor after Benois; *Jota Aragonese* with music by Glinka and décors by Andrieu; *Pulcinella* with music by Stravinsky and décors by Picasso; *Schéhérazade* with music by Rimsky-Korsakov and décor by Bakst.

1939

Ballets Performed by the Ballet Russe de Monte Carlo in Monte Carlo

April 4: *Le Lac des Cygnes, Bogatyri, Le Spectre de la Rose,* and *Gaîté Parisienne;* April 6: *Les Sylphides, Noble Vision* (Création), and *Le Prince Igor;* April 8: *Giselle* and *Le Beau Danube;* April 9: *Le Lac des Cygnes, Bogatyri,* and *Gaîté Parisienne;* April 11: *L'Épreuve d'Amour, Noble Vision,* and *Le Beau Danube;* April 13: *Coppélia* and *Gaîté Parisienne;* April 15: *Les Sylphides, Le Tricorne, L'Après-Midi d'un Faune,* and *Le Prince Igor;* April 16: *Giselle* and *Le*

Beau Danube; April 18: *Les Sylphides, Septième Symphonie,* and *Gaîté Parisienne;* April 20: *Giselle* and *Petrouchka;* April 22: *L'Épreuve d'Amour, Septième Symphonie,* and *Gaîté Parisienne;* April 23: *Les Elfes, Noble Vision, Le Spectre de la Rose,* and *Le Prince Igor;* April 25: *Carnaval, Septième Symphonie,* and *Le Tricorne;* April 27: *Les Elfes, Bogatyri,* and *Le Beau Danube;* April 29: *Petrouchka, Septième Symphonie,* and *Shéhérazade;* April 30: *Coppélia* and *Le Tricorne;* May 2: *Le Lac des Cygnes, Shéhérazade,* and *Le Beau Danube;* May 4: *Les Sylphides, Capriccio Espagnol* (Création), *L'Après-Midi d'un Faune,* and *Gaîté Parisienne;* May 6: *Les Elfes, Capriccio Espagnol, Igrouchka,* and *Le Prince Igor;* May 7: *Shéhérazade, Septième Symphonie, L'Après-Midi d'un Faune,* and *Capriccio Espagnol;* May 9: *Les Elfes, Noble Vision, Le Spectre de la Rose,* and *Capriccio Espagnol;* May 11: *Les Sylphides, Rouge et Noir* (Création), and *Gaîté Parisienne;* May 13: *Le Lac des Cygnes, Rouge et Noir,* and *Shéhérazade;* May 14: *Les Sylphides, Rouge et Noir, Igrouchka,* and *Capriccio Espagnol.*

NOTES

ABBREVIATIONS

Arts du Spectacle	Arts du Spectacle Library, Bibliothèque nationale, Paris.
Blum Homages	Marcelle Tristan Bernard, ed., *René Blum: 1878–1942* (Paris: Arts et Métiers Graphiques, 1950).
Monte-Carlo SBM	Archives Monte-Carlo SBM (Société des Bains de Mer), Monaco.
NYPL	Jerome Robbins Dance Division, New York Public Library for the Performing Arts, Lincoln Center, New York.

INTRODUCTION

1. Blum to Josette France, undated letter, translated by Anne-Sabine Nicolas, René Blum/ Josette France Collection, Arts du Spectacle.
2. A comprehensive view of the journal and its contributors has been written by Paul Bour- relier in *La Revue Blanche, une génération dans l'engagement 1870–1905*, Paris:Librairie Arthème Fayard, 2007.
3. Marcelle Tristan Bernard, ed., *René Blum: 1878–1942* (Paris: Arts et Métiers Graphiques, 1950).
4. Jean Cocteau, Blum Homages, 22.
5. Romain Coolus, Blum Homages, 26.

CHAPTER 1

Childhood and Youth: The Formation of an Intellectual Aesthete

1. William Logue, *Léon Blum: The Formative Years 1872–1914* (De Kalb: North Illinois University Press, 1973), 11.
2. Serge Berstein, *Léon Blum* (Paris: Librairie Arthème Fayard, 2006), 14.
3. Marc Vishniac, *Léon Blum* (Paris: Flammarion, 1937), 131.
4. Alistair Horne, *Seven Ages of Paris* (New York: Vintage Books, 2004), 294.
5. Colin Jones, *Paris: The Biography of a City* (New York: Penguin Books, 2004), 334.
6. Ibid., 343.
7. Alfred Cobban, *A History of Modern France*, Vol. 3: *1871–1962* (Middlesex, UK: Penguin Books, 1981), 43.
8. Jones, *Paris*, 345.
9. Vishniac, *Léon Blum*, 7.
10. Logue, *Léon Blum*, 13.
11. Jones, *Paris*, 348.

12. Lucien Blum, unpublished personal diary, July 14, 1940–December 1944, Francine Hyafil collection.
13. Ibid.
14. André Gide, *Correspondance avec sa Mère 1880–1895* (Paris: Gallimard, 1988), 57.
15. Jacqueline Lancrey-Javal, letter to Janet Rowson Davis, June 26, 1978. Janet Rowson Davis collection.
16. Lucien Blum, unpublished personal diary.
17. Ilan Greilsammer, *Blum* (Paris: Flammarion, 1996), 32.
18. When I visited Françoise, Georges' daughter, she delighted in showing us her father's piano, which she was able to retrieve after the Occupation from a German storage center filled with stolen pianos.
19. Georges Huisman, Blum Homages, 50.
20. Lucien Blum, unpublished diary.
21. Berstein, *Léon Blum*, 129.
22. Annette Vaillant, *Le Pain Polka* (Paris: Mercure de France. 1974), 113.
23. Ibid., 115.
24. Arthur Gold and Robert Fitzdale, *Misia* (New York: Alfred A. Knopf, 1980), 134.
25. Lucien Blum, unpublished personal diary.
26. Gregory Fraser and Thadée Natanson, *Léon Blum: Man and Statesman* (London: Victor Gollancz, 1937), 51–53.
27. Ibid., 37.
28. Jones, *Paris*, 348.
29. George D. Painter, *Marcel Proust*, 2 vols. (London: Chatto & Windus, 1989), 1:224.
30. Logue, *Léon Blum*, 99.
31. Moshé Catane, "The Dreyfus Affair," *Encyclopaedia Judaica* (1972), 6:227.
32. Logue, *Léon Blum*, 101.
33. Fernand Gregh, *L'Âge d'Or* (Paris: Grasset, 1947), 288.
34. Logue, *Léon Blum*, 105.
35. Vishniac, *Léon Blum*, 33.
36. Gregh, *L'Âge d'Or*, 290.
37. Painter, *Proust*, 1:223.
38. Ibid., 91.
39. Gregh, *L'Âge d'Or*, 168.
40. Painter, *Proust*, 1:228.
41. Ibid.
42. Ibid., 90.
43. Ibid., 169.
44. Ibid., 232.
45. Ibid., 2:31.
46. *The Journals of Andé Gide*, Vol. 1, translated and with an introduction and notes by Justin O'Brien (New York: Alfred A. Knopf, 1948), 110.
47. René Blum, Conference on Tristan Bernard, paper presented in Monte Carlo, December 20, 1924, 11.
48. André Gide and Jean Schlumberger, *Correspondance 1901–1950* (Paris: Gallimard, 1988), 698.
49. Gregh, *L'Âge d'Or*, 228.
50. Thadée Natanson, Blum Homages, 44.
51. J. P. Bihr, *Edouard Vuillard, les Nabis, La Revue Blanche, Séjour a Saint-Jacut*, Archives of the Musée d'Orsay, 250.
52. Belinda Thomson, *Vuillard* (Oxford: Phaidon Press, 1988), 93.

53. Logue, *Léon Blum*, 29.

54. Painter, *Proust*, 1:114.

55. Gregh, *L'Âge d'Or*, 157.

56. Ibid.

57. Painter, *Proust*, 1:115.

58. Perhaps Porto-Riche was homophobic at a time when many artists were engaged in homosexual affairs. Michael de Cossart, *Ida Rubinstein (1885–1960): A Theatrical Life* (Liverpool, UK: Liverpool University Press, 1987), 104.

59. Painter, *Proust*, 1:319.

60. Ibid., 295.

61. Ibid., 296.

62. Ibid., 297.

63. Marthe Bibesco, Blum Homages, 12.

64. Painter, *Proust*, 2:169.

65. Reboux, along with Charles Muller, edited *À la manière de Pastiche*, a collection of brilliant pastiches of many authors including Racine, Kipling, and Conan Doyle.

66. Paul Reboux, Blum Homages, 52.

67. Fernand Gregh, *L'Âge d'Airain: 1905–1925* (Paris: Bernard Grasset, 1951), 87.

68. Ibid.

69. Logue, *Léon Blum*, 29.

70. Romain Coolus, Blum Homages, 25.

71. Judith Thurman, *Secrets of the Flesh: A Life of Colette* (New York: Alfred A. Knopf, 1999), 104.

72. Ibid., 436.

73. Ibid.

74. Lynn Garafola, *Diaghilev's Ballets Russes* (New York: Oxford University Press, 1989), 356.

75. Ibid.

CHAPTER 2

René Blum, Man of Letters

1. Logue, *Léon Blum*, 190.

2. Jean Lacouture, *Léon Blum* (Paris: Éditions du Seuil, 1977), 99.

3. Belinda Thomson, *Vuillard* (New York: Abbeville Press, 1988), 78.

4. Ibid., 85.

5. Ibid., 96.

6. Annette Vaillant, *Bonnard: ou, Le bonheur de voir; dialogue sur Pierre Bonnard entre Jean Cassou et Raymond Cogniat; commentaires de Hans R. Hahnloser* (Neuchatel, Switzerland: Éditions Ides et Calendes, 1965), 136.

7. René Blum, "Polémique entre François de Nion et Théâtre Antoine," *Gil Blas* (October 9, 1903): n.p., clipping from Arts du Spectacle.

8. Maurice Charlot, *Gil Blas* (October 11, 1903): n.p., clipping from Arts du Spectacle

9. Henri Hertz, *Gil Blas* (October 11, 1903): n.p., clipping from Arts du Spectacle.

10. René Blum, *Gil Blas* (October 11, 1903): n.p., clipping from Arts du Spectacle.

11. René Blum, "Notre Enquête: Le Droit d'Adaptation," *Gil Blas* (February–March 1912): n.p., clipping from Arts du Spectacle.

12. Ibid.

13. Ibid.

14. Émile Faguet, *Gil Blas* (March 12, 1912): n.p., clipping from Arts du Spectacle.

15. Georges Courteline, *Gil Blas* (March 1, 1912): n.p., clipping from Arts du Spectacle.

16. Albert Guinon, *Gil Blas* (March 1, 1912): n.p., clipping from Arts du Spectacle.
17. Albert Grumon, *Gil Blas* (March 1, 1912): n.p., clipping from Arts du Spectacle.
18. Romain Coolus was a pseudonym for René Weil (1868–1952). He was Agrégé in philosophy, but abandoned teaching early on for a career in the theatre. A drama critic as well, he was the author of many plays that mirrored the ethos of his time. But today his works are lost to the public.
19. Romain Coolus, *Gil Blas* (February 2, 1912): n.p., clipping from Arts du Spectacle.
20. Paul Gavault, *Gil Blas* (February 2, 1912): n.p., clipping from Arts du Spectacle.
21. Albert Flament, *Gil Blas* (March 3, 1912): n.p., clipping from Arts du Spectacle.
22. Alfred Mortier, *Gil Blas* (March 9, 1912): n.p., clipping from Arts du Spectacle.
23. Canudo, *Gil Blas* (March 16, 1912): n.p., clipping from Arts du Spectacle.
24. Léon Blum, *Gil Blas* (March 17, 1912): n.p., clipping from Arts du Spectacle.
25. René Blum, *Gil Blas* (n.d.): n.p., clipping from Arts du Spectacle.
26. Other artists in the exhibition were Auguste Agero, Honoré Auclair, Raymond Du Champ-Villon, Pierre Dumont, Démétrius Galanis, Albert Gleizes, Rena Hassenberg, Alcide Le Beau, André L'Hote, Jean-Hippolyte Marchand, Louis Marcoussis, André Mare, Luc-Albert Moreau, Mean Metzinger, Eugène Tirvert, Tobeen, Henry Valensi, Paul Véra, Jacques Villon, Ernest-Frédéric Wield, Dunoyer de Segonzac, André Roger de la Fresnage and Georges Ribemont Dessaignes.
27. Salon de la Section d'or, October 10–30, 1912, *Catalogue avec une Préface de René Blum*, Paris, Galerie la Boétie, Musée du Louvre collection.
28. Ibid.
29. Ibid.
30. Ibid.
31. René Bergeret and Jean Pellerin, *Le Goût du Toc*, a comedy in one act, Antoine Malamoud collection.
32. *La Gazette du Bon Ton* was published by Émile Levy and edited by Lucien Vogel in the Librairie Centrale des Beaux-Arts, 13 rue Lafayette, Paris. No. 1, November 1912, Antoine Malamoud collection.
33. René Blum, "Le Goût au Théâtre," *La Gazette du Bon Ton*, no. 1 (November 1912): 23, Antoine Malamoud collection.
34. René Blum, "Le Goût au Théâtre," *La Gazette du Bon Ton*, no. 2 (December 1912): 57, Antoine Malamoud collection.
35. Ibid.
36. Ibid.
37. René Blum, "Le Goût au Théâtre," *La Gazette du Bon Ton*, no. 3 (January 1913): 91, Antoine Malamoud collection.
38. René Blum, *Gil Blas* (July 12, 1913): n.p., clipping from François Mitterand Bibliothèque Nationale, Tolbiac, Paris.
39. René Blum, "Le Gant," *La Gazette du Bon Ton*, no. 12 (October 1913): 374, Antoine Malamoud collection.
40. Ibid., 376.
41. René Blum, *Gil Blas* (March 10, 1914): n.p., clipping from François Mitterand Bibliothèque Nationale, Tolbiac, Paris.
42. René Blum, "Les Projets de Paul Gavault," *Gil Blas* (June 20, 1914): n.p., clipping from François Mitterand Bibliothèque Nationale, Tolbiac, Paris.
43. Ibid.
44. *Catalogue Général de la Librairie de France*, May 1925, 110 Bd. St. Germain. *Encyclopédie des Sports*, 2 vols. "Tous les sports étudiés au double points de vue, historique et technique par les critiques sportifs les plus éminents. Direction et Rédaction par René Blum."

45. Michael de Cossart, *Ida Rubinstein (1885–1960): A Theatrical Life* (Liverpool, UK: Liverpool University Press, 1987), 78.

46. René Blum, "Le Carnet du Bibliophile," *L'Amour de l'Art* 1, no. 7 (1920): 98–99, Janet Rowson Davis collection.

47. René Blum, "Le Carnet du Bibliophile," *L'Amour de l'Art* 1, no. 7 (1920): 252.

48. Ibid.

49. René Blum, "Le Carnet du Bibliophile," *L'Amour de l'Art* 1 (1920): 164.

50. René Blum, "Le Carnet du Bibliophile," *L'Amour de l'Art* 1 (1920): 128.

51. René Blum, "La Section du Livre Au Salon d'Automne," *L'Amour de l'Art* 2, no. 6, (November 1921): 365–67.

52. René Blum, *Conférence sur Tristan Bernard* (Monaco: Imprimerie de Monaco, 1925), 5.

53. Ibid., 6.

54. Ibid., 21.

55. Bernard was highly respected by his contemporaries. André Gide in his *Journals* (1880–1895) jotted down his favorable impressions after he returned from seeing Bernard's *Amants et Voleurs* (1:140), *Triple Patte* (1:164), and *Monsieur Codmat* (1:218).

56. René Blum, *Conférence sur Tristan Bernard*, 28.

57. Tristan Bernard, *Mathilde et ses Mitaines*, preface by René Blum (Paris: Albin Michel, 1929), François Mitterand Library, Paris.

58. René Blum, *Georges Courteline*, 1930, Société des Conférences, du Conférence du 23 décembre 1929, Instituée sous le Haut Patronage de S.A.S. Prince Pierre de Monaco, pour Paul Deudon, François Mitterand Library, Paris, 33.

59. M. André Corneau, *Journal de Monaco* (February 27, 1932): n.p.

60. *La Petite Illustration*, René Blum and Georges Delaquys, *Les Amours du Poète*, Revue Hebdomadaire, 13 rue Saint-Georges, Paris (February 27, 1932): 21.

61. Ibid.

62. Ibid.

63. Ibid.

64. Ibid.

65. Ibid.

66. Ibid.

67. Ibid., 7.

68. Ibid., 10.

69. Ibid., 13.

70. *Journal de Monaco* (January 4, 1936): n.p., Janet Rowson Davis collection.

CHAPTER 3

Proust and Blum: An Uncommon Friendship

1. Emily Eells, *Proust's Cup of Tea: Homoeroticism and Victorian Culture, Studies in European Cultural Transition*, Vol. 15, Martin Stannard and Greg Walker, general eds. (Burlington, VT: Ashgate, 2002), 204.

2. Marcel Proust, *Correspondance*, présenté et annoté par Philip Kolb, 21 vols. (Paris: Éditions Plon, 1971–1993), 12:94.

3. Frank Biancheri, *René Blum (1878–1942): D'Une Jeunesse Enthousiaste à "Nuit et Brouillard"* (Annales Monégasques, revue d'histoire de Monaco-Publication des Archives du Palais Princier, no. 20, 1996): 10.

4. Proust, *Correspondance*, August 17, 1902, 3:102.

5. Ibid.

6. Ibid.

7. Ibid., June 3, 1906, 6:99.

8. Ibid., April 8, 1907, 7:135.
9. Ibid., February 19, 1913, 12:77.
10. Quoted from Biancheri, *René Blum*, 10.
11. George D. Painter, *Marcel Proust*, 2 vols. (London: Chatto & Windus, 1989), 1:190.
12. *Banquet* was a short-lived literary journal created by Proust and his friends from the Lycée Condorcet.
13. Painter, *Proust*, 1:190.
14. Mina Curtiss, ed. and trans., *Letters of Marcel Proust*, with an introduction by Harry Levin (New York: Random House, 1949), 238.
15. Ibid., 241.
16. Ibid., 242.
17. Ibid., 243.
18. Ibid.
19. Ibid., 256.
20. Ibid.
21. Ibid., 257.
22. Ibid.
23. Evelyne Ender, *Architexts of Memory* (Ann Arbor: University of Michigan Press, 2005), 24.
24. Léon Pierre-Quint, *Proust et la Stratégie littéraire; Avec des lettres de Marcel Proust à René Blum, Bernard Grasset et Louis Brun* (Paris: Corrêa, 1954), 52.
25. Ibid., 53.
26. Ender, *Architexts*, 29.
27. Pierre-Quint, *Proust et la Stratégie littéraire*, 54.
28. *Gil Blas* (April 14, 1913): n.p., clipping from Arts du Spectacle.
29. Pierre-Quint, *Proust et la Stratégie littéraire*, 57.
30. Proust, *Correspondance*, mid-November 1913, 12:319.
31. *Gil Blas* (November 23, 1913): n.p., clipping from Arts du Spectacle.
32. Proust, *Correspondance*, 12: 319.
33. Painter, *Proust*, 2:231.
34. Ibid., 233.
35. Alan Sheridan, *André Gide: A Life in the Present* (London: Hamish Hamilton, 1998), 259.
36. Ibid., 260.
37. Ibid., 345.
38. Proust, *Correspondance*, May 30, 1916, 15:147.
39. Ibid., July 1916, 15:213.
40. Ibid., July 17, 1916, 15:224.
41. Ibid.
42. Ibid., August 14, 1916, 15:258.
43. Ibid., September 25, 1916, 15:302.
44. Ibid., January 31, 1917, 16:37.
45. Ibid., December 1919, 18:493.
46. Marcel Proust, *Correspondance*, présenté et annoté par Philip Kolb, vol. 1, 1880–1895 (Paris: Éditions Plon, 1975), 102–3.
47. Ilan Greilsammer, *Blum* (Paris: Flammarion, 1996), 23.
48. Marcel Proust, 1919 translation, *Within a Budding Grove, In Search of Lost Time*, Vol. 2, translated and edited by Scott Moncrieff and Terence Kilmartin, revised by D. J. Enright (New York: Modern Library Edition, 1992), 445.
49. Ibid.

50. Marcel Proust, 1913 translation, *Swann's Way, In Search of Lost Time*, Vol. 1, translated and edited by C. K. Moncrieff and Terence Kilmartin, revised by D. J. Enright, with an introduction by Jean Yves Tadié (London: The Folio Society, 2000), 91.

51. Pierre-Quint, *Proust et la Stratégie littéraire*, Introduction.

52. Letters from Blum to Pierre-Quint may be found in the Département des Manuscrits, Bibliothèque Nationale, Paris.

53. *Comment parut "Du Côté de chez Swann": Lettres de Marcel Proust*, introduction et commentaires par Léon Pierre-Quint (Paris: Éditions Kra, 1930).

CHAPTER 4

The Great War and René Blum

1. In his biography of the impresario Lincoln Kirstein, Martin Duberman wrote that Kirstein assisted his country during World War II. (*The Worlds of Lincoln Kerstein*, New York: Alfred A. Knopf, 2007) In 1945, serving with the U.S. Army in Europe, "Kirstein was central to the recovery of the Van Eyck 'Adoration of the Lamb,' which the Germans had stolen in 1942 and hidden in a salt mine in Austria" (*New York Times*, May 4, 2007: B30).

2. Commendation of René Blum, Janet Rowson Davis collection.

3. Serge Berstein, *Léon Blum* (Paris: Librairie Arthème Fayard, 2006), 155.

4. George D. Painter, *Marcel Proust*, 2 vols. (London: Chatto & Windus, 1989), 1:228.

5. Blum to Robert de Montesquiou, October 26, 1916, Département des Manuscrits, Bibliothèque Nationale, Paris.

6. René Blum, unpublished wartime journal, August 27–September 6, 1914, translated by Anne-Sabine Nicolas, Arts du Spectacle.

7. Blum to Robert de Montesquiou, May 24, 1916, Département des Manuscrits, Bibliothèque Nationale, Paris.

8. René Blum, unpublished wartime journal. All mentions of Blum's journal in Chapter 4 refer to this handwritten diary from the Arts du Spectacle collection.

9. George Wright, *Encyclopedia Britannica* (1972), 7:672.

10. Alistair Horne, *To Lose a Battle: France 1940* (Boston: Little, Brown and Company, 1969), 13.

11. Ibid., 15.

12. Lawrence H. Officer, "Exchange Rates Between the United States Dollar and Forty-one Currencies," *MeasuringWorth* [online], revised 2009. Available at http://www.measuringworth.org/exchangeglobal/.

13. Horne, *To Lose a Battle*, 13.

14. Ibid., 17.

15. Ibid.

CHAPTER 5

René Blum and the Théâtre de Monte-Carlo

1. Stanley Jackson, *Inside Monte Carlo* (London: W. H. Allen, 1975), 41.

2. Vladimir Fédorovski, *Le Roman de L'Orient Express* (Paris: Éditions du Rocher, 2006), 63.

3. Gunsbourg was the architect of the Archives du Casino de Monte-Carlo, where he deposited many letters, contracts, and photo materials.

4. Jackson, *Inside Monte Carlo*, 65.

5. Jean-Jacques L.Tur, *Notes et Études Documentaires* 2 septembre 1975, no. 4210 "Les Micro-États Européens: Monaco, Saint Marin, Liechtenstein" (Paris: La Documentation Française, 1975), 15.

6. Anne Edwards, *The Grimaldis of Monaco* (New York: William Morrow), 193. Edwards also cited the numerous North and South Americans who grew rich from mercantile ventures during World War I, as well as those who profited from Prohibition.

7. Renée Stein, *Trois Siècles de Ballet à Monte Carlo (1650–1950)* (Lausanne, Switzerland: Maurice Bridel, Librairie de Lausanne, 1968), 50.

8. Prince Louis, who had attended military school in Germany, fought in the French army during World War I, but was a friend of General Pétain and a German sympathizer during the Vichy regime.

9. Jackson, *Inside Monte Carlo*, 108.

10. Pierre Mortier, *Comoedia*, April 2, 1936, no page indicated.

11. All letters to and from René Blum at the Théâtre de Monte-Carlo may be found in the Archives Monte-Carlo, Société des Bains de Mer.

12. Sjeng Scheijen, *Diaghilev: A Life*, translated by Jane Hedley-Prôle and S. J. Leinbach (New York: Oxford University Press, 2010), 379.

13. Letter from René Léon, February 11, 1927, Monte-Carlo SBM.

14. Blum to René Léon, January 24, 1928, Monte-Carlo SBM.

15. Lynn Garafola, "In His Own Voice: Diaghilev in the British Press" (unpublished Article, 2008), 6.

16. Richard Davenport-Hines, *Proust at the Majestic* (New York and London: Bloomsbury, 2006), 59.

17. Georges Huisman, Blum Homages, 31.

18. Antoine Bibesco, Blum Homages, 9.

19. Marthe Bibesco, Blum Homages, 13.

20. Jacques Chabannes, Blum Homages, 20.

21. Colette, Blum Homages, 23.

22. Ibid.

23. Judith Thurman, *Secrets of the Flesh: A Life of Colette* (New York: Alfred A. Knopf, 1999), 351.

24. Romain Coolus, Blum Homages, 26.

25. Georges de Lauris, Blum Homages, 34.

26. Roland Dorgelès, Blum Homages, 29.

27. Frank Biancheri, *René Blum (1878–1942): D'Une Jeunesse Enthousiaste à "Nuit et Brouillard"* (Annales Monégasques, revue d'histoire de Monaco-Publication des Archives du Palais Princier, no. 20, 1996): 16.

28. Ibid., 18.

29.

Year	FF	$
1914	5	1
1924	23	1
1938	34	1

30. Alain Corneau, the chief critic for the *Journal de Monaco*, was a member of the Commission des Beaux-Arts (as was René Blum) and wrote criticism for some thirty years.

31. Souvenir Program, Théâtre du Monte-Carlo, 1927.

32. Jean-Jacques Bernard, the son of Tristan Bernard, was imprisoned with Blum by the Vichy government and the Nazis, and would witness and write about Blum's last days in the Drancy concentration camp in *The Camp of Slow Death*.

33. Michel W. Pharand, *Bernard Shaw and the French* (Gainesville: University Press of Florida, 2000), 276.

34. Ibid., 158.

35. See Lynn Garafola, *Diaghilev's Ballets Russes* (New York: Oxford University Press, 1989), 118.

36. In the past few years, it has been refurbished with plush red seats and a red velvet curtain with gold cupids and plaster decorations over the proscenium arch. It catered to a fancy, middle-class crowd that liked a good time in the theatre. When movies took over at the Mogador, the likes of Douglas Fairbanks and Jeannette MacDonald graced the screen.

37. Pierre Michaut, "Ballet and the Cinema in Paris," in *Ballet Annual*, edited by A. Haskell (London: A. & C. Black, 1953), 108.

38. *Daily Telegraph*, April 22, 1925, Janet Rowson Davis collection.

39. *Daily Telegraph*, April 29, 1925, Janet Rowson Davis collection.

40. *Daily Telegraph*, April 21, 1925, Janet Rowson Davis collection.

41. Bengt de Törne, *Apollo* 2 (1925): 177.

42. Ibid., 178.

43. Ibid., 123.

44. Ibid., 304.

45. Sotheby Parke Bernet & Co., Catalogue Boris Kniaseff (34–35 New Bond Street, London, 15/16 December, 1969), n.p.

46. Marcel Pagnol: Programme Officiel du Théâtre de Monte-Carlo, Saison Comédie et Operette, 1929–1930.

47. Henry Bernstein: Programme Officiel du Théâtre de Monte-Carlo, Saison Comédie et Operette, 1929–1930.

48. Jackson, *Inside Monte Carlo*, 156.

49. *Journal de Monaco*, January 11, 1934.

50. Georges Lecomte, Introduction to the Souvenir Program Season, 1927–1928.

51. Henry Malherbe, Program of Saison Opérette-Comédie 1927–1928.

52. *Journal de Monaco*, January 26, 1928.

53. Michael de Cossart, *Ida Rubinstein (1885–1960): A Theatrical Life* (Liverpool, UK: Liverpool University Press, 1987), 77.

54. Ibid., 46. This story about Ida Rubinstein and Diaghilev was written in an article by Louis Thomas as told by Léon Bakst, "Le Peintre Bakst parle de Madame Ida Rubinstein," in *Revue Critique des Idées et des livres*, vol. 36, no. 221 (February 1924), 103.

55. Cyril Beaumont, *The Monte-Carlo Russian Ballet: Les Ballets Russes de Col. W. de Basil* (London: CW Beaumont, 1934), 7.

56. Blum to René Léon, October 7, 1929, Monte-Carlo SBM.

57. Ibid.

58. Ibid.

59. Ibid.

60. Quote from Shankar's Souvenir Program, April 1931.

61. Ivor Guest, *The Paris Opéra Ballet* (Alton, Hampshire, UK: Dance Books, 2006), 82.

62. Ibid., 81.

63. Bernard Taper, *Balanchine: A Biography* (New York: New York Times Books, 1984), 125.

64. Guest, *Paris Opéra*, 82.

65. See Ninotchka Bennahum's *Antonia Mercé: La Argentina, Flamenco and the Spanish Avant-Garde* (Hanover, NH: University Press of New England, 2000).

66. Program, *Danses Espagnoles de Vicente Escudero*, April 23, 1931.

67. Kathrine Sorley Walker, *De Basil's Ballets Russes* (London: Hutchinson, 1982), 6.

CHAPTER 6

René and Josette

1. Unless otherwise noted, all correspondence cited in Chapter 6 is from the René Blum/Josette France Collection, Arts du Spectacle, and English translations are by Anne-Sabine Nicolas. Almost all of the Blum/France letters are undated.
2. Short paragraph written on Josette France in Introduction to the Inventaire, René Blum/Josette France collection, Arts du Spectacle.

CHAPTER 7

The Resurrection of the Ballets Russes

1. Vicente Garcia-Marquez, *The Ballets Russes: Colonel de Basil's Ballets Russes de Monte-Carlo 1932–1952* (New York: Alfred A. Knopf, 1990), 5.
2. Ibid., xi.
3. In the course of this research, many people cited Blum's generosity toward dancers and theatre people who had no means of survival.
4. Charles Richter, *Le Figaro*, February 16, 1932.
5. Pierre Michaut, *Le Ballet Contemporain* (Paris: Éditions Plon, 1950), 62.
6. Charles Richter, *Comoedia*, May 4, 1932.
7. Henry Malherbe, *Feuilleton du Temps*, June 15, 1932.
8. Henry Prunières, no title of publication, July 2, 1932, Janet Rowson Davis collection.
9. Serge Lifar, *Histoire du Ballet Russe* (Paris: Éditions Nagel 1950), 245.
10. Ibid.
11. In his book on the Ballets Russes, Garcia-Marquez offers very detailed accounts of the choreographies of this period.
12. Tamara Tchinarova Finch, "Les Ballets 1933," the *Dancing Times* (March 1988): 532–34.
13. Tamara Tchinarova Finch, letter to the author on November 7, 2000.
14. Bernard Taper, *Balanchine: A Biography* (New York: New York Times Books, 1984), 136.
15. Kathrine Sorley Walker, *De Basil's Ballets Russes* (London: Hutchinson, 1982), 23.
16. Garcia-Marquez, *Ballets Russes*, 6.
17. Boris Kochno, *Christian Bérard*, translated by Philip Core (New York: Panache Press, Random House, 1988), 34.
18. Irving Deakin, *Ballet Profile* (New York: Dodge, 1936), 143.
19. Quoted in Sorley Walker, *De Basil's Ballets Russes*, 9.
20. A. V. Coton, *Prejudice for Ballet* (London: Methuen, 1938), 76.
21. P. W. Manchester, "Conversations with P. W. Manchester," *Ballet Review*, Part 1, vol. 6, no. 3 (1977–1978): 65.
22. Tamara Toumanova, "A Conversation with Francis Mason," *Ballet Review*, vol. 24, no. 3 (Fall 1996): 41.
23. Ibid.
24. Deakin, *Ballet Profile*, 143.
25. Sorley Walker, *De Basil's Ballets Russes*, 12.
26. Manchester, "Conversations with P. W. Manchester," 64.
27. Pierre Michaut, *Histoire du Ballet*, Que sais-je? 177 (Paris: Presses Universitaires de France, 1948), 98.
28. Ibid.
29. Toumanova, "A Conversation with Francis Mason," 42.
30. Ibid.
31. Ibid.

32. The following is a list of all the operas with ballets that Balanchine choreographed: January 21, 1932, heralded the opening of the opera season with *Tannhauser*, which was repeated January 23; January 24, *Tales of Hoffmann*; January 26, *Le Prophète*; February 2, *Une Nuit de Venise*; February 9, *Lakmé*; February 11, *Samson and Dalila*; Febraury 13, *Faust*; February 20, *Patrie*, an opera ballet by Émile Paladilhe; February 20, Act III of *Hérodiade*, by Jules Massenet; February 21, *Turandot*; February 23, *Rigoletto*; February 28, *Manon*; March 3, *La Traviata*; March 6, *Roméo et Juliette*; March 8, *Fay-Yen-Fah*; March 19, *Aïda*; March 24, *Carmen*; March 31, *La Périchole*.

33. Deakin, *Ballet Profile*, 143.

34. Irina Baronova, *Irina* (Gainesville: University Press of Florida, 2005), 80.

35. Tamara Tchinarova Finch, *Dancing into the Unknown* (Alton, UK: Dance Books, 2007), 66.

36. Taper, *Balanchine*, 139.

37. Ibid.

38. Deakin, *Ballet Profile*, 144.

39. Garcia-Marquez, *Ballets Russes*, 8.

40. Sorley Walker, *De Basil's Ballets Russes*, 21.

41. Deakin, *Ballet Profile*, 144.

42. Ibid.

43. Manchester, "Conversations with P. W. Manchester," 57.

44. Sorley Walker, *De Basil's Ballets Russes*, 21.

45. Ibid.

46. Sol Hurok, *S. Hurok Presents: A Memoir of the Dance World* (New York: Hermitage House, 1953), 106.

47. Manchester, "Conversations with P. W. Manchester," 77.

48. Ibid.

49. André Eglevsky, "The Ballet Russe de Monte Carlo," *Harper's Bazaar* (October 1938): 86.

50. Ibid., 127.

51. Nathan Milstein, the great violinist who was a close friend to Balanchine, wrote disparagingly of de Basil. He recalled Balanchine's early employment with the Blum/de Basil company and spoke pejoratively about de Basil's leadership. Milstein wrote: "Balanchine worked for a crook, who pompously called himself Colonel de Basil. That scoundrel was no Colonel with the Cossaks and he was no de Basil, either." In truth, de Basil was a colonel with the Cossak army. Milstein continued: "In Paris he'd gotten a third-rate job in Prince Alexis Zeretelli's émigré opera enterprise, and suddenly he surfaced pretending to be a Russian aristocrat, and a rich one at that! Getting the 'de' and a false military rank was not hard in those days. But where did he get his money? I think I've figured out his little secret: the money didn't belong to de Basil, or to Zeretelli, his backer. The star soprano in Zeretelli's opera enterprise was Galina Kuznetsova, and all the money came from her, or rather, from her incredibly rich patron. De Basil used Balanchine and then threw him out. Luckily George met a young visionary, the wealthy American Lincoln Kirstein," quoted in "My Friend George Balanchine," *Ballet Review* (Fall 1990): 25. Sol Hurok also impugned de Basil's motives. In his *Impresario: A Memoir in Collaboration with Ruth Goode*, he spoke about "not getting on with him" (p. 201), and in his *Hurok Presents: A Memoir of the Dance World*, he offered that de Basil "was one of the most difficult human beings I have ever encountered in a lifetime of management" (p. 109).

52. Martin Duberman, *The Worlds of Lincoln Kirstein* (New York: Alfred A. Knopf, 2007), 162.

53. July 7, 1933, Monte-Carlo SBM, 1.

54. Blum to René Léon, July 25, 1933, Monte-Carlo SBM.

55. Blum to René Léon, September 19, 1933.

56. Manchester, "Conversations with P. W. Manchester," 73.

57. Lynn Garafola, "Astonish Me! Diaghilev, Massine and the Experimentalist Tradition," unpublished paper (2008): 11.

58. Sorley Walker, *De Basil's Ballets Russes*, 23.

59. Coton, *Prejudice for Ballet*, 81.

60. Program for *Les Présages*, April 13, 1933.

61. Leigh Wichel, *Ballet Review* (Summer 2007): 12.

62. Ibid.

63. G. E. Goodman, "Notes on Décor," the *Dancing Times* (August 1933): n.p.

64. The Sitter Out, the *Dancing Times* (August 1937): 556.

65. Ibid.

66. Ibid.

67. *Daily Mail*, Paris, June 2, 1933.

68. Louis Schneider, *New York Herald Tribune*, June 12, 1933.

69. Louis Léon Martin, *Paris Midi*, June 14, 1933.

70. *L'Echo de Paris*, June 19, 1933.

71. Letter from Blum to René Léon, June 13, 1933.

72. Manchester, "Conversations with P. W. Manchester," 63.

73. Letter from Blum to Georges Reymond, July 4, 1933.

74. Duberman, *Worlds of Lincoln Kirstein*, 167.

75. André Levinson, "The Duel of the Ballets Russes Companies," *Candide*, no date and no page indicated, Janet Rowson Davis collection.

76. Duberman, *Worlds of Lincoln Kirstein*, 200.

77. George Dorris, review of *The Art of the Ballets Russes: The Serge Lifar Collection of Theater Designs*, by Alexander Schouvaloff, *Dance Chronicle*, vol. 21, no. 3 (1998): 490.

78. Baird Hastings, "Massine's Symphonic Ballets," *Ballet Review* (Spring 1995): 88.

79. Ibid., 89.

80. Manchester, "Conversations with P. W. Manchester," 67.

81. Louis Schneider, *New York Herald*, June 1, 1934.

82. Irving Schwerke, *Chicago Daily Tribune*, June 2, 1934.

83. *Menton News*, November 18, 1933.

84. Janet Rowson Davis, "Les Ballets Russes," *Dancing Times* (October 1983), 41.

85. Letter from Michèle Thomas, February 27, 1978, Librarian, Arts du Spectacle to Janet Rowson Davis.

86. Sorley Walker, *De Basil's Ballets Russes*, 35.

87. Tchinarova Finch, *Dancing Into the Unknown*, 79.

88. Alexandra Danilova, *Choura: The Memoirs of Alexandra Danilova* (London: Dance Books, 1984), 135.

89. Irina Baronova, *Irina* (Gainesville: University Press of Florida, 2005), 135.

90. Ibid., 141.

91. Jack Anderson, *The One and Only: The Ballet Russe de Monte-Carlo* (New York: Dance Horizons, 1981), 37.

92. Ibid.

93. *Dance Observer*, editorial page (May 1934): 38.

94. Ibid.

95. S. D. [Sophia Delza], *Dance Observer* (May 1934): 44.

96. Ibid.

97. *Dance Observer*, editorial page (August/September 1934): 62.

98. Ibid.

99. Ibid.

100. Ibid.

101. Sorley Walker, *De Basil's Ballets Russes*, 50.

102. Blum to Alfred Delpierre, August 22, 1934, Monte-Carlo SBM.

103. Ibid.

104. *Menton News*, no date, Janet Rowson Davis collection.

105. *The Times*, London, February 2, 1935.

106. *The Times*, London, March 5, 1935.

107. Blum to George Balanchine, November 5, 1935, NYPL.

108. Ibid.

109. George Balanchine to Blum, November 21, 1935, NYPL, quoted by permission of the George Balanchine Trust. BALANCHINE is a trademark of the George Balanchine Trust.

110. Ibid.

111. Ilan Greilsammer, *Blum* (Paris: Flammarion, 1996), 339.

112. *Paris Soir*, April 26, 1937.

CHAPTER 8

Blum Brings Michel Fokine into the Fold

1. George Wright, "France, a History," in *Encyclopedia Britannica* (Chicago: William Benton, 1974), 7: 671.

2. Kevin Passmore, *Modern France: 1880–2002*, edited by James McMillan (New York: Oxford University Press, 2003), 57–59.

3. Blum to Alfred Delpierre, March 3, 1936, Monte-Carlo SBM.

4. See Dawn Lille's article "Michel Fokine, Choreography of the Thirties," *Proceedings Society of Dance History Scholars*, North Carolina School of the Arts, February 12–14, 1988, 194–99.

5. Jack Anderson, *The One and Only: The Ballet Russe de Monte Carlo* (New York: Dance Horizons, 1981), 14.

6. Lille, "Michel Fokine, Choreography of the Thirties," 197.

7. *Dancing Times* (June 1936): 243.

8. Ibid.

9. *L'Illustration*, May 2, 1936.

10. A. V. Coton, *Prejudice for Ballet* (London: Methuen, 1938), 113.

11. Cyril W. Beaumont, *Complete Book of Ballets* (New York: Grosset and Dunlap, 1938), 555.

12. Adda Pourmel, telephone interview with the author, June 2006.

13. Adda Pourmel, letter written to Janet Rowson Davis, September 12, 1988, Janet Rowson Davis collection.

14. Ibid.

15. Ibid.

16. Pourmel, telephone interview with the author.

17. Ibid.

18. Ibid.

19. Ibid.

20. Alfred Henderson, *Le Petit Niçois*, April 30, 1936.

21. Ibid.

22. *L'Éclaireur du Soir*, no date or month.

23. *L'Illustration*, signed V. or Vuillermoz, May 2, 1936.

24. The Sitter Out, *Dancing Times* (June 1936): 248.

25. Ibid.

26. Coton, *Prejudice for Ballet*, 113.
27. *Dancing Times* (April 1963): no page number, Janet Rowson Davis collection.
28. Blum to Josette France, undated letter, translated by Anne-Sabine Nicolas, René Blum/ Josette France collection, Arts du Spectacle.
29. *The Times*, London, June 26, 1936.
30. *The Spectator*, May 22, 1936.
31. Carmen Callil, *Bad Faith: A Forgotten History of a Family, Fatherland and Vichy France* (New York: Alfred A. Knopf, 2006), 141.
32. Ibid.
33. Ibid.
34. *The Times*, London, August 25, 1936.
35. No name or date on clipping, Janet Rowson Davis collection.
36. Ibid.
37. Letter from Delpierre to Blum, September 15, 1936.
38. *The Star*, Johannesburg, October 6, 1936.
39. *The Star*, Johannesburg, October 27, 1936.
40. Stanley Judson, *Dancing Times* (December 1936): 262.
41. Pourmel, telephone interview with the author.
42. Letter from Blum to Delpierre March 18, 1937.
43. Francis Savage, *Dancing Times* (May 1937): 151.
44. Ibid., 152.
45. Ibid., 153.
46. Ibid.
47. Ibid.
48. *The Times*, London, June 28, 1937.
49. *Dancing Times* (July 1937): 409.
50. Letter from Jean Cerrone to Janet Rowson Davis, 1985. Janet Rowson Davis collection.
51. *L'Éclaireur de Nice et du Sud-Est*, April 1, 1937.
52. *L'Eclaireur du Soir*, April 2, 1937.
53. Ibid.
54. Renée Stein, *Trois Siècles de Ballet à Monte Carlo (1650–1950)* (Lausanne, Switzerland: Maurice Bridel, Librairie de Lausanne, 1968), 52.
55. L. Gerbe, *Le Petit Marseillais*, April 6, 1937.
56. Vicente Garcia-Marquez, *Massine: A Biography* (New York: Alfred A. Knopf, 1995), 244.
57. Martin Duberman, *The Worlds of Lincoln Kirstein* (New York: Alfred A. Knopf, 2007), 658n.
58. Jacques Barraux, *L'Intransigeante*, May 17, 1937. Another approach to Fokine's ballets was written by the musicologist Constantin Photiadès, in a lengthy article presenting his personal appreciation for Fokine's new work in the *Revue de Paris* (June 15, 1937: 921–32).
59. Marcel Reichenecker, *Paris Soir*, April 26, 1937.
60. George Wright, *Encyclopedia Britannica*, "France, A History" (1974): 673.
61. Georges D. De Givray, *Chronique Théâtrale* (June 13, 1937): n.p.
62. Émile Vuillermoz, *L'Illustration*, June 5, 1937.
63. Clipping from the Bibliothèque du Musée de l'Opéra, Paris. The title of the newspaper and the critic's name are not included in the cutting.
64. Jean Dorcy, *La Tribune de Danse*, May 20, 1937.
65. *The Times*, London, June 25, 1937.
66. *The Times*, London, June 1, 1937.
67. *The Times*, London, June 9, 1937.
68. *The London Observer*, June 27, 1937.

69. Letter from Jean Cerrone to Janet Rowson Davis, 1985, Janet Rowson Davis collection.

70. Francis Savage, *Dancing Times* (November 1937): 147.

71. Frederick Franklin, interview with the author in Franklin's apartment, New York City, October 10, 2001. Garafola noted that Franklin may not have remembered correctly, as it was well known that Massine's *Coq d'Or* was a huge success.

72. Blum to Josette France, August 14, 1937, translated by Anne-Sabine Nicolas, René Blum/Josette France, Arts du Spectacle.

73. Ibid.

74. Ibid.

75. Franklin, interview with the author.

CHAPTER 9

The New World Calls! Blum Sells the Company to Americans

1. The World Art, Inc. correspondence is collected in the Blum/Denham correspondence, NYPL. In addition to Denham and Fleischmann, other correspondents in the Blum/Denham collection include Clyde Smith, Denis Milner (an Englishman who loaned Blum money), David Libidins, Jacques Rubinstein, Watson Washburn (a lawyer), Henri Gautrin, Sol Hurok, and Leonide Massine.

2. Vicente Garcia-Marquez, *Massine: A Biography* (New York: Alfred A. Knopf, 1995), 253.

3. A. V. Coton, *Prejudice for Ballet* (London: Methuen, 1938), 149.

4. Blum to Serge Denham, March 1, 1937, Blum/Denham correspondence, NYPL.

5. *Dancing Times* (May 1937): 139.

6. Adda Pourmel, letter to Janet Rowson Davis, September 12, 1988. Janet Rowson Davis collection.

7. Bringing the financial aspect of the transfer of power into focus, Blum told Denham in the March 1, 1937, letter how much must be paid for choreographer's rights to certain ballets each year; that is, for *L'Epreuve d'Amour* 2,000 francs (and 15,000 francs when performed in America and England) and for *Coppélia*, 400 francs per concert. He also mentioned problems with the young Eglevsky—that the young dancer was "blackmailing" him because his mother, acting as her son's adviser, was a disturbing influence. In spite of Eglevsky's great talent, Blum was prepared to let him go.

8. Blum to Serge Denham, March 1, 1937, Blum/Denham correspondence, NYPL.

9. Ibid.

10. In this long saga, we are reminded that Blum was not the only lead player discouraged by de Basil's continuously egregious activities. Massine became "restless" and, in the spring of 1937, or even earlier, began to meet with David Libidins, an English concert manager, and other potential patrons. In Massine's 1934 contract, de Basil was only willing to grant Massine the title "collaborateur artistique—" by no means equal footing. Therefore Massine sought the support of several wealthy and influential financiers who adored ballet. Jack Anderson, *The One and Only: The Ballet Russe de Monte-Carlo* (New York: Dance Horizons, 1981), 4.

11. Another letter followed in which Blum wrote Denham (c/o of the Guaranty Trust Company of New York) that he had not paid all his debts to his English creditors, in the sum of 1650 pounds with 5 percent interest. "If you pay this debt, then you will receive 5 percent interest on the money that you lent me." In the final letter on August 2, Blum declared that if the two agreed to the company transfer on February 1, 1938, then Denham must give Blum two months notice (in other words, by December 1) so that Blum might better prepare for this event.

12. Letter from Blum to Delpierre, August 3, 1938.

13. Jack Anderson, *The One and Only: The Ballet Russe de Monte-Carlo* (New York: Dance Horizons, 1981), 7.

14. "M. Massine and His Ballets," *The London Daily Telegraph* (July 24, 1937). Cited in Anderson, *One and Only*, 7.

15. Ibid.

16. *Edinburgh Evening News*, September 16, 1937.

17. Ibid.

18. Ibid.

19. *The Bulletin*, Edinburgh, September 17, 1937.

20. Ibid.

21. *Edinburgh Evening Dispatch*, September 17, 1937.

22. Ibid.

23. Ibid.

24. Ibid.

25. Blum to Serge Denham, October 10, 1937, Blum/Denham correspondence, NYPL.

26. Ibid.

27. Blum to Serge Denham, November 25, 1937, Blum/Denham correspondence, NYPL.

28. Blum recoiled at the idea that he was not consulted when M. Etienne de Beaumont was brought in as an advisor, and he found it intolerable that Mme. de Noailles would be creating ballets. "How absurd!"

29. René Blum, *Manchester Daily Dispatch* (November 5, 1937), n.p., clipping from Bibliothèque du Musée de l'Opéra, Paris.

30. Ibid.

31. Ibid.

32. *Brighton Supplement*, November 13, 1937, n.p., clipping from Bibliothèque du Musée de l'Opéra, Paris.

33. Ibid.

34. Ibid.

35. *New York Times*, November 20, 1937.

36. Alicia Markova, *Markova Remembers* (London: Hamish Hamilton, 1986), 69.

37. Ibid.

38. Letter from Blum to Maria Ruanova, December 30, 1937.

39. Ibid.

40. Blum's personal contract with World Art, Inc., NYPL.

41. Ibid.

42. Ibid.

43. Blum to Serge Denham, February 16, 1938, Blum/Denham correspondence, NYPL.

44. Ibid.

45. Blum to Serge Denham, April 23, 1938, Blum/Denham correspondence, NYPL.

46. Blum to Serge Denham, February 27, 1938, Blum/Denham correspondence, NYPL.

47. Blum to Julius Fleischmann, August 2, 1938, Blum/Denham correspondence, NYPL.

48. Ibid.

49. Ibid.

50. René Blum to Léon Blum, March 27, 1938, Archives Léon Blum, Centre d'histoire Sciences Po, Paris.

51. Marcel Reichenecker, *Le Petit Niçois de Nice*, March 1938.

52. Ibid.

53. Natasha Krassovska, interview with the author, Dallas, Texas, April 29, 2001.

54. Frederick Franklin, interview with the author in Franklin's apartment, New York City, October 10, 2001.

55. Jean Cerrone, letter to Janet Rowson Davis, no month, 1985. Janet Rowson Davis collection.

56. *Dancing Times* (May 1938):158.

57. Ibid.

58. Ibid.

59. Baird Hastings, "Massine's Symphonic Ballets," *Ballet Review* (Spring 1995): 90.

60. Ibid.

61. Ibid.

62. Quoted in Anderson, *One and Only*, 19.

63. Blum to Josette France, undated letter, translated by Anne-Sabine Nicolas, René Blum/ Josette France collection, Arts du Spectacle.

64. Jack Anderson, "The Enduring Relevance of Léonide Massine," paper delivered May 20, 2009, as part of "The Spirit of Diaghilev" academic conference, May 18–21, Boston University.

65. Anderson, *One and Only*, 26.

66. Ibid.

67. *The Times*, London, July 27, 1938.

68. Anderson, *One and Only*, 26.

69. Visa for René Blum, Janet Rowson Davis collection.

70. *New York Times*, December 22, 1938, n.p., Janet Rowson Davis collection.

71. Serge Denham to Blum, December 7, 1938, Blum/Denham correspondence, NYPL.

72. Albertina Vitak, *American Dancer* (May 1939): 22.

73. Ibid.

74. Ibid.

75. George Wright, "France, A History," *Encyclopedia Britannica* (1974): 674.

76. Blum to Serge Denham, January 18, 1940, Blum/Denham correspondence, NYPL.

77. René Blum, "Letter of Protest," *Dance* (April 1940): 31.

78. Ibid.

79. Ibid.

80. Ibid.

81. Ibid., 48.

82. Alfred Delpierre to Blum, December 16, 1940, Monte-Carlo SBM.

83. Kathrine Sorley Walker, *De Basil's Ballets Russes* (London: Hutchinson, 1982), 95.

84. Ibid.

85. Ibid.

86. Franklin, interview with the author, October 10, 2001.

87. Serge Lifar, *Ma Vie* (Paris: Editions Juilliard, 1965).

88. Serge Lifar, letter to Janet Rowson Davis, May 24, 1978. Janet Rowson Davis collection.

89. Ibid.

90. Ibid.

91. Ibid.

92. Sorley Walker, *De Basil's Ballets Russes*, 80.

93. Lifar, letter to Janet Rowson Davis, May 24, 1978.

94. Nathan Milstein, "My Friend George Balanchine," *Ballet Review* (Fall 1990): 25.

95. Jean Cerrone, letter to Janet Rowson Davis, 1985. Janet Rowson Davis collection.

96. *Dancing Times* (May 1938): 139.

97. John Martin, "The Dance: Ballet Russe," *New York Times*, September 8, 1940.

98. Franklin, interview with the author, October 10, 2001.

99. Ibid.

100. Ibid.

CHAPTER 10

Blum's Final Days

1. Georges Wellers, *De Drancy à Auschwitz* (Paris: Editions du Centre, 1946), 109. Wellers dedicated a chapter to René Blum in this book.
2. René Bruyez, Blum Homages, 18.
3. Ilan Greilsammer, *Blum* (Paris: Flammarion, 1996), 410.
4. René Blum, unpublished journal, May 19–23, 1940, Arts du Spectacle.
5. Ibid.
6. A letter found in the New York Public Library Performing Arts Collection from J. Kohn, June 1, 1966, also mentioned the fact that Blum worked through 1940 and 1941 on the Molière film.
7. Police Report, August 6, 1941, Archives de la Préfecture de la Police.
8. Daniel Mendelsohn, *The Lost: A Search for Six Million* (New York: Harper Perennial, 2006), 197.
9. Wellers, *De Drancy à Auschwitz*, 125.
10. Today there is a memorial plaque on the outside of the military school remembering these 743 prisoners.
11. Wellers, *De Drancy à Auschwitz*, 128.
12. Ibid., 109.
13. Ibid., 81.
14. Ibid., 134.
15. Anonymous letter regarding Gregory Sedoï, November 22, 1961, NYPL.
16. Ibid.
17. Ibid.
18. Ibid.
19. Ibid.
20. Ibid.
21. Jean Jacques Bernard, *The Camp of Slow Death*, translated by Edward Owen Marsh (London: Victor Bollancz, 1945), 40.
22. Ibid., 41.
23. Ibid., 42.
24. Ibid., 43.
25. Ibid.
26. Ibid., 102.
27. Ibid., 103.
28. Wellers, *De Drancy à Auschwitz*, 136.
29. Ibid., 137.
30. Ibid.
31. Ibid.
32. Ibid., 143.
33. Ibid., 145.
34. Ibid.
35. Ibid.
36. Ibid., 147.
37. Ibid.
38. Greilsammer, *Blum*, 517.
39. Ibid.
40. Ibid., 518.

EPILOGUE

1. Interview with Francine Hyafil, Paris, September 10, 2005.

SELECT BIBLIOGRAPHY

RENÉ BLUM'S PUBLICATIONS

Blum, René. "Polémique entre François de Nion et Théâtre Antoine." *Gil Blas* (October 9, 1903).

———. "Notre Enquête: Le Droit d'Adaptation." *Gil Blas* (February–March 1912).

———. [René Bergeret, pseud.], and Jean Pellerin. "Le Goût du Toc." *Comedy in one act*. October 12, 1912, Théâtre Fémina, Paris.

———. "Préface au Salon de la Section d'Or du 10–30 october 1912." *Catalogue avec une préface de René Blum*. Paris: Galerie de la Boétie, 64 rue de la Boétie.

———. "Le Goût au Théâtre." *Gazette du Bon Ton*, no. 1 (November 1912).

———. "Le Goût au Théâtre." *Gazette du Bon Ton*, no. 2 (December 1912).

———. "Le Goût au Théâtre." *Gazette du Bon Ton*, no. 3 (January 1913).

———. "Le Gant." *Gazette du Bon Ton* (October 13, 1913).

———. Editorial Column. *Gil Blas* (July 12, 1913).

———. Obituary for Adrien Bernheim. *Gil Blas* (March 10, 1914).

———. Interview with Paul Gavault, Artistic Director of the Odéon Theatre. *Gil Blas* (June 20, 1914).

———. Unpublished journal, August 27, 1914, to September 6, 1914, Arts du Spectacle, Paris.

———. Unpublished journal, August 27, 1915, to September 6, 1915, Arts du Spectacle, Paris.

———. "Le Carnet du Bibliophile." *L'Amour de l'Art*, vol. 1(1920). Year of 1920 Alphabetical Index shows René Blum on pp. 98, 128, 164, 219, and 252.

———. "L'Art du Livre." *L'Amour de L'art*, no. 10: 320.

———. "La Section du Livre au Salon d'Automne." *L'Amour de l'Art*, vol. 2, no. 6 (November 1921): 365–67.

———. "Conférence sur Tristan Bernard." *Monte Carlo: Imprimerie de Monaco* (1925): 1–28.

———, ed. and compiler. *Encyclopédie des Sports*. 2 vols. Paris: Librairie de France, 1925.

———. Préface. In Tristan Bernard, *Mathilde et ses Mitaines*. Paris: Albin Michel, 1929.

———. "Georges Courteline" 1930 (Société des Conférences, du Conférence du 23 décember 1929, Instituée sous le Haut Patronage de S.A.S. Prince Pierre de Monaco, pour Paul Deudon), 1–43.

———. [René Bergeret, pseud.]. *Le Capitaine Fracasse*, a comédie lyrique with new compositions by Mario Costa, adapted from the picaresque novel by Théophile Gautier. This light comedy opened on December 9, 1930, at the Théâtre de Monte-Carlo.

———, and Jean Sarment. *Le Plancher des Vaches*, comédie en trois actes par Jean Sarment et René Blum. November 21, 1931, Théâtre de Monte-Carlo.

———, and George Delaquys. *Les Amours du Poète*. January 5, 1932, Théâtre de Monte-Carlo. *La Petite Illustration*, publiant des pieces de théâtre. Paris: Éditions de "L'Illustration," February 27, 1932.

———. "René Blum Writes a Letter of Protest, to the Editor." *Dance*, vol. 7 no. 5 (1940): 31, 48.

———. Unpublished journal, May 19–23, 1940, Arts du Spectacle, Paris.

OTHER WRITINGS

Anderson, Jack. *The One and Only: The Ballet Russe de Monte-Carlo*. New York: Dance Horizons, 1981.

———. "The Enduring Relevance of Léonide Massine." Paper presented at the Centennial Conference on the Ballets Russes at Boston University, June 2009.

Baronova, Irina. *Irina*. Gainesville: University Press of Florida, 2005.

Beaumont, Cyril W. *The Monte Carlo Russian Ballet: Les Ballets Russes de Col. W. de Basil*. London: CW Beaumont, 1934.

———. *Complete Book of Ballets*. New York: Grosset and Dunlap, 1938.

Bennahum, Ninotchka. *Antonia Mercé,"La Argentina": Flamenco and the Spanish Avant Garde*. Hanover, NH: University Press of New England, 2000.

Bernard, Jean Jacques. *The Camp of Slow Death*. Translated by Edward Owen Marsh. London: Victor Bollancz, 1945.

Bernard, Marcelle Tristan, ed. *René Blum (1878–1942)*. Paris: Arts et Métiers Graphiques, 1950.

Berstein, Serge. *Léon Blum*. Paris: Librairie Arthème Fayard, 2006.

Biancheri, Frank. *René Blum (1878–1942): D'Une Jeunesse Enthousiaste à "Nuit et Brouillard."* Annales Monégasques: Revue d'histoire de Monaco-Publication des Archives du Palais Princier, no. 20, 1996.

Bourrelier, Paul. *La Revue Blanche, une génération dans l'engagement 1870–1905*. Paris: Librairie Arthème Fayard, 2007.

Callil, Carmen. *Bad Faith: A Forgotten History of a Family, Fatherland and Vichy France*. New York: Alfred A. Knopf, 2006.

Cobban, Alfred. *A History of Modern France*. Vol. 3: *1871–1962*. Middlesex, UK: Penguin Books, 1981.

Cossart de, Michael. *Ida Rubinstein (1885–1960): A Theatrical Life*. Liverpool, UK: Liverpool University Press, 1987.

Coton, A. V. *Prejudice for Ballet*. London: Methuen, 1938.

Danilova, Alexandra. *Choura: The Memoirs of Alexandra Danilova*. London: Dance Books, 1984.

Davenport-Hines, Richard. *Proust at the Majestic: The Last Days of the Author Whose Book Changed Paris*. New York and London: Bloomsbury, 2006.

Deakin, Irving. *Ballet Profile*. New York: Dodge, 1936.

Detaille, Georges, and Gérard Mulys. *Les Ballets de Monte Carlo: 1911–1944*, preface by Jean Cocteau. Paris: Arc-en-ciel, 1954.

Dorris, George. Review of *The Art of the Ballets Russes: The Serge Lifar Collection of Theater Designs*, by Alexander Schouvaloff. *Dance Chronicle*, vol. 21, no. 3 (1998): 489–93.

Duberman, Martin. *The Worlds of Lincoln Kirstein*. New York: Alfred A. Knopf, 2007.

Edwards, Anne. *The Grimaldis of Monaco*. New York: William Morrow, 1992.

Eells, Emily. *Proust's Cup of Tea: Homoeroticism and Victorian Culture*. Studies in European Cultural Transition, vol. 15. Burlington, VT: Ashgate, 2002.

Ender, Evelyne. *Architexts of Memory*. Ann Arbor: University of Michigan Press, 2005.

Finch, Tamara Tchinarova. *Dancing into the Unknown*. Alton, UK: Dance Books, 2007.

Fraser, Gregory, and Thadée Natanson. *Léon Blum: Man and Statesman*. London: Victor Gollancz, 1937.

Garafola, Lynn. *Diaghilev's Ballets Russes*. New York: Oxford University Press, 1989.

———. "In His Own Voice: Diaghilev in the British Press." Unpublished article, 2008.

———. "Astonish Me! Diaghilev, Massine and the Experimentalist Tradition." Unpublished paper.

Garcia-Marquez, Vicente. *The Ballets Russes: Colonel de Basil's Ballet Russes de Monte Carlo, 1932–1952.* New York: Alfred A. Knopf, 1990.

Garcia-Marquez, Vicente. *Massine: A Biography.* New York: Alfred A. Knopf, 1995.

Gide, André. *The Journals of André Gide.* Vol. 1, translated and introduced by Justin O'Brien. New York: Alfred A. Knopf, 1948.

———. *Journals: 1880–1895.* Paris: Gallimard, 1988.

———. *Correspondance avec sa mère 1880–1895.* Paris: Gallimard, 1988.

———, and Jean Schlumberger. *Correspondance 1901–1950.* Paris: Gallimard, 1993.

Gold, Arthur, and Robert Fitzdale. *Misia.* New York: Alfred A. Knopf, 1980.

Gregh, Fernand. *L'Age d'Or.* Paris: Bernard Grasset, 1947.

———. *L'Age d'Airain: 1905–1925.* Paris: Bernard Grasset, 1951.

Greilsammer, Ilan. *Blum.* Paris: Flammarion, 1996.

Horne, Alistair. *To Lose a Battle: France 1940.* Boston: Little. Brown and Company, 1969.

———. *Seven Ages of Paris.* New York: Vintage Books, 2004.

Hurok, Sol. *Impresario: A Memoir by S. Hurok, in Collaboration with Ruth Goode.* New York: Random House, 1946.

———. *S. Hurok Presents: A Memoir of the Dance World.* New York: Hermitage House, 1953.

Jackson, Stanley. *Inside Monte Carlo.* London: W.H. Allen, 1975.

Jones, Colin. *Paris: The Biography of a City.* New York: Penguin Books, 2004.

Kochno, Boris. *Christian Bérard.* Translated by Philip Core. New York: Panache Press, 1988.

Lacouture, Jean. *Léon Blum.* Paris: Éditions du Seuil, 1977.

Lifar, Serge. *Histoire du Ballet Russe.* Paris: Éditions Nagel, 1950.

Logue, William. *Léon Blum, The Formative Years: 1872–1914.* DeKalb: Northern Illinois University Press, 1973.

Markova, Alicia. *Markova Remembers.* London: Hamish Hamilton, 1986.

McMillan, James, ed. *Modern France: 1880–2002.* New York: Oxford University Press, 2003: 57–92.

Mendelsohn, Daniel. *The Lost: A Search for Six Million.* New York: Harper Perennial, 2006.

Michaut, Pierre. *Histoire du Ballet, Que sais-je? no. 177.* Paris: Presses Universitaires de France, 1948.

———. *Le Ballet Contemporain.* Paris: Plon, 1950.

Mulys, Gérard. *Vie des Ballets de Monte-Carlo,* Direction René Blum. Vue par Detaille, photographe. Monte-Carlo: G. Detaille, 1947.

Painter, George D. *Marcel Proust.* 2 vols. London: Chatto & Windus, 1989.

Pharand, Michel W. *Bernard Shaw and the French.* Gainesville: University Press of Florida, 2000.

Pierre-Quint, Léon. *Comment parut "Du côté de chez Swann." Lettres de Marcel Proust.* Paris: Éditions Kra, 1930.

———. *Proust et la stratégie littéraire; Avec des lettres de Marcel Proust à René Blum, Bernard Grasset et Louis Brun.* Paris: Corrêa, 1954.

Proust, Marcel. 1913 translation. *Swann's Way, In Search of Lost Time.* Vol. 1, translated and edited by C. K. Moncrieff and Terence Kilmartin, revised by D. J. Enright, with an introduction by Jean Yves Tadié. London: Folio Society, 2000.

———. 1919 translation. *Within a Budding Grove, In Search of Lost Time.* Vol. 2, translated and edited by Scott Moncrieff and Terence Kilmartin, revised by D. J. Enright. New York: Modern Library Edition, 1992.

———. *Letters of Marcel Proust.* Translated and edited by Mina Curtiss, with an introduction by Harry Levin. New York: Random House, 1949.

———. *Correspondance.* 21 vols. Présenté et annoté par Philip Kolb. Paris: Éditions Plon, 1970–1993.

Scheijen, Sjeng. *Diaghilev: A Life.* Translated by Jane Hedley-Prôle and S. J. Leinbach. New York: Oxford University Press, 2010.

Sheridan, Alan. *André Gide: A Life in the Present.* London: Hamish Hamilton, 1998.

Sorley Walker, Kathrine. *De Basil's Ballets Russes.* London: Hutchinson, 1982.

Stein, Renée. *Trois Siècles de Ballet à Monte Carlo (1650–1950).* Lausanne, Switzerland: Maurice Bridel, Librairie de Lausanne, 1968.

Stokes, Richard L. *Leon Blum: Poet to Premier.* New York: Coward McCann, 1937.

Taper, Bernard. *Balanchine: A Biography.* New York: New York Times Books, 1984.

Thomson, Belinda. *Vuillard.* New York: Abbevile Press, 1988.

Thurman, Judith. *Secrets of the Flesh: A Life of Colette.* New York: Alfred A. Knopf, 1999.

Vaillant, Annette. *Bonnard: ou, Le bonheur de voir; dialogue sur Pierre Bonnard entre Jean Cassou et Raymond Cogniat; commentaires de Hans R. Hahnloser.* Neuchatel, Switzerland: Éditions Ides et Calendes, 1965.

———. *Le Pain Polka.* Paris: Mercure de France, 1974.

Vishniac, Marc. *Léon Blum.* Paris: Flammarion, 1937.

Walker, Kathrine Sorley. *De Basil's Ballets Russes.* London: Hutchinson, 1982.

Walsh, T. J. *Monte Carlo Opera 1879–1909.* Dublin: Gill and Macmillan, 1975.

Wellers, Georges. *De Drancy à Auschwitz.* Paris: Editions du Centre, 1946.

INDEX

Bold page numbers indicate a photograph.